Twayne's United States Authors Series

Sylvia E. Bowman, *Editor*

INDIANA UNIVERSITY

Mary N. Murfree

MARY N. MURFREE

By RICHARD CARY

Colby College

Twayne Publishers, Inc.   ::   New York

To the Memory
of My Mother

MANUFACTURED IN THE UNITED STATES OF AMERICA BY
UNITED PRINTING SERVICES, INC.
NEW HAVEN, CONN.

Preface

SEVENTY-FIVE YEARS AGO a little lady who called herself Charles Egbert Craddock stood on the loftiest uplands
of popular favor. Today not one of Mary N. Murfree's twenty-
five books is in print. Like the literary movement of which she
was a consequential part, she fell victim to changing times and
tastes. Her reputation, now down to the point where only scholars
of regional writing can name more than five of her titles, survives in the local-color chapters of omnibus anthologies of American literature. In these books, where deserving tribute is usually
paid to Harte, Hay, Eggleston, Joaquin Miller, Jewett, Freeman,
Cable, and Kate Chopin, one finds Miss Murfree's "The Dancin'
Party at Harrison's Cove," "The 'Harnt' That Walks Chilhowee,"
"Over on the T'other Mounting," or selections from *The Prophet
of the Great Smoky Mountains* or *In the "Stranger People's"
Country*.

The impression gained is that Miss Murfree wrote nothing
but novels and short stories about Tennessee mountaineers. This
view is unjust to her actual range and versatility. When the passion for local color paled, she turned her hand to tales of Tennessee pioneers and Indian wars, then to modes and manners
in the Mississippi Delta country. An adolescent during the Civil
War, she later made it the hub of two novels and of a number
of shorter fictions. She composed effective social satire and provided thrills and pieties for the juvenile market.

In 1941 Edd Winfield Parks published the first and, to this
date, only biography of Miss Murfree, a highly competent account from primary sources. Herein he notes all of these phases
in their chronological occurrence and evaluates what he considers her major works. He did not take as his task—nor could
he have been expected to—a complete analysis of her output.
None exists, and the handful of articles devoted to her are in the
main not usefully critical. For the student unwilling or unable
to seek out hundreds of book reviews in newspapers and
periodicals scattered over a period of more than forty years
there has been no recourse. This book endeavors to rectify that
shortcoming.

After the first chapter, which scrutinizes chief events in Miss Murfree's life and influences on her sensibility, each of eight chapters explores and interprets a specific facet of her prismatic writings: early social criticism, materials and methods in her mountain construct, mountain novels, mountain short stories, Civil War, frontier Tennessee and Indians, Mississippi, juveniles. The final chapter ponders the historical assessment and potential longevity of her achievement. It is hoped that these chapters constitute serviceable signposts to the forgotten artistry in Miss Murfree's varied domain, now largely *terra incognita*.

Miss Murfree was first to appropriate the Tennessee mountains as an exclusive literary property. She worked her lode perhaps too energetically and, toward the end, gave more slag than gold. Nevertheless she is still unrivaled in the depiction of this region and its people. Although a leading exponent of local color, and a proficient practitioner in several other fields, she never attained first rank in the list of American authors. So, in this day of read and run, the few snippets of her stories in academic anthologies may be as much as the student may look forward to. Yet it becomes growingly important—as mass communications media inexorably standardize our speech, clothes, customs, manners, and thoughts—to mark and cherish the diversities that went into the making of the American heritage. Miss Murfree's mountaineers are one of the indispensable cases in point, for esthetic as well as sociological reasons.

RICHARD CARY

Ocean Point, Maine

Contents

Chronology

1850   Mary N. Murfree born January 24, near Murfreesboro at Grantland, the family home facing Stone's River, the scene of *Where the Battle Was Fought*.

1854   Stricken with fever, resulting in partial paralysis and slight permanent lameness.

1855   For fifteen consecutive years spends summers in the family cottage at Beersheba Springs in the Cumberland Mountains.

1857   Family moves to Nashville where she attends Nashville Female Academy.

1861   At outbreak of Civil War, father attempts to get family to one of his plantations in Mississippi. Prevented by military hazards, they stop for a short interval at Grantland, then return to Nashville.

1862   During battle of Stone's River, Grantland destroyed.

1867   Attends Chegary Institute, a finishing school for girls in Philadelphia.

1869   Returns to Nashville.

1872   Family occupies New Grantland. She begins writing with publication in view.

1874   "Flirts and Their Ways" published in May *Lippincott's*, under the pseudonym of R. Emmet Dembry.

1876   Sells her first two mountain stories, "Taking the Blue Ribbon at the County Fair" and "The Panther of Jolton's Ridge," to *Appleton's Weekly*, but they are not published until 1880 and 1885, respectively.

1878   "The Dancin' Party at Harrison's Cove" published in May *Atlantic Monthly*, under the pseudonym of Charles Egbert Craddock.

1879   First juvenile short stories appear in *Youth's Companion*.

1881   Family moves to St. Louis.

1884   Eight of her mountain stories from the *Atlantic Monthly* published in *In the Tennessee Mountains*, her first volume.

1884   *Where the Battle Was Fought*, a Civil War novel written before any of the mountain stories, now published.

1885   Travels to Boston with her father and sister to reveal her identity to Thomas Bailey Aldrich, editor of the *Atlantic Monthly*.

1885   *The Prophet of the Great Smoky Mountains* published.

1890   Family returns to live at New Grantland.

1893   Helps to establish and build St. Paul's Episcopal Church in Murfreesboro.

1898   Joins the Daughters of the American Revolution. Does extensive research on Tennessee pioneers and Indians.

1899   *The Story of Old Fort Loudon*, her first historical novel, published.

1902   *The Champion*, a juvenile novel with a city setting—her only use of St. Louis in fiction—published.

1903   Moves to Murfreesboro.

1908   *The Fair Mississippian*, her first novel about the Delta country, published.

1912   Elected state regent of the Daughters of the American Revolution.

1914   *The Story of Duciehurst*, her twenty-fifth and last volume, published.

1921   "Muscle Shoals in Colonial Days," her last published article, appears in December *Youth's Companion*.

1922   Awarded honorary Doctor of Letters degree by the University of the South.

1922   Died July 31 in Murfreesboro.

1930   Her last novel, *The Erskine Honeymoon*, published serially in the Nashville *Banner* from December to March, 1931.

Mary N. Murfree

CHAPTER 1

The Soil, the Seed, and the Flower

MARY NOAILLES MURFREE was to the manor born. Except for one ebullient eddy at midpoint, her extraordinarily placid life coursed through its allotted threescore and twelve years trailing laurels and civilities appropriate to a Southern gentlewoman and best-selling author. She arrived in a decade marked by national agitation over the Fugitive Slave Law, the Compromise of 1850, the Kansas-Nebraska Bill, the Dred Scott decision, and John Brown's assault on Harper's Ferry in 1859; she spent her adolescence within the smell of cannon fire during the war between the States; and she matured in the Reconstruction atmosphere of a sector whose basic loyalty never positively evolved. Withal, she was singularly unscarred by her natal environment and made little use of it for literary purposes beyond the customary first autobiographical novel. Strong as her tendency toward self-dramatization was, she confined it resolutely to the domestic arena. True to contemporary traditions of her class and sex, she remained aloof from the enticements of large publishing centers and the hurly-burly of public adulation. She determined her own roles and with serene assurance adopted such modifications as seemed personally useful to her against the wider urgencies of a shifting social, economic, and literary scene. Not the last spasms of a dying era nor the metallic screech of a new one could divert Mary Murfree from her chosen way as a woman and a writer.

I *Childhood at Grantland*

With characteristic circumspection, Mary Murfree chose her ancestors from promising stock—the emergent, civic-minded, landowning middle class with a taste and a capacity for higher gratifications. Her great-grandfather Colonel Hardy Murfree, a vigorous, wealthy, expansive man, lent his patronymic to two towns in North Carolina and Tennessee. For his services in the Revolution he was awarded a grant of land in Tennessee, some thirty miles southeast of the frontier settlement of Nashville, where in 1807 he built a house, aptly named Grantland, and came to live. His son and heir William Hardy, a competent attorney, Congressman, and gentleman farmer, followed him sixteen years later and firmly established Grantland as the primary homestead of the Western Murfrees.[1]

Grantland was a comely twelve-hundred acre tract of woods and meadows, cotton and tobacco fields, and extensive fruit orchards. The main house, a dark-red brick structure in the colonial fashion, enveloped by a grove of venerable oak and hickory trees, stood on a rise overlooking Stone's River. Two rooms on the upper story were lined entirely with books,[2] the continuing heritage of Mary's grandparents on both sides. At the rear of the mansion lay a miscellany of utility buildings and living quarters for a full complement of slaves who tended the vegetable and flower beds, the herds of cows and sheep, the prize hogs and race horses.

Mary was fortunate in her parents. From these two sensitive, attentive people she derived not only the fitting combination of qualities but also the incitement to give artistic expression to her childish thoughts and feelings. Her father, William Law Murfree—lawyer, linguist, editor, and author—early stressed activities favorable to her development as a writer. Her mother, Fanny Priscilla Dickinson, played the piano several hours daily and inculcated the predilection for music so evident in Miss Murfree's life and works.

Mary, born on January 24, 1850, was four years younger than her sister Fanny Noailles Dickinson and four years older than her brother William Law, Jr. The sisters, strikingly compatible in temperament and intellect, shared identical social and esthetic interests. They were inseparable until Mary died.

Mary heard her first songs and stories from the lips of a black singing nurse in a gaily-papered room, where Mary had her own pigmy bookcase. Before she was five she could write with exceptional facility and had begun to read voraciously. At this juncture she was struck by a fever and by a partial paralysis which left her with a noticeable permanent lameness. The frisky child was reduced for a period to a sedentary indoors life, but the ailment failed to retard her spirit or imagination. She read more intensely, improvised many merry tunes, and cast herself as heroine of innumerable romantic dramas in which a totally conceptual Henri Beauchamp figured as her habitual deliverer. So powerful was her creative aptitude that she once persuaded her brother they had another sister away at school—after, no doubt, convincing herself that it was true.

Two retorts, one tinged with infantine defiance and the other with teen-age rationalization, demonstrate her unyielding conviction that she was born to achieve. Asked by a lady if it made her sad not to run like other children, she replied, "No, that's all they *can* do. I can spell 'Popocatepetl.' " And when she had grown to courting age, she explained with perhaps forced animation that she did not mind sitting out dances "for she could talk to twenty men at a time while other girls could dance with only one man at a time."³ Since she clasped the old-world supposition that physical deformity is a sign of divine esteem, Mary was sure from the beginning that her limp had a special portent.

The South before the Civil War was not ideal soil upon which a woman could hope to flourish in any occupation outside that of fiancée, wife, or mother. Least of all was the South likely to consider the arrantly public and intellectual function of author. Moreover, with the tradition of the leisured gentleman strongly in force, it was difficult even for a man to make his way in the profession of letters. The hermetic plantation system did not encourage either innovation or open inquiry. Conversations were more apt to revolve around the merits of a blooded horse than those of a recent novel or opera. Standards were stagnant; culture inert. In 1857 Edmund Quincy demanded querulously: "What book has the South ever given to the libraries of the world? What work of art has she ever added to its galleries?"⁴ And as late as 1866 James Russell Lowell complained that "There were no public libraries, no colleges worthy of the name; there was no art, no science, still worse, no literature but Simms's;— there was no desire for them."⁵

The private library accumulated by the Murfrees indicated wealth, enlightened appetite, and the paucity of municipal facilities decried by Lowell. Its contents reflected the reading trends of the day: *The Spectator*, the Waverley romances, Austen, Thackeray, Dickens, Wilkie Collins, Bulwer-Lytton, Dumas, Fenimore Cooper. *Jane Eyre* headed the list of Gothic favorites. Among the poets, Scott, Byron, Moore, and Tennyson predominated. Earlier periods were represented by Shakespeare, Milton, Bunyan, Richardson, and Edward Young.⁶ The Greek and Latin classics were more revered than read. Of these and of all the other books she encountered in her steady march through the massed titles in the upstairs rooms, Miss Murfree expressed deepest contentment with Scott, Dickens, Thackeray, George Eliot, and the Brontes. Progressively, their techniques and themes invaded her sensibility and became visible attributes of her subsequent art.

II *Nashville and Beersheba*

In 1857 Mr. Murfree moved the family to Nashville to expand his law business and to provide larger educational opportunities for his children. A city of some twenty thousand, the state capital encompassed—*mirabile dictu*—a bookstore said to contain "a better collection of recent literature, on sale, than is to be found elsewhere in the United States."[7] The girls acquired their first formal schooling at the Nashville Female Academy, which offered the usual academic staples of penmanship, mathematics, Latin, Greek, French, and mythology, as well as courses in drawing, painting, fancy needlework, and music, both vocal and instrumental. Upon her own insistence, Mary was assigned to Fanny's grade and, precociously, led all her older classmates. "A certain very smug smile would wreathe" her face when ranks were announced each week to an admiring assembly of parents.[8]

Nashville remained the family base for over sixteen years. There were frequent excursions to Grantland and sundry trips to Mr. Murfree's three plantations in the Mississippi Delta, a region whose somnolent menace Mary was to re-create in her last substantial writing. But most pleasurable—and fundamentally most important to Mary's emergence as a writer—were the vacations spent during fifteen summers at Beersheba Springs. This resort in the Cumberland range, about one hundred miles southeast of Murfreesboro, was described as "one of the most delightful and fashionable watering places in the South,"[9] and was patronized by affluent Southern families. The rambling, white frame hotel had a front porch with pillars in a long row, a Bachelor Quarter, bowling alleys, a ballroom, observatory, bandstand, and plank walks.[10] Miss Murfree later reproduced it with remarkable fidelity as the New Helvetia Springs Hotel in several of her mountain stories. Here, in the beginning, the Murfrees came to stay, but shortly before the war Mr. Murfree built a comfortable cottage, which he called Crag-Wilde, not far from the hotel.

For Miss Murfree the overwhelming allurements of the place were the landscape and the natives. The magnitude of the mountains seized her imagination, and she could never have enough of the spectacle. Fanny once wrote: "The view of the heights and valleys from the great rock in front of the cottage has been declared by travellers to be the most beautiful prospect on earth. . . . [Mary] used to gaze upon that scene for hours, wanting but the joy of looking upon it."[11] For additional perspectives Mary drove around in a jersey wagon and, despite her handicap, walked indefatigably. With her sister she visited the meager mountain homes, ostensibly to buy chickens, fruits, and vegetables. In this manner she became acquainted with the men, women, and children of the section; with the interiors of their cabins; with their talk, habits, and values. From these impressions she wrought her finest novels and short stories.

III   *The Civil War and Chegary*

Two other experiences invoked palpable effects in Miss Murfree's earliest endeavors as author: the destructive proximity of the war and her tenure at a cosmopolitan finishing school. At the outbreak of fighting, Mr. Murfree thought to salvage his Mississippi cotton. He packed up the whole family and started toward Fairoaks, one of his plantations. Upon arriving at Murfreesboro, he learned that the levees along his property had collapsed. He turned in at Grantland, where the family stayed for several peaceful weeks until Buell's troops attracted Confederate forces into the area. When a clash of arms appeared imminent in the vicinity, Mr. Murfree returned to Nashville.

Life in this garrison city lacked few of the amenities of a capital in ordinary times. There were books and music, the theater, military dances, and ladies' groups. The girls enjoyed seeing infantry drills and hearing the bands play. As manifested in Mary's *The Storm Centre*, the presence of an occupation army inspired no perceivable animus.

The certitudes of war were driven much more sharply into Miss Murfree's soul by the cataclysm at Grantland. During the bloody encounter at Stone's River between the armies of Rosecrans and Bragg (December 31, 1862 to January 2, 1863), Grantland was levelled, the furniture dismembered, the books burned. The defoliated orchards, the rusted fragments of bayonets, the shallow graves, all reappear dourly in *Where the Battle Was Fought*.

Two brief years after the war the sisters attended Chegary

Institute in Philadelphia, a school dedicated to turning young girls into charming young ladies. The prevailing sentiment of the day had it that culture should be foreign, preferably Continental, but in any instance not American. As one of the better Northern schools catering to the daughters of Southern proprietors, Chegary invested every aspect of its curriculum with a pronounced Gallic accent. However, it was the music program that afforded Miss Murfree her profoundest fulfillment. She played, sang and composed rapturously. During this interval she also wrote some of the very few poems she was ever to produce.[12]

The Misses Murfree returned to Nashville in 1869, to a gay atmosphere of parties and picnics, music and literary clubs, croquet. They moved smoothly in the upper circles of polite society, sparkled at dinners and dances, dropping now a discreet foreign phrase into the conversation, now an allusion to the latest play, now a devastating pun. At these gatherings Mary watched avidly the tactics of belles and beaux as they maneuvered intricately for advantage. These observations formed the core of her first two published pieces.

IV *Literary Situation in the South*

The South as a producer of estimable literature before the war was subject to the contempt of its own most influential editors. James DeBow rose to inquire in a mocking paraphrase of Sydney Smith: "Who of the North reads a Southern book?" Excluding Simms and Hayne, DeBow's point is defensible. This failing was usually excused on the score of the diffusive, agrarian, highly individualized civilization, and upon the absence of literary centers, prestigious local publishers, and strong literary magazines. The paroxysms of war inflated these factors or effected significant changes in them.

Military occupation by the North exerted intolerable pressures upon the old ideals. Suddenly and shockingly, an alien philosophy of industry, commerce, and urbanization overspread every recess of daily activity. The vast plantation—the heart of the economy—became overnight financially impracticable without slave labor. The Southern social and economic system, already undermined by decades of self-doubt, tottered. A mutation of pattern, born out of distress and accommodation, was inevitable. For Southerners who remained in the South, resuscitation of their once burgeoning domain resolved itself into a struggle between generations: the intransigent plantation aristocracy who lived only for the evacuation of Northern interlopers and restoration of *status quo ante* versus the younger element who stopped grieving over the sundered past and started matching the material success of the industrialized North. As the latter group prevailed, plantations were carved into manageable fractions, and scientific farming and business methods replaced the old princely waste. Trade and manufacture assumed respectability. The mind of the South took on a cast more conformable with the approaching century.

In the early years of the aftermath, young writers coming upon the scene did not, of course, find this change an accomplished fact. They had to distinguish delicately between tradition and innovation in flux. Since publishing houses and periodicals were even scarcer than before the war, Southern authors wrote on sufferance of Northern editors—a predicament which led to retreat from reality or to unconscious compromise in the work of Thomas Nelson Page and others no longer regarded as representative of their time and place.

In at least three respects the war itself instigated new writing. First, mobilization of the South into a temporary nation had created a sense of personality which, now disintegrated, required analysis and explanation from within. Second, this proud self-consciousness, flawed by defeat and subjugation, called for reinstatement of image beyond its own borders. Third, the general financial depression spurred many Southerners to seek a livelihood by way of the pen. Authorship joined the growing list of occupations acceptable even for the erstwhile purely ornamental gentlewoman.

Between 1860 and 1870 Southern writers on Southern themes could expect no haven in Northern magazines. The citadel *Atlantic Monthly* opened its doors only to conservative expatriates. Paul Hamilton Hayne, who had appeared in its pages before the war, gained no entry again until 1872. *Lippincott's, Peterson's,* and *Godey's Lady's Book* were among the few of note to print contributions in the new vein. They were soon emulated by *Galaxy* and *The Round Table*, but not until 1873-1874 did *Harper's* and *Scribner's* enlarge their policies of acceptance so that Southerners could dispatch their manuscripts with confidence. *Century* and the *Atlantic Monthly*[13] fell in step, and the last resistance vanished. The wished-for reconciliation was engrossed.

This new school of writers—principally comprised by Richard

Malcolm Johnston, George Washington Cable, Thomas Nelson Page, Constance Fenimore Woolson, Joel Chandler Harris, and Miss Murfree—turned away from the florid, stylized romanticism of their predecessors and confronted more or less realistically the phenomena peculiar to their own sections. The coast, plantation, foreign quarter, and back country were depicted in prodigal detail. The Cracker, Creole, Negro, and mountaineer issued vividly as types in their own right. But nostalgia and a desire for national approbation hampered completely reliable presentation. An uninhibited account of relations between whites and blacks, for instance, would have drawn disfavor from both Northern and Southern contingents.

V *First Writings*

At the beginning of this fertile literary decade the Murfrees were in parlous economic condition. The war had depleted Mr. Murfree's properties, and his railway investments foundered. He built a New Grantland within riding distance of the old, gutted location, and in 1872 moved back to the Murfreesboro area. Straitened finances and sobered postwar spirits had cut down the number of social events; as a result, the family was thrown more conclusively on its own resources. At this time Miss Murfree began to put words to paper in impressive quantities, at first for domestic entertainment, then with publication in mind.

The background for a literary career bestowed upon her by Mr. Murfree and his unabating impulsions to that end must be reckoned important forces in her ultimate determination. The impress of his character and occupation is detectable everywhere in her work. Her fictional lawyers, military officers, and retired gentlemen have more than a touch of his grace and eloquence. Her plots devolved on legal quiddities, she resorted to prolonged court scenes, her terminology was frequently at one with Blackstone's. Mr. Murfree had seen to it from the first that his home was a center of excellence in books, paintings, and music; he taught Mary Latin, Spanish, the classics, and hired an instructress for French. He read to her hour upon hour from Scott, Dickens, Thackeray—and forthwith she adopted them as her own. An adroit mimic, Mr. Murfree amused her with countless anecdotes in Irish, Negro, and mountaineer dialect. And always he importuned her to write. "Mary, stop sewing," he would say. "Anyone that can write has no business sewing."[14] In a duplication of Fenimore Cooper's experience with his wife, Mr. Murfree may well have nudged Mary to the edge of publication. He was reading a story aloud to the family. Unimpressed by the unnamed author's ability, Mary murmured that she could do at least as well herself. "Why don't you, then?" he retorted;[15] and the die was cast.

In May, 1874, *Lippincott's* published an impish little essay, "Flirts and Their Ways," by R. Emmet Dembry—Miss Murfree's first pseudonym. Another story-essay in similar vein published the following year concluded this brief phase of her writing— social satire. Later she made use of her pointed insights into behavior, but never again as a primary motif.

It is difficult to disentangle from existing evidence precisely what mode she gravitated to next.[16] *Alleghany Winds and Waters*, an incomplete manuscript novel of early, indeterminate date, contains a hodgepodge of Civil War-mountaineer-Mississippi elements, each of which assumed a separate design in the fuller fabric of her career. From this unpublished work she extracted the name of a minor character, Egbert Craddock, appended Charles, and thereby created the *nom de plume* which she retained until the end of her writing days. Much could be made in this day of psycho-consciousness of her penchant for male aliases and the exaggerated masculinity of her handwriting,[17] but Fanny's simple explication—Mary was "Modest, timid, shrinking, she knew how the woman author was yet regarded, and that there would be an advantage in a masculine penname"[18]—seems an accurate key to her sister's motivation.

It is unquestionable that her novel of the Civil War, *Where the Battle Was Fought*, was written around 1875 (although not published until 1884). Of greater import in the long run, however, was the acceptance by *Appleton's Weekly* in 1876 of two short stories with mountain locale and characters. Although they did not appear in print until 1880 and 1885, by then her salient trend was marked: she had published fifteen adult and juvenile stories of the Tennessee mountains.

VI *Local Color*

"The Dancin' Party at Harrison's Cove" appeared without fanfare in the *Atlantic Monthly* for May, 1878. It won instantaneous acclaim and established her as a sturdy portrayer of the raw mores of a remote, anarchic enclave. This shift in manner and matter, so drastic for a lady so seemly bred, bears inquiry. Miss Murfree expounded her choice of subject to Thomas Bailey Aldrich with prosaic directness: "I struck upon the mountaineers as a topic at hap-hazard, perhaps because I was myself greatly interested by them; but I did not then appreciate how very little was known of them elsewhere. I was early familiar with their primitive customs, dialect, and peculiar views of life, for I used to spend much time in the mountains long before I knew of the existence of such a thing as 'literary material.' "[19]

Parks believes that her inclination may have been fed by "The Yares of the Black Mountains," a mountain-dialect story by Rebecca Harding Davis in the same issue of *Lippincott's* (July, 1875) that carried Miss Murfree's "My Daughter's Admirers."[20] His assumption has some standing since this story embraces a primitive area, summer tourists, an expressive baby, talk of camp meeting, a woman ploughing, a yellow-haired maiden spinning, a sallow old woman in calico and bare feet, a pig in a kitchen, and soft-spoken giants. Miss Murfree may well have been intrigued at this time, for this number also contained "The Romance of Birdseye" by Chauncey Hickox, a tale dealing with another sequestered section, in Pennsylvania, which "has never known the echo of a steam-whistle." The wilderness is primeval; there are shabby cabins, a sawmill, a lithe young girl with blonde hair, a young man who will grow prematurely old, and other constituents of Miss Murfree's mountain chronicles.

The most forceful influence upon her, however, must have sprung from the elementary fact that, for a quarter-century following Bret Harte's "The Luck of Roaring Camp" in 1868, local-color writing monopolized literary imagination (and markets) in the United States. A number of factors conspired to bring about and sustain this domination. Among these, the Civil War with its enormous dispersion of persons increased awareness of cultural peculiarities in various segments of the country and roused curiosity to know more. As factories and railroads proliferated, spreading uniformity of standards and tastes into once isolated zones, champions of the past rushed in to record the environmental essence before it was completely dissipated. In this era of irremediable dilution, the uniqueness of the land and the people was most notably documented by Harte, Twain, and Joaquin Miller in the West; by Edward Eggleston and John Hay in the Midwest; and by Sarah Orne Jewett and Mary Wilkins Freeman in New England.

The South, with its magnified sense of despoliation, rallied an imposing battalion against the inroads of modernity. Out of love, memory, and defensive egoism, Johnston, Cable, Page, Woolson, Harris, and Murfree (soon to be flanked by Kate Chopin and Grace King) released a flood of stories and sketches redolent of the particular terrain each had appropriated as his own. Clamor for a distinctive indigenous literature and ravenous demand by Northern publishers quickened their disposition to commemorate local myth and substance.

As a genre, local color exploits those characteristics of a people and a region which differentiate them from the ordinary. Concentration is upon the oddities of topography, customs, folkways, dress, habits of speech, thought, and deportment within, usually, a remote sector immured from the winds of change. The local colorists of this period tended to stress not the basic universalities of human nature and experience but the picturesque and idiosyncratic manifestations. The general result was a superficial realism of detail glossed over by a benevolent romanticism of feeling.

Reacting to a triad of common incentives—practicality, nostalgia, and sectional loyalty—Miss Murfree produced a spate of novels and short stories depicting the singular scenes and happenings in out-of-the-way Tennessee mountain communities as yet untouched by urban blight. As Charles Egbert Craddock, she rode the crest of the local-color wave. Between the years 1878 and 1897 she wrote exclusively about this area, publishing twenty-eight short stories (all but one of which were collected in four volumes), and eight novels (two of them juveniles). After a sojourn of ten years in other literary fields, she returned to the mountains for two more novels and ten short stories. *In the Tennessee Mountains* (1884), her first collection, inaugurated her national reputation; *The Prophet of the Great Smoky Mountains* (1885) secured it. Her books ran to many editions and were reviewed extensively.

VII *The Great Revelation*

In 1881 the Murfrees had moved to St. Louis, where William, Jr., was firmly ensconced in the practice of law. The sparsity of published stories during her first two years of residence here suggests that Miss Murfree may have been temporarily distracted in this center of quiet culture, with its university, Museum of Fine Arts, active Philosophic Society, and summer opera. For years now she had submitted her manuscripts with the by-line Charles Egbert Craddock and signed her letters ascetically M. N. Murfree. No editor suspected that *M* stood for Mary, least of all the one who is said to have sent her a smoking jacket for Christmas. Critics soberly extolled Mr. Craddock's power and energy.

Miss Murfree's justification for this continued masquerade is vague and seems evasive: "I assumed a pseudonym because I wanted to do the best work of which I am capable, without self-consciousness and unhampered by personal considerations."[21] Her deeper reasons undoubtedly involved her as a product of Southern gentility bending to the dictum that woman's place was in the home, at the musicale, or at the spa.

In any case, she might have concealed her true identity indefinitely but for a contretemps which occurred after serialization of *The Prophet of the Great Smoky Mountains* had begun in the *Atlantic Monthly* for January, 1885. Versions of the great revelation which took place in March, 1885, are innumerable, and all differ. The account obtained by Mary S. Mooney in an interview of Fanny Murfree is probably the most authentic. When Nashville newspapers, supposing the initials to be in error, gave credit for the novel to Mr. Murfree, he decided that the time had come to disclose the truth. Mary journeyed to Boston with her father and sister, and in the office of the *Atlantic Monthly* she abruptly divulged to the editor that *she* was Charles Egbert Craddock. When Aldrich recovered from his amazement, he pledged Mary to silence until next evening. At a dinner he arranged for Oliver Wendell Holmes, Lawrence Barrett, Mrs. Annie Fields, and others, the news evoked a flurry of disbelief, indignation, and hilarity.[22]

The public sensation generated by this dramatic unmasking had no equal since the days it became known that George Sand, Currer Bell, and George Eliot were women. The bold handwriting and the robust élan of Miss Murfree's stories had presumed a tall, tough, laconic male who strode or rode, gun at hand, over a rugged, lawless territory without fear or fatigue. It took some time for editors and readers alike to reconcile this conception with a limping slip of a woman, who was chic, gentle, and bookishly witty. After three months of amiable visits with her several editors and literary friends in the East, she returned to St. Louis.

VIII *The Historical Interlude*

During the St. Louis years, Miss Murfree's name appeared regularly in the pages of the *Atlantic Monthly, Harper's, Harper's Weekly, Youth's Companion, Wide-Awake,* the *Christian Union;* she published four volumes of mountain stories for adults, two for young people, and the first of her Civil War novels. The vogue of local color was ascendant, and the public looked forward to each succeeding episode in her anthology of humble life in the highlands. In 1890, the family moved back to New Grantland, where Mr. Murfree died two years later. Miss Murfree was literally stunned by the loss; he had been not only father but mentor, motivator, comrade, critic, and confidant.

Her popularity progressed unabated until 1895, through the publication of *The Phantoms of the Foot-Bridge.* Nothing of hers appeared in 1896; in 1897, a collection of mountain stories for juveniles, and *The Juggler,* only marginally concerned with mountain motifs, were published. The lode of local color had run out. The tightly circumscribed areas had been thoroughly probed and laid bare in the first, fine, fresh years. Now repetition, with whatever hyperbolic variants, palled. In the face of expanding indifference in editors and readers, the veteran local colorist could either quit writing or move on to another mode.

The alternative for Miss Murfree was either to intensify her realistic strain and march with the upcoming naturalists—Stephen Crane, Jack London, Hamlin Garland, E. W. Howe, and Frank Norris—or to give way to her romantic propensity and take a seat in the school of historical fiction newly raised by Charles Major, Mary Johnston, S. Weir Mitchell, Paul Leicester Ford, and their English compeer Anthony Hope. Because she had an ineradicable sense of regional allegiance, because she had a flair for research, because the good historical novel called for authoritative re-creation of time and place, because she was at heart reactionary, and perhaps because she remembered Scott so well, Miss Murfree chose the latter course. But because she had so long observed and recorded the actualities of scene and character, she did not go the way of flamboyant costume mummery. Instead, she took up the soberer tradition of her fellow Southerners John Esten Cooke and William Gilmore Simms. In this decision she was assisted by the house of Macmillan which, in 1897, invited her to submit a novel on the pioneer days of Tennessee. After ferocious investigation of every relevant source,

Miss Murfree wrote *The Story of Old Fort Loudon*. It was published in 1899, a time when many Americans were willing to lose themselves in glamorous antiquity as a relief from the afflictions of a nation lately at war, now grappling with international complications in the Philippines and China, and harassed internally by problems of monopolies, wholesale bankruptcies, labor unions, and strikes.

In the next six years she turned out three more novels and several short stories about colonial frontiersmen and Indians, but without the consistency of purpose or the popular response she had enjoyed with her mountaineer series. In 1902, she wrote *The Champion*, a juvenile novel with the only metropolitan setting she was to draw from her St. Louis experience. In 1905, *The Storm Centre* reverted to the scene and era of her very first novel about the Civil War. In 1907, after a lacuna of ten years, she came back to the mountains in *The Windfall*. In a world that had grown away from her, she could find no sure landmark. So she thrashed about somewhat helplessly as she groped for a touchstone that would restore her to leadership in the lists of living writers.

Her next venture was a combination of local color and social analysis. *The Fair Mississippian* (1908) derived from impressions gained on vacations in the Delta in her girlhood and from the sensitivity to manners she had shown in her embryonic Dembry essays. In the backwash of these early memories she vacillated for the remainder of her active years, contriving one more mountain novel, one more collection of mountain stories, one more Mississippi novel—*The Story of Duciehurst* (1914), her last published volume.

IX *The Culminating Phase*

Miss Murfree's writing methods encompassed two extremes: she was overzealous in laying out her groundwork and volatile about putting it into final form for publication. No amount of drudgery could dissuade her from the pursuit of data which would give the ring of reality to her fiction. She pored over legal commentaries, played poker grimly day after day, measured the contentions of religion versus science, pondered colonial documents and annals, studied the instruments and ingenuities of war, the dialect of mountaineers, the etymologies of Indian speech, all lore and legends pertaining to her region, and the complexities of camp meetings, moonshining, river piracy, and legislative procedures. When cautioned about overdoing this research, she answered in Scott's words: "I love to be particular."

If she had any system of composition, it was not apparent to those around her. Sister Fanny said: "As far as I can judge, she had no recognized method. She made no plan beforehand. . . . When a magazine installment came to a close, she would often cease writing entirely. Days would go by when she played the piano, or drove around a little, made a few calls or went to the theatre. . . . At last, when the time for forwarding the manuscript had almost arrived, she would seat herself at her desk . . . then complete an installment of eighteen or twenty thousand words with incredible rapidity and freshness."[23] She depended upon mystic surges to see her through to the end of any current project. Like as not, she had lost the trend of plot or development of theme—demonstrable in several of her novels—but she was of the Dickensian persuasion that a novel is as good as the sum of its parts. Her fitful way with a manuscript was the despair of editor Aldrich. With impeccable discretion he would remind her that she was late with an installment. Just as impeccably, she would promise to reform. She never did.

For ten years after 1890, Miss Murfree lived at New Grantland, giving some time to friends, music, and church service. Mostly, however, she wrote. In the middle of this decade it was borne upon her that the rage for local color was on the wane. A letter from Horace E. Scudder, then editor of the *Atlantic Monthly*, informed her that he preferred to see her new serial before committing himself to publication. Before, she imperiously affirmed or declined all offers; her manuscripts were to be accepted sight unseen. While Houghton Mifflin did capitulate in this instance, it signalized the beginning of the end for Miss Murfree as a major name on the American literary scene.

After the death of Mrs. Murfree in 1902, the sisters took a rented house in Murfreesboro. In an atmosphere of dwindling repute and dwindling royalties, Miss Murfree persevered at her desk. Now she wrote on invitation of editors, along such lines as *they* deemed interesting. In 1910, Houghton Mifflin, her consistent publisher over the years, rejected her proffers of a novel and a collection of stories.

Purchase of a large house around this time aggravated her financial discomfort. As though in compensation, honor of a different kind was conferred upon her. In 1912 she was elected state regent of the Daughters of the American Revolution which she had joined during her historical research interlude. For two years she traveled and lectured in numerous small towns throughout the state, extracting immense pleasure from this renaissance of her former buoyancy. World War I seemed not to have meaning for her except as a souvenir of the dim conflict that had brushed against her long ago in a beleaguered city. From 1916 to 1921 she published six articles in *Youth's Companion* and a short story in the *Southern Review*.

In latter years her lameness bound her to a wheelchair, and eye trouble obstructed her efforts to write. An operation failed, and she lost her sight completely, but her spirit survived unaffronted. She dictated to Fanny one last valiant novel, which ran posthumously as *The Erskine Honeymoon* in the Nashville *Banner* from December, 1930, to March, 1931. In June, 1922, the University of the South awarded her the honorary degree of Doctor of Letters *in absentia*. The illness that prevented her attendance at the presentation was terminal. She died on July 31, 1922.

As a woman, Mary Murfree wavered demurely between the practical and the ideal. She moved in a proper world properly, too wise to rattle the norms of her social and intellectual establishment. Yet she was alert to the compulsions of an intangible self. "There is an immense gulf between me and my mind," she once said. Inventive and theatric in childhood, she devised eyries to which she could thereafter escape with her illusions. As a writer, she saw the uglier elements surrounding her but used an astonishing vocabulary to avoid reporting them. She gilded time and distance to suit heart's desire, skirting the absolutes of esthetic integrity in order to serve congenially a considerable number of her contemporaries. She may have had genius, but she appealed only to her talents. Her art is a reflection of her disparate selves.

Girl's-eye View of Society

IN THE FIVE YEARS between the age of nineteen (when she began to take writing seriously as a possible vocation) and twenty-four (when her first publication occurred), Miss Murfree ventured into at least three spheres she was to explore more fully in her maturer years. Each of these—the strategies of social interchange, the tramp of the Civil War around Grantland, and the allure of unspoiled mountaineers—is autobiographical in conception although all are presented indirectly. In the whole canon of her works she chastely eschews the first-person posture.

I "Flirts and Their Ways"

The social subject was probably uppermost in her mind during the early 1870's, for she had lately returned from Chegary Institute, already described as an inculcator of Continental elegance. Freshly enlightened in the latest graces, Miss Murfree noted with sharper appreciation the covert struggles for precedence which were going on in the coils of society around her. Her position on the sideline, enforced by her inability to dance, provided a vantage as point of view; fostered contemplation of the elaborate maneuvers; and gave her orderly brain opportunity to classify, enumerate, and adjudicate. But these intervals of inescapable aloneness also colored her conclusions with a stain of sour grapes.

"Flirts and Their Ways" (1874) is her initial public expression of observations and feelings on the duplicities of young females in their unending war for the attention of young males. Diverging neatly from the dictionary definition of flirt, she then disposes the varieties "like early potatoes" into several categories. The dashing flirt dances, rides, and talks with exhaustless gusto; the demure flirt, feminine but no feminist, screams, clutches, and objects to reading because it might unsex her; the musical flirt is a *prima donna assoluta*, playing the piano and harp, and singing; the literary flirt has never written anything although she has the supposed capability of a Francis Bacon, memorizes her bon mots carefully, is skilled in Latin and logic; the pious flirt goes about with downcast eyes and sweetly pensive face inducing young men to attend church, to forego dancing, billiards, the theater, opera, and other devices of Satan; the sympathetic flirt, confidante par excellence for men with wounded hearts, elicits tales of unrequited attachment and recitals of poetry; the sentimental flirt favors vine-clad porches, promenades on shady lawns, boat rides in moonlight, and tête-à-têtes on beaches.

Miss Murfree unfolds this classification of specific types systematically, expands and illustrates each, submits a comparison of their relative merits, and then concludes with the cynical admonition to "Buy a hogshead of prayer-books and do the pious flirt." One might have expected her to lean to the literary flirt, whose method it is to "sit on a mountain and bob for whale" instead of trapping minnows. Here the psychology of her limitation intervenes. Doomed by her disability at an age when physical attractiveness is a sovereign asset, she takes refuge in aloofness and scorns to play the petty game. It is her brag of spelling Popocatepetl revised to an older application. Her sympathy here is patently with the victimized young fops rather than the scheming young butterflies. Indeed, more frequently than not throughout her books, maidens fail to get their men.

She displays a fine sense of organization and an eye for infinitesimal detail. The prose is not nearly so congested as it was to get in her descriptions of landscape. It suffers, however, from a surfeit of French, Latin, and Italian phrases dropped at regular intervals with a show of schoolgirlish offhandedness. Under the broad irony courses a flippant iconoclasm surprising in so staunch a churchgoer—Reverend Yawn-your-head-off is one of the impaled supernumeraries. As a dissection of social mores this essay hangs on the dilettante level, faintly recalling Thackeray's *Book of Snobs,* Jane Austen's wry sport with the nefarious craft of ensnaring a husband, or Addison's way with the foibles of a special group.

"Flirts" has a material significance far outweighing its slender value as literature. Miss Murfree related to Aldrich that—after having her first sketch accepted, paid for, and published, and enjoying the notice it brought her—"I grew to have a definite

literary intention."[1] It was the opening shot of a career that reverberated for over forty years. It gave her the momentum she needed.

II   *"My Daughter's Admirers"*

Fourteen months later Miss Murfree's second piece appeared in print. Not purely an essay nor wholly a story, it is a hybrid comedy of situation containing dialogue, a modicum of plot and conflict, exposition of character, and a psychological resolution. "My Daughter's Admirers" is narrated by the father; nevertheless, Miss Murfree's attitudes on a theme similar to that of "Flirts" is strongly discernible. In fact, in its major respects "Admirers" may be regarded as a pendant to "Flirts."

In a domestic circumstance not too different from the Murfrees' own, the father, mother, grandmother, and brother sit at a game of cards while eligible gentlemen call on the young lady of the house, Miss Emmy (a diminutive of Miss M?). The "variety of genus *beau*" is codified less punctiliously and in fewer species than the flirts but to analogous effect. There is a dashing "horse horsey, turf turfy, and dog doggy" sportsman. Mr. Sparkle is both musical and literary; he sings German and Scotch ballads, recites on cue, and has written a book *nearly* ready for press. Mr. Crichton, who is primarily literary, reads Greek and speaks a dozen languages; and he also sings. Miss Murfree turns her analytic eye to the opposite sex and as wickedly exposes its basic pretensions. While this sketch has not the coördination of the first, the satire pinches quite as keenly.

The tone is more frivolous than before, with one consolation that the shower of foreign phraseology is reduced to four drops. Characters strain to be clever and succeed in being dismal. The nomenclature is bad Thackeray: Lyon is a hunter; John Doe, a lawyer; Mr. Sparkle sparkles (or tries to); there is a Professor Thumbscrews; and Reverend Yawn-your-head-off returns. Two deeper themes emerge, however. The first of these is presumably Miss Murfree's youthful horror of spinsterhood, expressed through the father's ruminations about "a dreadful thing, a shocking thing, to be an old maid!" He brands such a state "an anomaly in nature." Perhaps Miss Murfree had not totally given up hope that she might fulfill the expectations of her place and class.

The second theme carries Freudian implications of the surpassing love between daughters and fathers. Miss Emmy talks over her suitors' qualifications with her father and accords with all his objections even though she specifies trivial reasons of her own. His first reactions are annoyance and a threat to veto their visits. Next, he recoils from the repugnant idea of Emmy as a rich old solitary. Finally, he oscillates back to his original position, sinking back into smug gratification when all the suitors are gone. Miss Murfree seems to mimic her own condition—defensive ridicule of young men and subconscious flight to father-love to compensate for stinted ability to capture a husband. This may have sufficed as catharsis. When in 1885 a Boston newspaper hinted her engagement to an unnamed male, she rebutted airily that she was "wedded to her art."

III *Social Critic Manqué*

Parks is relieved that Miss Murfree so soon abandoned the manner exhibited in these essays.[2] There is no question about their puerility of mood and expression. This quality, however, may be discounted as imprudence due to inexperience. What seems regrettable in her premature withdrawal to another genre is the possible loss of a social critic of some consequence.

The inherent literary worth of these pieces is in sum negligible. The indicative factor lies in their revelation of a mind meticulous in its scrutiny of individual behavior within a complicated framework of rules. This was her first predilection and may thus have been her most natural faculty. There is minuteness and acuteness in her perceptions and enough promise of depth and variety in her presentation to justify anticipation of better to come. She had an instinct for the motives that underlay manners and could pierce unerringly to them. Given time to sharpen and develop this bent, she might have achieved the subtlety of a Jane Austen or a Henry James. She had Thackeray's gift of espying the typical in the personal, and she had a touch of his drollery.

One can build on more than mere conjecture. Despite the fact that her mountain stories deal predominantly with people whose norms of deportment admit no such elaborate shams, she accurately confirmed such amenities and priorities as existed among them. To the extent that valley and town folk differed in their usages, she also observed these. Her Civil War stories consider the rigidities of outworn aristocratic modes persisting in an era of callous disregard. And the most convincing evidence that her earliest preoccupation was not a passing conceit is its full-fledged reappearance in *The Fair Mississippian* (1908), where she places two social climbers at the edge of the next level and records their futile attempts to hoist themselves over it. Again in *The Story of Duciehurst* (1914) she shows through a rift the calculated barbarities practiced behind a screen of propriety. (These two books are examined in Chapter VIII, under the category of regional novels about the Mississippi.) In this last novel—when Paula Rosney watches Hildegarde Dean's way with men and snidely designates it as "the universal fascination-system"—Mary Murfree comes full circle. She had used that identical phrase in her very first publication.

Her pristine urge to probe and expose the core of social hypocrisies, diverted by the stronger urge to please a wider latitude of readers, murmured inertly for over three decades and then raised its voice again, too weakly and too late. In Miss Murfree, a superior novelist of manners died before being born.

Brown Jeans and Homespun

AFTER HER BRIEF FLING as a social satirist, Miss Mur-free turned with verve to the rising fashion of American fiction—the depiction of local color. With satisfying rapidity she sold two stories of this class to *Appleton's Weekly* in 1876. To her disappointment they were shelved when this periodical sud-denly perished. She had to wait four years and then five more years before "Taking the Blue Ribbon at the County Fair" and "The Panther of Jolton's Ridge" found their way to print in other sources. So it came about that her introduction to the nation as a portrayer of life in the Tennessee backland was delayed until "The Dancin' Party at Harrison's Cove" appeared in the *Atlantic Monthly* for May, 1878. To all intents this was a fortunate stroke for, as analysis reveals, neither of the earlier stories has texture or complexion as attractive as "Dancin'," which launched her unconditionally as a master of her medium.

I   *Color of the Country*

Local color had its origin in the first storyteller who pledged himself to accurate rendition of indigenous scenes, characters, and customs. In Europe it received fullest expression in the exotic productions of French romantics such as Hugo and Meri-mée and in Taine's conjecture of *race, milieu,* and *moment*. Across the English Channel it affected Defoe, Fielding, Dickens, Scott, and Bulwer-Lytton, the last two grandly. Its American beginnings may be read in the Knickerbocker and Tarrytown chronicles of Washington Irving, in the contortive Down East humors of Seba Smith and Artemus Ward, and in the frontier tales featuring Davy Crockett, Daniel Boone, Mike Fink, and Paul Bunyan. To all of these traditions and to contemporary factors, local-color literature owes its great surge of popularity during the 1870's in the United States.

This particular offshoot of local color, sired by Bret Harte, un-covered its most appealing properties in immured rural districts still in the handcrafts stage and practically devoid of a money economy. The better writers achieved understanding of the milieu, interpreting character, setting, and manners as a complex of interacting forces which sustained little worlds sufficient unto themselves; the lesser writers settled for caricatures, extraordinary backgrounds, and mannerisms whose charm lay in oddity or in a spurious quaintness. Where local color becomes an end in itself, realism—its instructing impulse—is debased by romance and sentimentality. By and large this debasement permeated the American movement of that day.

Mary Murfree, self-styled "a voracious reader," absorbed the effects of imported local color, especially the scenic grandeurs of Scott and the idiosyncrasies of character in Dickens. More immediately, she was in conjunction with a line of Southern authors whose work, though not then called local color, was assuredly within its intent. It is reasonable to believe that Miss Murfree was cognizant of at least three of these antecedents. Augustus Longstreet, Johnson Hooper, and Joseph Baldwin were already classics of anecdotage in the South during her childhood, their reputations so widespread and their books so well-read that they could not seemingly have escaped her. Longstreet, for example, was a reigning favorite of her father, who must have recited his milder tales with relish. In the work of these three Southerners can be descried components of language, activities, people, place, themes, and treatment which crop up in her own stories later.

All three were highly educated men, all were jurists, and Longstreet was also a college president. Each turned the full resources of his culture upon the folk tradition and transfigured it with a style or point of view too sophisticated for the material. None, however, softened the outlandish dialects, the curt brutalities, the rough buffooneries of the natives he depicted. In *Georgia Scenes, Characters, and Incidents* (1835), Longstreet presented representative men and occurrences along the state's frontiers. Fox hunts, horse races, shooting matches, fights, and gander pulls of unspeakable crudity are garlanded in drawing-room diction by "an eye and ear witness of them." Individual exploits of pinewoods farmers and bear hunters are larded with expedient preachments and served up with unleavened realism.

Johnson J. Hooper created a coarsely comic hero in *Some Adventures of Captain Simon Suggs* (1845) who went about gulling innocents in the Old Southwest. Graphic among the scenes in this book are the cardplaying sessions and the impassioned camp meetings. Joseph G. Baldwin accoutered *Flush Times of*

Alabama and Mississippi (1853) with Simon Suggs, Jr., who prolonged the epic of braggarts, gamblers, and other seedy denizens of these unfledged territories. Humor was the object of Longstreet, Hooper, and Baldwin—the raw, unfeeling jocularity of a male-oriented society. From their elevated station these authors imposed a pedantic overlay of satire and piety which now seems less a desire to correct than a pretext to dabble in matters usually eschewed by the shielded readers of their generation.

Remarkable analogies can be drawn between Miss Murfree and these men. She grew up in an atmosphere of higher learning, her father and brother were jurists, she had firsthand knowledge of untutored natives, she utilized many of the same episodes in her narratives, and she satirized and moralized quite as complacently. Only in degree of realism did she differ. Her sex and upbringing would not permit the inordinate vulgarities brought into play by her predecessors.

Few stories had been published about detached mountain communities before Miss Murfree discovered them as opulent grounds for literary exploration. Simms and Cooke, J. T. Trowbridge, Harden Taliaferro, and John B. Lamar had made occasional forays into the Virginia and North Carolina ranges. In *Tiger-Lilies* (1867) Sidney Lanier painted an idyllic picture of a resort in the Great Smoky Mountains not dissimilar to Beersheba Springs. The first writer to offer a nominal representation of Tennessee mountains and mountaineers was George Washington Harris, a Tennessee River steamboat captain. *Sut Lovingood Yarns* (1867) concerns a bluff, hard-drinking practical joker in a number of typical situations—wedding parties, quiltings, funerals, camp meetings, dances—perpetrating outrageous japes and gloating over his victims in lusty vernacular. Here again sadism and scatology are enframed by a gentlemanly surrogate. Miss Murfree's brother continually recounted and endorsed Sut's escapades to her. Lovingood is little more than a farcical caricature of a mountaineer, and the mountains are never pointedly local. But the area had been breached and was ready for more serious penetration.

II *The Tennessee Mountains*

The rapidly moving westward frontier of the United States left "quiet pools in the mountains of Virginia, North Carolina, Kentucky, and Tennessee."[1] There is general agreement that "time

has lingered in the Appalachians,"[2] and that even in the twentieth century the Southern mountaineer was a "distinct remnant
of Colonial times."[3] Thus it would seem a relatively simple task
to measure off one of these static zones and to render place and
people with utter fidelity. Where change is a stranger and where
every stranger is as flagrant as a horse in a parlor, a gifted ob-
server is not troubled by the transmutations and complications of a metropolis. Withal, the microcosm that Mary Murfree
carved out of the living rock of Tennessee was an incongruous
composite.

At Beersheba Springs in the fairly low Cumberland range she
came to know the men, women, and children who populate her
stories of mountain life. The vicinity of the resort was not in fact
an isolated, benighted section, nor did it suffer from rampant
illiteracy. The railroad connected the coal mines with the county
seat, and the University of the South (founded in 1857) was in
the adjacent county. "The growing town [in 1874] at the coal
mines, as well as the spring, affords a splendid market for everything raised for sale, and instead of hunters and a half civilized
backwoods people, the population is coming to be an industrious
and thrifty people, who, are beginning to look with as much
interest to the question of churches and schools as any people
in the State."[4] Miss Murfree was willing to extend to all mountaineers the primitivism and ignorance she found in those who
most interested her.

Situated near the headwaters of three rivers, Beersheba was
at the heart of wild and glorious country overspread by cliffs,
caves, cataracts, and titanic evergreens. Yet it is barely a match
for the wilder splendors of the Great Smoky Mountains about
a hundred miles distant. In the autumn of 1885, and several times
thereafter, Miss Murfree took an extended trip to Montvale
Springs in the Great Smokies (the opening scene of Lanier's
Tiger-Lilies). The grander aspects of landscape, the cruder self-
sufficiency of the natives, and their more rarefied dialect impressed her unforgettably. Her next novel, *In the Clouds* (1886),
may be said to reach a new peak in ecstatic mountain descriptions. (She had written *The Prophet of the Great Smoky Mountains* without having known the Great Smoky Mountains.) From
this time on she creates a kind of montage in which mountaineers of the Beersheba district are arranged against a Great
Smokies backdrop.[5] She invests the middling Cumberlands with
Great Smokies dimensions but gives no intimation of the long

stretch that actually separates the two. Neither does she compensate properly for variations in the characters and customs of the two regions.

In defense of Miss Murfree, it can be pointed out that the differences were those of degree rather than kind. The inhabitants of both ranges were, overwhelmingly, descendants of seventeenth-century British emigrants to America, freedomloving Scot borderers and Irish Presbyterians in religious dissent of James II. Originally settlers in Virginia and North Carolina, the majority crossed over in small groups and established solitary homes on the sides of mountains or congregated in loose, uncommitted roadside centers. Among them was a strong proportion of wanderers from the southerly provinces of Longstreet and Baldwin, essentially of the same ancestry, if somewhat less governable. A sprinkling of Huguenots (the Noailles in Miss Murfree's line) virtually completes the ethnic order. By mixing their traits and ways as seemed advisable in each instance, she gave the impression that a uniform type spanned all the mountains in Tennessee. In time, she was horrified to see her mountain friends twisted into identification with the poor white, but unwittingly and unwillingly she had established the concept of the mountaineer as a perennial loafer living in a tumble-down cabin with a slatternly wife and a horde of small children.[6]

Not everyone feels that Miss Murfree distorted unconscionably. H. A. Toulmin, a sociologist with psychological overtones, declares unequivocally that "she embodied a faithful reproduction of the actual conditions with little perversion for artistic purposes" and, further, that "Her books are laboratory records of a distinctive investigation in generic psychology which gives her the credit of a genuine contribution to the science of the social organization as well as to the creation of an artistic and literary success."[7]

Toulmin is perhaps too easily satisfied. Generic psychology and sociology are one thing, art another; and no one can pretend that strict adherence to the imperatives of one is equivalent to success in the other. Local color, ineluctably a combination of realism and romanticism, thrives as much on the use of imagination and artistic emphasis as it does on fidelity to details of environment, character, and custom. In the choice between literal transcription and verisimilitude, Miss Murfree leaned to the latter—unconsciously, in the first place, for she was by nature creative; consciously, in the second, for Northern editors at this time were demanding more and more color. If the end result is not unadulterated truth, as Toulmin avers, it is at least nearer the reality of place and thought than most local-color writing of her period. Whatever the merit of these distinctions, Miss Murfree's mountain fiction must be judged on its substantive value as literature—not as scientific verification.

III   *First Two Stories*

The first of Miss Murfree's mountain stories was written sometime after 1872, sold in 1876, published in 1880, and collected fifteen years later. "Taking the Blue Ribbon at the County Fair" is a pleasant georgic of love and rivalry recited by a spectator slightly to the side of the action; obviously not a native, he is amusedly sympathetic with countryfolk. The story has faults of structure, characterization, point of view, and a lack of depth which eliminate it from consideration as a piece of work worthy in itself. As a harbinger of Miss Murfree's future materials and methods, it repays analysis.

The plot hangs on a slender string. Jacob Brice is in disfavor with Jenks Hollis, a mountaineer whose one ambition is to win the horsemanship contest at the Kildeer County Fair. He has trained tenaciously and is expected to prevail. When his daughter Cynthia refuses to marry Brice, he enters the competition. As the hour of decision approaches, it becomes apparent that Brice is ahead. During the intermission he promises Cynthia to withdraw if she will elope with him. She consents. Hollis is awarded first place, learns of their flight, chases them, but arrives too late to prevent the marriage. On the day he takes the coveted prize, he has the mortification of losing his daughter. The story closes on the faint irony that—*amor vincit omnes*—it is Brice who captures the real blue ribbon.

Miss Murfree simultaneously develops the horsemanship and courtship motifs. The action is complete before the overlong pursuit, which becomes merely an appendage with secondary function. As in many later stories, Miss Murfree seems unsure of how many horses to mount or in how many directions to ride them at once. She dawdles between a comedic quirk (be sure to lock the stable while the horse is out) and a firmer theme of sectional diversities (town versus country).

The fair that takes place on the outskirts of Colbury, the county seat, draws attendance from three sectors: residents of

the town, well-to-do outlying farmers, and rustics from Old Bear
Mountain. Miss Murfree sets up an opportunity for more complex comparisons than she provides later—when she usually
restricts herself to mountain-valley[8] *or* to mountain-city confron-
tations. Here she avoids direct entanglement by taking the less
rigorous path of comic intrigue. She mentions "a bitter and
deeply rooted animosity" cleaving "the country people of Kildeer
County and the citizens of the village of Colbury" but sidesteps
its profounder implications by pointing the contest as a battle
between champions of the "townies" and the "mounting" men.
These mountaineers are far tamer than her forthcoming prototypes, and the farmers are indistinguishably "hand-in-glove with
the town's people."

In other respects the story fails. There is clumsiness in the
presentation of the courting scene between Jacob and Cynthia,
a too broad naïveté for even such bucolic lovers. And Miss Murfree's insertions of homily, apothegm, satire, data, stage directions, and opinion demolish tone and continuity. People and
place, however, offset these defects. Piquant rather than powerful, they nevertheless emanate a sense of freshness and uniqueness. The county fair is redolent with details of athletic prowess
and skill in husbandry. Jenks's cross-country dash contributes a
view of the landscape between town and mountains—fields of
Indian corn, wheat, and crab grass; translucent streams; white
frame houses with vine-grown verandas, well-tended gardens,
and groves of oak, beech, and hickory trees. This setting is succeeded by a glimpse of blue mountains against the indefinable
tints of the horizon and finally of the humble log cabins and
dingy little store at the Cross-Roads settlement.

All persons of any prominence in this story are precursors of
staple Murfree types. Hollis is slim and long-legged, wearing the
standard uniform of too-short brown jeans with ill-adjusted
patches, a loose-fitting coat out at the elbows, and a droopy old
white wool hat. He has a dejected air about him, the very picture of sloth. With him, Miss Murfree introduces the theme of
common humanity. "His inner life—does it seem hard to realize
that in that uncouth personality concentred the complex, incom-
prehensible, ever-shifting emotions of that inner life which, after
all, is so much stronger, and deeper, and broader than the material? Here, too, beat the hot heart of humanity. . . . He had
his hopes, his pleasure, his pain, like those of a higher culture,
differing only in object, and something perhaps in degree."

Mrs. Hollis is spare, her gaunt face prematurely lined and old. She dresses in blue and white checked homespun; her scanty hair is in a tidy knot on the top of her head. She has a veritable brood of youngsters; nevertheless, she keeps her house scrupulously clean. Outside she has cultivated a fine vegetable garden and maintains an abundance of poultry. With her, Miss Murfree introduces the theme of the indomitable feminine spirit. "These simple belongings were the trophies of a gallant battle against unalterable conditions and the dragging, dispiriting clog of her husband's inertia." A "group" of tow-headed, grave-faced, bare-footed, well-scrubbed children make mudpies; and the inevitable sedate, bald-headed baby lies wide awake in a wooden cradle.

Cynthia's complexion is of "singular purity and transparency," her dark eyes slumbrous, her brown hair curling. She wears a brilliant yellow dress, and a row of black beads on a shoestring around her neck, yet has a sobriety of demeanor "almost portentous" in a girl of seventeen. Jacob Brice, her suitor, is the exemplar of younger mountaineers—a tall, muscular, languid hunter in patched and stained brown jeans suit, with no estate and no fondness for physical work.

Not one of these characters rises to individuality in his or her own right. They move to the narrator's gesture, illustrate conditions, and play out the plot. Miss Murfree's feeling for them, avouched in her contemplation of Hollis, is one of subconscious condescension which persists throughout her work despite evident compassion and sincere efforts to confirm them as correlative human beings.

She writes with comparative simplicity here. Her prose, while formal, is flexible, stripped of the strained cosmopolitanisms of her essays. The reader notes a thin resemblance to Washington Irving's "The Legend of Sleepy Hollow" in the reflection of rural types and activities, the precipitous flight across country, the light ironies, and the aura of localized myth.

"The Panther of Jolton's Ridge," published in 1885 and collected in 1899, was written about the same time as "Taking the Blue Ribbon" and was sold with it in 1876. But it is a decided advance in the presentation of mountain environment and characters, and it revolves around two fundamental preoccupations of the region—religion and moonshining. Mark Yates, a cheerful mountain lad, forms the habit of going to the still-house of the Brice brothers, not so much to drink as to take in the stories about Indians, feuds, and hunting. One evening John Brice, the panther, implies that he is going to revenge himself on the preacher for ousting the Brices from church membership, thereby adversely affecting their sale of liquor. Yates had been inspired by the concept of a community churchhouse and had worked mightily during its erection. He warns the irascible panther against any drastic action, and they part in anger. The church bursts into flame that night. Brice, apprehended leaving the scene, tries to escape via a railroad bridge, encounters a train midway, plunges into the waters far below, and is never found. Yates races immediately to investigate the fire. Known to be friendly with the Brices, he is suspected of having had a hand in setting the blaze. His explanation is ostensibly accepted in the settlement, and it is tacitly agreed thereafter that he is a fine fellow—even though he did help the panther fire the church.

Again Miss Murfree enjoys some patent ironies. Yates's reconciliation with his fellows comes about not through belief in his incorruptible love of the church but through a mood of indulgence toward his non-existent sin. The Brices feel "that they had experienced the most unexpected and disastrous catastrophe possible in nature" when ostracized by the preacher, not because of any moral obloquy but because they depend upon the goodwill of the churchgoers to sell them illicit whisky. Out of such social and ethical anomalies is constructed an efficient contrast between horseback and Pullman-coach cultures.

The railroad train is the chief instrument of the contrast. Loaded with city people, it represents civilization which "offered no recompense to the few inhabitants of the gorge. . . . It passed swiftly far above them, seeming to traverse the very sky. They had no share in the world; the freighted trains brought them nothing—not even a newspaper wafted down the wind; the wires flashed no word to them." The exalted position of the railroad invests it with symbolic superiority—a mechanistic, dispensing deity. As in Auden's "Musée des Beaux Arts," the detached, careless city passengers turn away "quite leisurely from the disaster," completely unaffected by the ignorance and isolation below. The fire is a paramount event to the mountaineers. "Only a little church on fire," says the conductor. The panther, at odds with native principles, is destroyed by the pitiless progress of an urban way of life. Miss Murfree forsees the inevitable dissolution of the Yates-Brice world, partly by its self-ravaging violence, partly by the infringements of an unwanted new mode. In her sympathies she remains indeterminately between the gorge and the bridge.

Like Lucifer, John Brice attacks an ineffable verity and is consigned to infernal waters. The power of religion in the mountains is thus effectively demonstrated. But it too is susceptible to craft in observance. "Perfessin'" piety endows social distinction and is often more important than practicing. Moreover, the preacher's insistence on a "personal and practical religion" is looked upon as interference in the affairs of the congregation. Yet the moral position must not be subjected to direct or external assault. The eternal war between good and evil is allegorized in the still-house run by Brice and the churchhouse built by Yates. Yates falters between the two, as do other parishioners. In the moment of absolute choice, however, he and they have no doubt about their convictions. Brice suffers orthodox punishment, and the still falls into desuetude. The story is finally an illustrated sermon on the need for right discriminations.

Scene and people, as well as themes and tone, begin to take on more pronounced particularity. The action unfolds in "a certain wild chasm, cut deep into the very heart of a spur of the Great Smoky Mountains," forlorn log huts cling to the ledgy slopes, the still is revealed in somber light, the moon makes a prominent appearance, and several folk songs set the mood of irreverent conviviality. Yates is too dedicated and naïve to be typical, but the four burly Brice brothers are molds of the mountain moonshiner: big, glowering, vicious, and vengeful, nothing loath "ter git the skin o' one o' these hyar brethren an' nail it ter the door like a mink's ter a hen house." Mrs. Yates's sarcastic wit prepares us for a long succession of talkative crones. The preacher, a "skimpy saint" who comes "like a whirlwind, sweeping the chaff before him," is the first of many inflamed evangelists whom the mountaineers respect and ridicule by turn. There is no lovely young heroine.

A number of other Murfree practices are discernible in the germ here. The opening paragraphs are given to a survey of massive mountain surroundings. By way of democratic equation she suggests that noteworthy tragedies and comedies of existence are played out as graphically in these small backward communities as in the spotlight of great metropolises. Appropriately to her subject, she allots Biblical names to all principals (Mark, John, Joel, Aaron, Peter, Joseph, Moses), pits the preacher as

David against hulking Goliaths, and frequently simulates Old
Testament rhythms. She sprinkles *obiter dicta* and satiric observations through the text, and she assigns to Mrs. Yates and Moses
Carter witticisms beyond their level. She employs a favored
device of silhouetting figures athwart the sky, and another of
prefiguring events (the panther's innuendoes about the church).
Brice's disappearance gives birth to a local ghost legend. The
loose ends of narrative are neatly tied together, and the didactic
intent is compactly summarized in a superfluous coda.

In all, Miss Murfree's point of view in this story is unsteady;
she stalls the forward motion with periodic digressions and cannot keep her sights on a main purpose. While displaying a
stronger grasp of the essential materials, "The Panther" has the
same flaws of conception and execution as "Taking the Blue
Ribbon." Although neither is worth more than passing notice
for its own sake, they expound her formative period in fiction
and denote with amazing precision the trail she was to break
through the haunted forests and beetling crags of the eastern
Tennessee mountains. With "The Panther" her short apprentice-
ship comes to a close.

CHAPTER 4

Mystique of the Mountains

THE FIRST STORY to be printed under the name of Charles Egbert Craddock, "The Dancin' Party at Harrison's Cove," was originally intended as the opening chapter of a novel that Miss Murfree and her sister had planned to write. After the customary family reading, it was decided that this segment had a unity of its own and should be sent to the *Atlantic Monthly* as it stood. Howells published the story in May, 1878, and in the next six years Miss Murfree sold seven others of the same stripe to the *Atlantic*. On Aldrich's recommendation Houghton Mifflin gathered these eight stories and issued them in 1884 under the title of *In the Tennessee Mountains*. "The Dancin' Party" had revealed Miss Murfree to the elite of the eastern seaboard as an invigorating artist in local color. The collected volume captured the entire country and ran into more than a dozen editions within two years. Edward J. O'Brien, dean of short story anthologists, reports its "reception rivaled that of *The Luck of Roaring Camp*," and opines that Craddock's book "marked another important milestone in regionalist writing."[1]

One anonymous critic voices objections to the slightness of the heroines, the prolixity, and the tendency to explicate; but he links Craddock with some impressive contemporaries. "His" situations are more intense, as unpretentious, mellow, and quiet as Sarah Orne Jewett's; "his" gift of close observation recalls Thomas Hardy; "his" effects are less pointed, "his" pathos less deep than George Washington Cable's; "he" is less artificial in method; "he" is truer to the dialect and general possibilities of the region than Bret Harte is to the Pacific slope.[2] At this stage these imputations are, on the whole, overly generous. However, applied in specific instances, the comparisons are supportable.

The eight stories that comprise *In the Tennessee Mountains* have an aura of unity gained through homogeneity of landscape, language, folklore, names of people and places, morals, tone, and point of view. Details differ from one crossroads settlement to another; activities and seasons vary; but the essential similarity is sturdier than surface diversity. Day to day and year to year a sense of cycle operates through individual lives and incidents, blending them into an endless, unresisting continuity. Generations of unchanged outlook, reconciled to the magnanimity of the mountains and to the meagerness of man's lot, have formed grooves within which lives may run their course without friction. The immense general sameness is a condition of existence; the contrast between nature and human nature is minimized and no longer effective as inspiration to the natives.

Miss Murfree catches this quality all too consciously and projects it with an array of techniques sometimes too awkward to convey a reality of either life or art. At fault is her inability to dissociate her own place and position with the ruder ones she is considering. It delimits her view, raises a barrier between subject and reader, and in the final assessment precludes that necessary fusion of intimacy and detachment which informs all perdurable fiction. As a totality in itself, *In the Tennessee Mountains* affords a convenient unit for study of Miss Murfree's evolving methods. Subsequent short stories and novels about the mountains will be reviewed in relation to and as an extension of this first really long step upward.

I *The Mountain Scene*

The overwhelming central fact of life in Miss Murfree's tales of Tennessee are the mountains. Their presence is felt within the first page of all but one of these eight stories. Isabella Harris has counted eighty-nine descriptive passages of paragraph length in the 322 pages of this volume. Variety would seem hard to achieve through so many iterations, but Toulmin believes that Miss Murfree rivals Swinburne in the galaxy of expressions she musters. Although relatively chary with chromatic depiction in the short story, as against the novel, she has been scored for repetition and floridity. Miss Harris asserts that she "lugs in description by the ears . . . because she has never recovered from the awe of a summer visitor at the scenery about her."[3] Undisturbed, Milton T. Adkins considers this "a venial fault" and cites Wordsworth as her peer.

The effect of the mountains is unquestionably pervasive, for Miss Murfree has marvelous evocative powers. Yet, even in this collection, the press of too many recurrences and too many adjectives becomes onerous. She fails not in fidelity to detail so much as in artistic balance. Often she breaks off in the middle of a crucial dialogue or dramatic action to take still another glimpse at a rugged vista. She said in extenuation of this defect that "one observes most keenly and remembers most vividly in a crisis."[4] Be that as it may, it is not always the beauties of landscape that catch the sense.

Miss Murfree sets one of these stories in the Cumberlands, another in a wild spur of the Alleghenies, a third in the Great Smoky Mountains. These are purely nominal designations. The prospect is all of a piece, with infinitesimal variations. The sky by day is lustrously blue and changes to crimson, purple, gold, and saffron as evening verges into night, then makes way for moons of every phase and hue. In the vast phalanxes of towering ranges, majestic summits intercept the horizon. A wilderness of dark evergreens and deciduous trees casts dense shadows over sheer precipices, great projecting ledges, treacherous chasms, and unexplored caverns. Cataracts spurt out of immense fissures and smash tumultuously against giant boulders. Stony roads curve downward to basin-like valleys. Birds, foxes, wolves, deer, and an occasional bear slip lightly through thick foliage, which is deeply colored in keeping with the season. "Her Tennessee mountains are purpler, bluer, and yellower than any other," wrote one critic in exasperated disparagement.[5]

Undeniably, Miss Murfree accentuates to the point of affectation the exquisite aspects of landscape. However, all does not fall within Addison's dictum that "we find the works of nature still more pleasant, the more they resemble those of art." She is most successful when allying external nature with man in his obscurer moods and meditations, when man merges with environment in harmonious acceptance of the mystery of existence. This inexpressible coordination, here best demonstrated in "Over on the T'other Mounting" and in "The 'Harnt' That Walks Chilhowee," is given full tribute by William Malone Baskervill: "Her description, too, serves a literary purpose, now expressing the fitting sentiment, anon developing the appropriate passion. She seizes and interprets physical features and natural phenomena in their relation to various aspects of human life with at times unerring precision, vigor, and dramatic force. Indeed, the scenery of the mountains is essential to the comprehension of the gloom of the religion, the sternness of the life, the uncouthness of the dialect, and the harshness of the characters presented in her stories."[6]

This effect of interrelationship she accomplishes in part by adducing Gothic horror as an ever-present concomitant of loveliness in nature, illustrating the duple sides of man's nature and influencing his thoughts and actions. Among the over-all sublimities a peak "beetles" bare and grim. Gigantic walls of rock loom "gloomy and sinister" over denuded forests of desolate black-branched trees. "Grisly yawning abysses" lay in wait for unwary riders, and the primeval magnificence is shrouded in somber neutral hues. When offered in apposition to dour expectations or emotions, these atmospheric details become more than mere geographic adjuncts, more than mere local color. They serve as true portents and indices of human sensitivity.

Less abstruse in its application is the use of metaphor to substantiate the invisible affinity of man and nature. Lifting his gaze to a star or to a mountaintop, man feels his soul and imagination lifted. Watching empty nights succeeding empty days ratifies his own loneliness; hearing foxes bark in a moonlit autumn wood relieves it. The grace of a woodland flower is reflected in that of a young girl. Man's imperceptible aging mimics erosion in nature, and his misery is not unlike that of a freezing bird or a wounded deer. A creek disappearing into a mountain recess is seen as a human life lost in the eternal enigma. The calm of the forest restores the calm of a harassed heart and spirit.

The moon, which later contends with the mountains in frequency of appearances, calls attention to itself in five of the stories. Everyone has had his little joke about "Mary's moon," as her mother dubbed it; but most reviewers condemn it offhand as a meretricious stage prop. "She was often accused of hauling the moon over the Tennessee Mountains too often and too lingeringly and in one instance, if we remember rightly, of causing it to rise in a part of the sky never intended by nature for moonrise," noted the *Outlook*. "As somebody has said, she works her moon too hard," echoed the *Atlantic Monthly*.[7] This is irrefutable but, as in other facets of Miss Murfree's writing, there is more here than meets the uncritical eye. In her preoccupation with the moon she is a true "lunatic" with, however, method in her madness.

When not hung out purely as decoration, the moon's major function is to act as a spotlight. In a district devoid of central artificial lighting, what more natural way exists to illuminate outdoor drama at night? Miss Murfree utilizes moonglow strategically to focus the area of action and to pick out imperative details of topography. She turns the rays on people's faces to expose emotions or significant changes of expression. A "drowning" moon accompanies the bitter reflections of a misfit over his persistent failures, a "sinking" moon corresponds with sudden fright, and a "red" moon shines on a ruffian, hands dripping with blood, who is running from the forest. Like Hawthorne, she causes the moon to obscure as well as to elucidate, casting ambiguous beams on elements to be disclosed later. Like him, she also certifies the moon as a moral agent. It smiles "right royally" on the jocund dancing party and withholds approval of the outlaw band which rides into "the gloom of the shadows."

In this breathless domain of "clifty heights" the typical abode is a log hovel clinging uncertainly to the mountainside. A vagrant path leads to the rickety fence upon which perches a motionless man. Hounds, calves, "soprano pigs," chickens, and horses roam the yard—but the hounds and chickens are as often in the house. The porch is occupied by broken chairs, cooking utensils, discarded garments. In the fireplace, which takes up almost one side of the house, a hickory fire is usually burning. The rough, uncovered floor, with one or two loose puncheons, supports inverted washtubs and splint baskets used for seats, a bedstead with sagging mattress and patchwork calico quilt, some rush-bottomed chairs, perhaps a spinning wheel. From the rafters dangle strings of bright red peppers, ears of corn, hanks of woolen and cotton yarn, bunches of medicinal herbs, brown gourds, and little bags of seeds. Ranged on shelves along the walls are pots, pans, and drinking vessels. Miss Murfree stresses the marked cleanliness of these interiors.

A store and a blacksmith's shop may be found at road junctions together with a smattering of cabins within walking distance of one another. Often just called "Cross-Roads" or "the Settlemint," these hamlets epitomize the extent of mountain community. By reverting to such generic names—and others such as Big Injun Mountain and Colbury, the county center—throughout these stories, Miss Murfree creates a sense of unbroken tissue. Each story becomes a separate incident in a protracted, haphazard epic of life in this beautiful, violent, backward country.

II   *The Mountain People*

The mountain men and women seen briefly in "Taking the Blue Ribbon" and in "The Panther of Jolton's Ridge" take on added dimensions in *In the Tennessee Mountains*, and we are introduced to several other basic types. Notwithstanding, Miss Murfree restricts her range to a small segment of the variegated mountain populace. She knew best those she met around Beersheba Springs and concentrates on those along the lowest social-economic margin, ignoring the better educated, the more affluent and adaptable citizens with minor appeal to far-off magazine readers. Mountain aristocrats were too much like their upcoming town counterparts, so she exploits the Boeotian qualities of the unaltered rustics. She achieves a tiring repetition before she leaves them for other fields, but there exists sufficient testimony that she faithfully retained most of the realities within her narrow bailiwick.[8]

Men dominate the forefront. They hunt, fish, fight, loaf, or disport themselves with primal disregard for domestic obligations. All are congenitally shiftless although some work sporadically around their depressed homesteads. The smith, the miller, and the moonshiner seem the only ones who apply themselves steadily. Fierce independence and a fine contempt for the law are promiscuous. Only a minority, however, are actually lawless. Of these the representative in "The Dancin' Party" is horse-thief and brawler Rick Pearson, who is an outgrowth of the panther, John Brice. His person, with some scant deviations, foretokens a long line of intrepid, immoral, blunt, bluff, not unattractive demiheroes to follow.

> He was dressed, like the other mountaineers, in a coarse suit of brown jeans somewhat the worse for wear, the trowsers stuffed in the legs of his heavy boots; he wore an old soft felt hat, which he did not remove immediately on entering, and a pair of formidable pistols at his belt conspicuously challenged attention. He had auburn hair, and a long full beard of a lighter tint reaching almost to his waist; his complexion was much tanned by the sun, and roughened by exposure to the inclement mountain weather; his eyes were brown, deep-set, and from under his heavy brows they looked out with quick, sharp glances, and occasionally with a roguish twinkle; the expression of his countenance was rather good-humored,—a sort of imperious good-humor, however,—the expression of a man accustomed to have his own way and not to be trifled with, but able to afford some amiability since his power is undisputed.

The more tractable male adults are listless, recurrently drunk, wear a grave mien, talk in a monotonous drawl, see ghosts, abuse their wives, indulge their beasts. Younger men have tremendous build and strength, are quicker to anger, livelier in banter, and tenacious in courting.

There are three ranks of females in this masculine realm: the young maiden, the young wife, the older woman. The young mountain maiden expands into a highly controversial figure later in Miss Murfree's work. In five stories in *In the Tennessee Mountains* the lineaments of the larger portrait begin to emerge. The young mountain girl before marriage is extraordinarily beautiful, has the grit and determination of her forebears, a propensity for misfortune in love, and a strong strain of resignation.

Mandy Tyler is least characteristic, with black hair and too much vivacity. As yet an unbridled coquette, she plays practical jokes with impunity on her clumsy swains. Clarsie Giles is a step closer to the composite. Although also a brunette and untameable, she is tall, lithe, with "delicately transparent complexion" and large, liquid eyes. She turns out to be the norm of mountain girls who marries the norm of mountain boys. Celia Shaw is the first full step toward the ultimate mountain-flower type. One of the mountaineers pictures her succinctly: "She's a mighty good, saft-spoken, quiet sort o' gal, but she's a pore, white-faced, slim little critter." Obviously alien to her own world, she is incapable of entering the one above her. Puzzled neighbors dismiss her as "teched in the head." She has a fair, ethereal face, bronze hair, opaline eyes, and a voice with the cadence of autumn winds. Miss Murfree calls her a "woodland flower." Selena Teake is her immediate complement: delicate crimson lips, limpid eyes, and —a salient feature hereafter—masses of yellow hair. Cynthia Ware combines the spunk of the first pair with the pulchritude of the second. Her brilliant auburn hair is accounted a defect by the mountaineers; it sets her aside as "different." She sacrifices valiantly for love, loses, and takes her medicine without rancor.[9]

The general run of mountain girl, who does not share the pluck, the radical beauty, or love-tragedy of the mountain-flower type, marries early, settles into an unsightly shanty, produces a troop of children, and sinks into the muck of immutable routines. It does not take long to enter the next stage. The mother of Clarsie Giles is "a slovenly, indolent woman, anxious, at the age of forty-five, to assume the prerogatives of advanced years. She had placed all her domestic cares upon the shapely shoulders of her willing daughter, and had betaken herself to the chimney-corner and a pipe." The married mountain woman quickly becomes thin and sallow, with deeply sunken eyes, jutting cheekbones, and a set expression of hopeless melancholy. At an entertainment in Boston a gentleman objected to the apparent incongruity of such unlovely mountain mothers and such enchanting daughters. Miss Murfree retorted *sotto voce*, "Look about you, sir, look about you."[10] Startling authentication of this very point is contained in the closing lines of John Crowe Ransom's "Blue Girls":

> Practice your beauty, blue girls, before it fail; . . .
> It is so frail.
> For I could tell you a story which is true:
> I know a lady with a terrible tongue,
> Blear eyes fallen from blue,
> All her perfections tarnished—and yet it is not long
> Since she was lovelier than any of you.

As often as not the women work in the fields, more industriously than their husbands. Pitiably, they are caught between the forces of contending men and frequently suffer the brunt of the consequences. In time, however, they establish for themselves a kind of hearthside immunity. From this vantage the older crones release incessant streams of shrewd, shrewish comments on affairs of the home or around the Settlemint. They interrupt and derogate everyone. Aggressive, crisp in judgment, they enjoy astonishing toleration from their menfolk. Once in a while a garrulous grandfather arrogates this role, but he inclines to be minutely anecdotal and less caustic. Children do not usurp the center of attention as they do in many subsequent Murfree stories. When noted at all here, they are peripheral groups of "boisterous tow-headed children."

Another cementing element in Miss Murfree's encircled world is its peculiarities of speech. As with the landscape, she amalgamates impressions from several sections. She also pretends that mountaineers of every class consistently speak one dialect. At first Charles Forster Smith, most vigilant critic of her usages, exhorted her indiscriminate mixing of localisms and arbitrary coinages. Later he admitted being too pedantic and placed her with Joel Chandler Harris and George Washington Cable as the best dialect writers of the South.[11]

The base of mountaineer language in the time of her stories was a combination of Anglo-Saxon and Celtic, with Chaucerian overtones; but Miss Murfree incorporated no great number of esoteric expressions. The reader is seldom jogged by utterly unfamiliar locutions, for she favors recognizable words, idioms, and similes from conventional contemporary English and American sources.[12] Whatever her distortions, she succeeds in producing verisimilitude through reproductions of the slow, dry, digressive drawl of the region, deceptively somnolent yet barbed with pungent country wisdom. She employs it patently and excessively, but her most grievous error lies in cacography—the inelegant misspellings accepted by her generation as genuine transcription of colloquial speech and as a legitimate form of humor. Piquant to begin with, it grows tiresome as all unabated idiosyncrasy does. Before long it nullifies much of its value as a characterizing device.

In three of these stories she uses vernacular to dynamic advantage in the opening sentence—a native statement which immediately sets tone, gives an inkling of custom, and points the direction of plot. The best example is her first: "Fur ye see, Mis' Darley, them Harrison folks over yander ter the Cove hev determinated on a dancin' party." For the rest, she falls back on only two words that may give pause ("chouse," "cymlin'") and two that are determinable in context (a mountain range runs "spang up into Virginny," and "plumb catawampus"). Mild malapropism occurs when a mountaineer "hev hed the insurance" to associate with townspeople. "Drag me through hell an' beat me with a soot-bag" has the tune and stride of backland lingo, but "tuk ter the work like a pig ter carrots" and "perlite an' smilin' ez a basket of chips" smell of professional polish.

Despite the exceptional freedom to talk granted the people in these stories, not many escape Miss Murfree's possessive grip and take shape as personalities on their own power. In the manner of earlier nineteenth-century novelists, she furnishes full formal credentials with each character at initial entry into the action. Some few are anticipated by remarks of their familiars, but this introduction does not obviate summary treatment afterward. She overdoes the method of *oratio oblique*, arriving at antecedent and internal determinants of character from an external third-person stance. A man's attributes and psychological development are described in so many words. Looks are equated with qualities. Her nobler people *look* different, *i.e.*, the mountain-flower type. Also, a mountain lad turned lawyer has chiseled Grecian features. There are now and then people with subsurface rumblings, persons with problems not amenable to solution by intoxication or physical violence. While Miss Murfree indicates her belief in a double self and permits some introspection, she continually reverts to exposition rather than self-revelation.

The characters in *In the Tennessee Mountains* are largely

stereotypes. Less than half a dozen can be recalled as individuals. Rick Pearson in "The Dancin' Party" is merely picturesque; Kenyon, a showcase of blunt moral and physical manliness. Mandy Tyler raises expectations of conflict and comedy, but she fades out both as a personality and an activator. Rufus Chadd emerges from the massed background of types as a man torn by inner tumult. "A harrassing sense of doubleness" invests him with vitality absent in the host of mountain mothers and mountain-flower girls who acquiesce mutely to their condition of social and emotional bondage. "The 'Harnt' That Walks Chilhowee" contains three figures who reveal levels of consciousness which go deeper than their narrative and environmental functions: Simon Burney with his awkward, fruitless courtship of a much younger girl, his tender concern for Clarsie's lawbreaking, and his thankless philanthropy; Mrs. Giles with her acidulous tongue, invented folklore, and crafty usurpation of decision-making in the household; Reuben Crabb with his deprived, lonely soul and presumptuous acceptance of gratuities as though they are his due—all give suggestions of subterranean currents, of complexities and contradictions conducive to speculation. Budd Wray undergoes a psychological dilemma, but the hand of Miss Murfree too heavily guides the outcome. Every city man and woman is to some degree a mouthpiece of Miss Murfree's attitudes and opinions—the women keen but shallow, the young men particularly leaden.

III *Mountain Mores*

The powers of routine, inertia, and ignorance shape most of the activities and attitudes of Miss Murfree's mountaineers. So positive are these influences that not even those who leave the mountains are exempt from their dictation, but one notable exception is the opportunist Evander Price who shakes himself clear to his own irreparable injury. The two most noticeable traits of these mountaineers are their sloth and their pride. Completely content with things as they are, the men pass from one day to another as English squires might: hunting, racing horses, drinking, shooting for prizes, telling and retelling tales of their exploits. Only dire emergency can move them to more practical exertion. Intensely individualistic, they carry pride to inordinate lengths; and they are undisposed to combine in enterprise except for avoidance of liquor taxes, which they regard as an intervention in their personal affairs. They acknowledge no superiors, social, moral, or physical, and will resist with their lives any attempts at domination.

Pride infiltrates family feeling, potent and unspoken. Respect for the aged is second nature, and solidity of clan is demonstrated in a supper where four generations—ranging from two to eighty years of age—sit together in unceremonial communism. The effect is one of continuity and homogeneity, visible in their absorption with events of the past (possibly as compensation for the scanty happenings of the present) and in xenophobia. The latter takes on two contrary semblances. Stemming from their insulated existence, they view every unaccounted stranger with suspicion, if not hostility; anyone may be a revenue agent or an informer in the pay of the government. No questions are asked and none answered. Even the nearby valley people are held to be "cur'ous critters," and the mountaineers become "sifflicated" in lowland air. Yet, stemming from family pride, they respond with instant and total hospitality to all, including doubtful "furriners" who come to their door. Food, lodging, or aid is extended ungrudgingly. Guests get the best the house can offer and are accompanied by expressions of regret as they leave. Privacy of background is inviolate; a stranger need only tell as much as he chooses about himself.

Violence is the primary principle of reaction and a customary occurrence. Under the slow talk and the sluggish gestures throb currents of ungovernable emotions. Stabbings and shootings are conventional. Blood is no deterrent; passions run red. Revenge is a personal prerogative, and murder is planned as casually as one might review yesterday's weather. A mother foresees impassively the extermination of her son by a bandit gang: "They'll slaughter the boy." Women develop stoic acceptance of their place as chattel. Beaten and slashed by their drunken husbands, they loyally defend them from retaliation by male relatives. Any demonstration of courtesy or filial affection is out of order, and women traditionally refrain from displays of feminine delicacy in public. Spinsters are openly condemned and pitied, as are slight or redhaired women.

Originally Presbyterians, the mountaineers have gravitated to evangelical creeds propagated by the flamboyant circuit riders who seasonally breach their remote borders. Eagerly they await the next visitation and the "bloody-minded sermons." The mountaineers interpret Scripture literally and subscribe to Calvinistic predestination. The resultant of these periodic revivals is a moral code strict in statement, lax in observance, and relative in values. As against murder, a venial infraction, dancing and gambling are grave transgressions directly punishable by God. Murder contemplated over the stealing of a mere bay filly is censured, but "ef it war the roan three-year-old now, 'twould be different." In a conflict between earthly and heavenly criteria the response is overt piety and sly expediency. The mountaineers are careful not to jeopardize future reward for present profit—however, why not try for the best of both worlds? For the most part, all laws except those against bootlegging are obeyed. And with uncomplicated trustfulness they expect immunity from prosecution by the county attorney as their due for having elected him.

Fearless in physical pursuits, they are incorrigibly superstitious. Life in a state close to nature fraught with inexplicable movements, noises, and consequences has bequeathed a repository of lore about human "harnts," screeching owls, and prophecy by ritual. The devil is ubiquitous by night and to him is ascribed all prodigies and most mishaps. On the mountaineers' calendar the day of judgment has an indeterminate but rubrical place. Mrs. Harrison, for instance, fears that the house will fall on them as a reproof of their wickedness in dancing.

IV Contrast of Cultures

Out of this locale, these people, and their practices, Miss Murfree embodies a plausible world in which comedy, pathos, politics, grief, love, religion, and brutality intermix in proportions determined by the special temperament of this special generation. The stories in In the Tennessee Mountains contain only rudiments of her fuller construct, but they provide infallible guidelines to her subsequent manner. The materials, techniques, and themes of the stories that comprise this volume leave no doubt that she perceives the impelling forces of mountaineer life and that she sympathizes with her subjects. They also indicate that she could never be much more than a responsive stranger in a country too crude for her ingrained sensitivity.

The ruling method of management in five of these eight stories is a contrast of urban and rustic cultures. The first story, in point of publication, most nearly approximates her own experience. The central altercation in "The Dancin' Party at Harrison's Cove" occurs between two mountaineers, but it also involves directly and indirectly summer visitors from the resort hotel at New Helvetia Springs. Mrs. Johns, a mountain wife whose chief

occupation is to sell Indian peaches to the city vacationers, returns to the hotel one day to secure medicines for her ailing
husband. She goes into a long account of her son's imminent
danger—he insists on attending the dancing party in defiance
of Rick Pearson's threat to kill him if he does. Her sallow face,
expressionless voice, and shabby, faded calico are juxtaposed to
Mrs. Darley's plump round arms, flowing black dress ("all fur-
belows and flounces"), and animated manner. They make "a
wonderful contrast," says Miss Murfree, illustrating further the
enormous cleft that separates their speech and social discretions.
An intermediate standard is inserted later when the Harrison
girls enjoy a brush with sophistication at Cheatham's Cross-
Roads and develop a desire to emulate "fashion." Pitiful by Mrs.
Darley's estimation, the Cross-Roads is a filter through which the
most backward may acquire a modicum of metropolitan style.
Male qualities come under profounder scrutiny. Ambrose Kenyon, the city man who by raw physical courage prevents gunplay
between young Johns and Pearson, elicits respect from the mountaineers because they mistake him for a preacher—he is a lay
reader—and tally his dour visage and platitudinous moralisms
with those of a circuit rider. An outsider, he would probably
have been slain except that he stills the dissonance between town
and mountain by evincing an indigenous virtue: "He had grit
enough to belong to the gang." Pearson espies in him "a parallel
of his own belligerent and lawless spirit." Country courage in
whatever dress is country courage.

In "The Star in the Valley" Miss Murfree again favors the
ruder culture. Reginald Chevis, a sensitive city sportsman camp-
ing in the mountains, looks down on Celia Shaw "with a mingled
pity for her dense ignorance, her coarse surroundings, her low
station." He is appalled when she encourages her father and his
friends to drink to excess. When he learns later that she did so
in order to gain time enough to warn a man they intended to
murder, "he began to have a glimmering perception that despite
all his culture, his sensibility, his yearnings toward humanity, he
was not so high a thing in the scale of being." Miss Murfree
rates bedrock virtues above finishing-school manners, and she
is reasonably proud that "differences of caste are absolutely un-
known to the independent mountaineers." Chevis prides himself
on this humanity, Celia actually has it; he talks about it, she
acts. When she dies not long after her mission in the snowstorm,
she assumes, for Chevis, the symbolic status of a star.

Miss Murfree now embraces a wider scope of comparisons. In "The Star" Chevis' companion Ned Varney does not figure strongly enough to constitute an attitude, but in "The Romance of Sunrise Rock" John Cleaver and Fred Trelawney project two distinct reactions of the city to the country: Trelawney is sympathetic; Cleaver, inimical. In the byplay of development, the good and bad of both ways of life are weighed—and the simpler existence comes off better once more. The contrast begins on a deceptive note when the native is referred to as a "hairy animal" and Cleaver as "this fine young fellow." Within minutes, however, he drops his unexpressed disdain of country dullness, admitting that "Greek and Latin do not altogether avail." As for his elaborate edifice of education, why, the happy sheep-farmer does not need it. Through Selina Teake, a sad and lovely mountain-flower, the onus of frivolity is placed squarely on girls who pursue "society." Trelawney shrinks at what Selina might think of them, and Miss Murfree launches a long self-incriminating satire on the uselessness of fashionable education which enables city women "to interject commonplace French phrases into their daily conversation, and render their prattle an affront to good taste." (Like most dilettante ruralists, she derogates polite attainments while never really abandoning them; she feels secretly superior in her possession of them. In short order, ironically, she interjects a French and a Latin expression.) Regardless of paradox, she makes her overt point in the resolution of Trelawney and Cleaver. Trelawney decides to remain in the mountains, sheds the skepticism of his college days, and acquires calm and strength from his environment "very like the comfort of religion." On the other hand, Cleaver returns to the city, is surrounded by an envious crowd that disparages his success, and lives bleakly in the knowledge of their pettiness.

Using a *Tom Jones* technique of cross-sectioning society, Miss Murfree presents a new set of variants in "Drifting Down Lost Creek." Cynthia Ware's pilgrimage to Sparta to effect the release of Evander Price from jail permits views of life on the mountain, along the sparsely settled valley area, and in the county seat. The differences are less striking than those between mountain and metropolis; but Cynthia, in perfect harmony on the mountain, is the object of suspicion on the road and of pity in the town. Like all good mountaineers, she is out of place away from the mountain. By the time she arrives in Sparta, "all her grace and pliant swaying languor [are] lost in convulsive, awkward haste and a feeble, jerky gait." Only after she glimpses the mountain again does she feel "the supreme exaltation" and recover her poise. The lover she rescues rejects her, adopts town life, and marries a town woman. Once an ambitious inventor, he settles down to a routine job and is harassed by lurking doubts of his powers. He is proud of his wife's "school l'arnin'," but she considers him uncouth and depressing. On a brief visit back to the mountain he is no longer capable of seeing its beauties, only weather signs. He has lost the better girl and the more wholesome place. In the beginning the mountain "stands against the west like a barrier. It seemed to Cynthia Ware that nothing which went beyond this barrier ever came back again." Prophetically, this is the story of her loss. Evander crosses the barrier, grows hard and calculating. His native quality is totally vitiated.

In the return-of-the-native theme of "Electioneerin' on Big Injun Mounting," Miss Murfree sets up yet another scheme of contrast, buttressed by a psychological conflict. Rufus Chadd, a mountain dweller until he is twenty, moves to town, becomes a lawyer, and is elected district attorney. His native instincts and primal experiences help him outstrip city antagonists. Gradually, constant contact with the worst phases of human nature harden him; he becomes a pitiless prosecutor. When he returns to his old bailiwick to campaign for re-election, he discovers that his book talk and store clothes repel his former neighbors. He is attacked and almost killed by a vicious bully, Isaac Boker. When Chadd declines to identify Boker as his assailant and demands that he be freed, sentiment flows back in Chadd's favor. Like Kenyon in "The Dancin' Party," Chadd demonstrates an indigenous virtue and wins deference. Although a civil officer, he pays allegiance to the mountain code of silence. (His motivation goes deeper, but the mountaineers accept at face value his refusal to inform.) Such reversion to regional mores is proof sufficient to the mountaineers that Chadd is still one of them. He is the obverse of Evander Price for, in this struggle between old and new, the old prevails. Chadd is eventually re-elected by the heaviest majority ever polled on Big Injun Mounting.

Of the three remaining stories in *In the Tennessee Mountains* only "A-Playin' of Old Sledge at the Settlemint" offers no specific regional oppositions; in "Over on the T'other Mounting" Miss Murfree arbitrarily injects the opinion that the "magnificent pageant of the four seasons . . . was a gracious recompense for the spectacular privileges of civilization," thus aligning herself

again with the mountains. And she appends this clearly inconsequent aphorism as last paragraph to "The 'Harnt' That Walks
Chilhowee": "The grace of culture is, in its way, a fine thing,
but the best that art can do—the polish of a gentleman—is hardly
equal to the best that Nature can do in her higher moods."

V *Point of View and Diction*

One of the severely divisive factors in these stories is Miss
Murfree's inability to establish a point of view and thereafter
maintain it consistently or shift it strategically to best advantage.
Her principal perspective is that of a spectator on the perimeter
of the action who is obviously not autochthonous but acquainted
with the ways of the natives and inclined to appreciate their
finer, often invisible endowments. Her tendency in this role of
overseer is to manage people and affairs too firmly and to deny
them development in their own essential directions. When, as
in "The Dancin' Party," she permits a mountaineer to divulge
the basic situation, she invariably relegates this narrator to a far
corner and resumes control. The fracture that results is disturbing to the mood of unity, for Miss Murfree cannot refrain from
extraneous commentary about the characters or course of events.

As a literary artist she makes every conscious effort to enter
the nerve center of this strange world, but her training as a
Southern lady simply will not let her. The closest she comes is
arm's length. In a burst of spontaneous approbation, she exclaims: "Here are the true republicans!" or indeed, "Here are
the only aristocrats!" Yet this forthright glorification cannot can-
cel out the insidious reappearance of the phrase "these mountaineers"—and worse, "these people"—in her less guarded, less
rhapsodic moments. Frequently, she emits inadvertent condescension through surrogates such as Mrs. Darley in "The Dancin'
Party," Reginald Chevis in "The Star in the Valley," Rufus
Chadd in "Electioneerin' on Big Injun Mounting," and John
Cleaver in "The Romance of Sunrise Rock." Chevis, for instance,
reflects the attitude of patrician to pleb that creeps willy-nilly
into all Miss Murfree's mountain stories when he lifts his hat
"with that punctilious courtesy which he made a point of according to persons of low degree." Did Miss Murfree realize the import of her offhand remark that "even a 'mounting' woman is
susceptible of the sting of wounded pride," including the obloquy
of the single quotation marks? She approaches the brink of self-
analysis when she wonders whether Cleaver is a snob because

he sees the mountaineers as bull-headed, ludicrous, and unkempt. Soon, however, she is back regarding the scene as a stage and herself as an applauding spectator.

A second disjunctive practice is Miss Murfree's truly extraordinary use of formal language. O. Henry dabbles in grotesque polysyllables for the pure fun or irony they provide, but she sets them down in utter seriousness. Fairly sparing to begin with, she progressively increases the number of arcane words and phrases in later stories and novels. In these stories the reader stumbles over such horrendous Latinisms as "febrifuge," "interfulgent," "exercitations," "stellular," and a "fulvous-tinted" deer. French falls trippingly into the text and sits cheek by jowl with Italian: "stupendous alto-relievo in silver repoussé." Jogging country dancers are "votaries of Terpsichore." The academic resonance and the halting rhythms are incompatible with the coarse fluidity of native speech. The ornate adjectives only make natural splendor a gaudy spectacle.

The contrast of elevated and corrupt language undoubtedly helps to accentuate the great gap between the worlds of city and mountain, but its effect upon tone and continuity is destructive. In "Over on the T'other Mounting" a long vulgate passage runs without transition into a stylized depiction of "a subtile amethystine mist," and is succeeded by "Waal" and another expanse of dialect. Even more harsh is the collision of the first and second paragraphs of "The Romance of Sunrise Rock." "Moons waxed and waned; nations rose and fell; centuries came and went. And still it faced the east, and still, undimmed by storm and time, it reiterated the miracle and prophecy of the rising sun." This grandiose description of Sunrise Rock collapses abruptly against the jagged sharpness of Selina's, " 'Twar painted by the Injuns,—that's what I hev always hearn tell." The shock of disparity is out of proportion to any intended impression. Like melodrama, it tempts the reader to laugh in the wrong places.

VI *Themes*

Most of the stories in *In the Tennessee Mountains* portray the unrequited sacrifice of a patient, noble soul or the rise to moral heroism of others less worthy. Through the exercise of pity and terror, and through interpolated homily, all the stories seek to inculcate lessons of devotion and feelings of emulation. By far the dominant theme, however, is that of common humanity: the proposition that human nature is the same everywhere regardless of birth, condition, or degree of refinement. In "The Dancin' Party" Miss Murfree expounds this truism on three levels. (1) Mandy Tyler and her city counterparts are sisters under the skin —the prospect of a dance stirs "the same sentiments in her heart and mind as do the more ambitious germans and kettledrums" in lowland girls; Mrs. Darley apprehends the "absurd resemblance" between the social prattle of mountaineers and that of her own circle. (2) Mr. Harrison is as acutely aware of the need to provide opportunities for his daughters to meet eligible young men, as is any father at the fashionable watering-places. (3) In Kenyon's intrepid behavior Pearson acknowledges "a parallel of his own belligerent and lawless spirit."

Despite their diametric sensibilities of city and mountain, Varney and Bates in "The Star in the Valley" respond accordantly to Chevis' idealized "star." In Miss Murfree's own amateur way, Chevis notes the odd dress and appearance of the mountaineers, their grainy patois, their shiftlessness and mental poverty, and takes pleasure in watching "the development of the common human attributes in their peculiar and primitive state of society." In the end he discovers that "fine feelings" are as much the property of untutored instinct as they are of cultivated intellect.

In "The Romance of Sunrise Rock" Cleaver is shown to lack the touch of common humanity and foolishly pities Trelawney in his ultimate adoption of bucolic existence. In comic analogy to Judy O'Grady and the Colonel's lady, "the unsophisticated mother of the mountains" and "the expert tactician of a drawing-room" are declared to be equally adept in foiling the courting schemes of unapproved suitors in "Drifting Down Lost Creek." Pathos wields a heavy hand in reawakening Chadd's buried sympathies in "Electioneerin' on Big Injun Mounting": the horror-stricken eyes of Mrs. Boker, who is regularly beaten by her husband but remains dumbly loyal, recall a predicament Chadd once shared, and he does not incriminate Boker.

Miss Murfree plays a variation on the theme of the dreary, inarticulate, repressed, and resigned lives led by the mountaineers, with or without culture-contrast or common-humanity accompaniment. The traditional autocracy of the mountain male is deeply indoctrinated. Mrs. Johns epitomizes the mountain women whose mouths open to scream but no sound issues. Violence and abuse are their way of life, and they accept male supremacy with only occasional demur. Mrs. Johns takes the probable

murder of her son as a matter of course. Celia Shaw cannot protest effectively and therefore resorts to subterfuge—and dies.
Mrs. Peel, also the victim of a wife beater, stands heartstricken
between husband and vengeful brother. Mrs. Boker appeals
mutely for clemency for her brutish spouse. Cynthia Ware suffers emotional rather than bodily injury from the man she loves,
assimilating her abandonment without regret or resentment. In
these mountains, woman's lot is one of tragic suppression.[13]

Nobility is imminent in both sexes, although a crisis is usually
required to bring it out in the men. Pearson flaunts his with
bravado when faced down; Chadd reacts to pathos; Simon
Burney swallows his defeat in courtship and extends every
benevolence to surly Reuben Crabb; at the moment of long-
awaited retribution, Budd Wray disclaims his hatred and withholds punishment of his faithless former sweetheart. Three girls
demonstrate innate nobility through self-effacing sacrifice. Selina
Teake gives no indication of her true love until it is too late.
Both Celia Shaw and Cynthia Ware undertake pilgrimages in
which they accomplish moral victory but lose more than they
gain. Celia perseveres through a vicious storm to warn the Peel
family of coming danger to their lives and loses her life. After
a long journey reminiscent of Jeanie Dean's in *The Heart of
Midlothian*, Cynthia secures a pardon for her lover and loses
her love.[14]

"Electioneerin' on Big Injun Mounting" asserts through Rufus
Chadd that you can take the man out of the mountain but you
cannot take the mountain out of the man, while "Drifting Down
Lost Creek" illustrates through Evander Price that this does not
hold invariably. The theme of man's puny, transitory existence
as compared with nature's grandeur and permanence comes
through strongly in "The Star in the Valley," "The Romance of
Sunrise Rock," "Over on the T'other Mounting," and "Drifting
Down Lost Creek." "The Romance of Sunrise Rock" stresses the
helplessness of human beings in the hands of sportive, undeviating Fate: "What chaotic sarcasm in this mysterious ordering of
events."

While all the stories have appropriate lessons attached to
them, if not implicit in their unfolding, "A-Playin' of Old Sledge
at the Settlemint" has the lineaments of a morality play. Two
elderly men, like Old Testament prophets, try to ward off the
baneful consequences of card playing. They invoke Judgment
Day, the infernal fire and brimstone, call on the gamblers to

repent their ways, predict for them the downfall of Jonah. The storekeeper fills the role of the Voice of Reason, asseverating that they have gone too far and that it *must* be sinful. The drama of the obsessive card game is played out in a macabre atmosphere of unholy shrieks and echoes emanating from the dark forest, not unlike the arena of evil in Hawthorne's "Young Goodman Brown." This howling hell of terror and derision—signifying the forces of God and nature—has no more influence upon the contestants than the objections made by men. The infatuated gamblers move outdoors when the tallow dip flickers out and continue their mad card game by a pine-knot fire and the steady white glare of the moon—a scene recalling Wildeve and Diggory Venn passionately casting by the phosphorescent light of glowworms in Hardy's *The Return of the Native*. Miss Murfree roundly berates gambling and desire for revenge, but she ranks them among the lesser sins. Greed masquerading as love is more sordid and corrosive.

VII *Intonation and Structure*

The awesome immensity of the mountains fills these stories with a sense of infinite space and slow, timeless movement. Under eternal skies the natives live out drab lives, take without complaint the buffets of fate, and thank whatever God there be for their immortal souls. Not all, however, is wonder and gloom. Through the unwinding days and nights they find in their work and in their sport occasions to jest, to laugh. They make amusing analogies between themselves and their animals, domestic or wild. Coquettes twit their suitors unmercifully. Men and women jibe coarsely at each other. And their dialect, though natural to them, provides another dimension of comedy for the reader.

Rustic jocularity is not to Miss Murfree's own taste. She prefers the slimmer blade of drawing-room wit. Standing above and to one side of the defenseless mountaineers, she insistently jabs them with glittering ironies. She creates discordance by interposing remarks about the alleged superiorities of city over country, by coupling the potency of mountains with women's suffrage, by grinning over some yokel blunder. It is all kindly meant, and the irony heightens because she does not realize its end effect.

She develops irony of situation in the tensions of choice between mundane and spiritual values, in native rationalizations of crimes, in verifying the uselessness of bookish education in a rural plight, and in exposing a fearsome 'harnt' as a frightened, one-armed sniveler. She exploits irony of theme in "The Romance of Sunrise Rock" (Selina loves the wrong man and Cleaver never knows how happy Trelawney is); in "Electioneerin' on Big Injun Mounting" (the mountaineers vote for Chadd for the wrong reasons); in "A-Playin' of Old Sledge" (the community makes undeserved presumptions about Wray's renunciation of revenge); in "Over on the T'other Mounting" (Britt's attempt to murder Hoxie leads to reconcilement of their long-standing feud); in "The Star in the Valley" and "Drifting Down Lost Creek" (one girl dies and one girl recedes into herself while neither male protagonist ever comprehends their pathetic intensity). In this last category of ironic usage Miss Murfree succeeds in implementing her theme of common humanity least pretentiously.

Miss Murfree did not subscribe to Poe's conception of the short story as a vignette of single accumulating effect or a single incident with decisive impact upon character. Says Fred Lewis Pattee: "Strictly speaking, her short stories are not short stories at all save in the one element of shortness. She records simple, everyday incidents in their natural sequence and stops when the space allotted to her has been filled. She moves leisurely from incident to incident in a monotonous vacuity of mountain life, as a minutely written journal might move."[15] Sarah Orne Jewett, who used to "nibble all round her stories like a mouse," refers to Miss Murfree's "big" stories. They are in many cases, now and later, two stories indeterminately fused; they are aborted or condensed novels. The bastard term *novelette* would suit a good number. They offer excessive antecedent data, digress too far afield, and go on long after the unifying action is concluded.

"Drifting Down Lost Creek" is an outstanding example of Miss Murfree's disregard of prescriptive principles. It is less a short story, even in length (seventy-nine pages), than an attenuated novel. She does not focus on a single turbulent or understated incident for a flash of insight; instead, she presents a developmental chronicle of the changes wrought in the lives of two young lovers over the course of a decade. She imparts an appearance of unity to this domestic tragedy of Puritan stoicism by repeated correspondence of humanity and nature—Cynthia's life and the purposeless drift of leaves on the surface of Lost Creek—and through the cyclic effect of this basic symbol in the opening and closing paragraphs. But the prolongation of Cynthia's ordeal and Miss Murfree's obtrusive explanations diminish its power as a short story.

"The Star in the Valley" proceeds with deliberate, convincing intensification from a static scene of idealistic meditation to a static scene of realistic threats to a kinetic scene of escape and pursuit. Miss Murfree then allows the story to strangulate in turgid recapitulation and explication, rendered unnecessary by her fugal interplay of the "star" in the valley (Cynthia Ware), the "star" on the mountain (Reginald Chevis), and the first ascendant star of evening. "The Romance of Sunrise Rock" takes long in starting, progresses to an exciting height of hallucination, then similarly flags into a redundant epilogue.

Mrs. Johns's introduction to the evolving climax of "The Dancin' Party" constitutes a narrative frame which Miss Murfree might better have extended to infold the entire story or not have used at all. The vital, central duel is thus seen through the screen of an omniscient tenderfoot rather than through the eyes of an implicated, native witness. Suspense is capably broached and upheld in the manner of Hardy's "The Three Strangers" by a dynamic series of three contrastive entrances. Pearson and his armed comrades do not disturb the dancers, for they are all insiders. Kenyon gives momentary pause to the fiddler and the dancers, for he is an outsider who stirs conscience and raises discomfortable possibilities. His reassuring bromides restore equanimity and prepare the scene for a drastic dislocation. Johns's appearance at the door stops the music and brings the dancing to a standstill, for he carries the spark of abeyant catastrophe.

"A-Playin' of Old Sledge" is also based on a vivid central duel, but Miss Murfree somewhat bedims its vigor by distending it into a moral application. Wray's psychological reflexes, plausible in the card game, become improbable in his cancellation of revenge. Miss Murfree's proclivity to follow more than one thread in a short story is again visible in "The 'Harnt' That Walks Chilhowee," but she strikes a highly satisfying balance between the pathos of Reuben Crabb's life-in-death quandary and the comedy of a December-May rivalry in courtship. With its overlay of forest shadows, local superstitions, pithy characters, domestic genre details—and Miss Murfree's forbearance as narrator—it is in so many respects the best story in this volume.

Within its formal frame, "Over on the T'other Mounting" has

the loose weave, circuitous pattern, and primary colors of a folk tale. Miss Murfree adopts the anecdotal method of arriving at the core incident and leaves promise at the conclusion of further tangents to be explored. After accepting the first premise that witches fired T'other Mounting, the subsequent adventures and ironies follow as logically as any deadpan tomfoolery. Violence and hilarity blend with the supernatural and the vernacular in a tale without dominant didactic motive except for reasserting the inequality of power in the partnership of man and nature.

The resolution of "Electioneerin' on Big Injun Mounting" comes nearest to matching the type most frequently encountered in the contemporary short story. Miss Murfree relinquishes none of her ceremonious procedures, but cuts through cleanly to a throbbing nerve of motivation. Chadd's decision not to testify against his assailant Boker is determined by one fleeting glimpse of piteous Mrs. Boker standing in the doorway; his experience tears away the accretions of town life from his heart and opens a flow of restorative group memory. Neither the preliminary or posterior apparatus obscures the validity of this instinctive reversion, which marks a point of rare discernment in Miss Murfree's early interpretation of mountaineer behavior.

VIII   *Later Mountain Short Stories*

After *In the Tennessee Mountains* Miss Murfree published some fifteen stories in this category (three others with Civil War components are discussed under that head). Seven of the stories appeared in the period 1885-1895; the others, between 1908-1920. Although she introduces few new elements, she perceptibly strengthens her rhetorical and structural techniques. There is less emphasis on the contrast of cultures; she presents the mountaineers more often in situations undefiled by outside influences; and she more often dispenses with her *alter ego* commentator from the city. Although she continues to trespass as author-critic, she moves in point of view closer to her subjects; she is more the prober than the thrilled spectator. If anything, she is more persistently pietistic, and she inclines more readily to the hoax. After a decade of toiling in other literary vineyards, she returns to the mountains. In this last era she re-creates the scenic prodigies, the unorthodox natives, the romance and outlawry of the region; and she conjures up again the tinted names of the mountains, and Colbury, Cross-Roads, Kildeer County, Tomahawk Creek. Nevertheless, the feeling of strain in the stories is due to a manifest attempt to recapture the magic of the old, successful formula. Sadly, the once heady compound has lost its potency.

Five stories are informed with the spirit of Christmas and ring slight variations on the gospel of man's regeneration through love. They all turn on the same device of feud or ill-will melted by the sight of a Tennessee mountain recrudescence of the Child in the Manger. The repetitive quality of this determining scene and the excess of sentimentality is accounted for by the fact that each appeared in the December issue of a national periodical and was undoubtedly contrived with that specific occasion in mind.

The hatred of one man for another in "Way Down Lonesome Cove" (1885) feeds on rivalry in love and a stolen horse. The second circumstance rekindles the feud which had arisen over the first. Gunfighting ensues. When Luke Todd comes to kill Tobe Gryce, he discovers him hiding in an abandoned saltpeter cave with his little daughter and the horse. Todd's trigger finger is stayed by "A soft aureola with gleaming radiations, a low, shadowy chamber, a beast feeding from a manger, and within it a child's golden head." His heart gives a great throb: "Somehow he was smitten to his knees. Christmas Eve!" The objective correlative of child, animal, and holiday wreaks this somewhat disputable effect upon a hardened mountaineer bent on murder. The conversion is too abrupt to be convincing—Bret Harte's "The Luck of Roaring Camp" with a Christmas confection. Far more credible is the poignant confrontation between Mrs. Gryce, once an "azalea-like girl," now faded by unceasing work and worry, and the younger Mrs. Todd. Here Miss Murfree presents with unusual cogency two stages in the metamorphosis of a mountain-flower to a crone. Mrs. Gryce sees in Mrs. Todd a vision of herself when beautifully young; Mrs. Todd espies in Mrs. Gryce's face the forecast of wrinkles to come in her own. Another standby in many stories and novels—the monarch baby who tyrannizes everyone within the ken of his clenched fist and defiant stare—also makes a first full-fledged entrance in Gryce's daughter, the "Colonel," who is a cut more obstinate, imperious, and greedy than most of her breed. Knowing Miss Murfree's inveterate fondness for irony, one wonders at the utilization of this little Tartar as a Christ likeness, as well as the names Gryce (Christ) and Todd (God).

Sentimentality and stereotypes overwhelm this story. Miss Murfree lapses ineptly into the historical present tense. She reveals prior events through flashback conversation, a creditable technique except that Mrs. Gryce recalls the details to her mother, who must surely have been familiar with them. And yet this story has saving graces in the scene between the two wives and in such symbolic touches as the sinister light from the flares of the mob falling now and then on the holly bushes, a provocative inverse prefiguration of the happy denouement.

Discounting some minor changes, "His 'Day in Court'" (1887) is a facsimile of the foregoing story but is, perhaps, less believable. This feud has extended over several generations of killings and maimings, includes all members of the Quimbey and Kittredge families, and is currently bitter, whereas Todd and Gryce had never fought and Todd had not seen Mrs. Gryce in ten years. Renewing the Montague-Capulet heresy, Absalom Kittredge marries Evelina Quimbey. When they have a falling out, Absalom kidnaps their baby. Forced by court order to restore the boy to his mother, Absalom creeps up to the Quimbey home one night intent on stealing him back. Evelina had placed the golden-haired child temporarily in its piggin on the straw-covered ground in the stable, surrounded by cattle and sheep. The over-all grouping reminds Absalom that this night is Christmas Eve. He steals away quietly, the Nativity scene having had its due effect upon his vindictive heart.

Miss Murfree revives every cliché of Christmas magazine fiction, even alluding to the Babe in the Manger and the Star of Bethlehem; but again there are aspects of excellence. As in the preceding story, she brings her knowledge of legal technicalities skillfully into play; and she lifts the curtain on a fascinating, populous "underfoot world" of children, dogs, poultry, and other oddities on the kitchen floor only dimly significant to adults. Several short scenes, done with faultless restraint, have a power greater than the totality: the gurgling child captivating the huge, brute Quimbeys (like "The Luck" grabbing Kentuck's finger); old Quimbey's vilification of Absalom in the courtroom; the reunion of Evelina and her father, and his gentle, diplomatic threat of murder to mediator Joe Boyd. Old Mrs. Kittredge creates an unforgettable impression of classic tragedy and remorse after she permits Evelina to carry off the baby: "She was terrified by her own deed, and cowered under Absalom's wrath. . . . She flung her apron over her head, and sat still and silent—a monumental figure—among them."

"Who Crosses Storm Mountain?" (1908) is shallow anecdote

exemplifying the Christian lesson of peace on earth, goodwill toward men but this time in O. Henry farce-irony vein. The lost baby of one feudist, Gilhooley, is picked up by a drunkard, placed in a mail pouch (the presumptive manger), and then unknowingly adopted by the second feudist, Petrie. When identity is established, Gilhooley comes to claim the child. The two sworn enemies—mollified by his immaculate innocence—patch up their differences and are last seen on all fours, barking for the infant's delectation. Miss Murfree's disposition to pontificate, to give ex officio explanations of motive, and to underscore theme explicitly destroy movement and humor.

"The Riddle of the Rocks" (1886) is, by contrast, solemn in tone and embraces a fundamental concern of the mountaineers—prophecy based on signs. The feud, children, and Christmas Eve play habitual parts in the eventuation of this story; but all are subordinated to the arduous struggle of a man to regain his faith. Roger Purdee, a totally ignorant herder gifted with "the fires of imagination," is sincerely confident in his ability to read the Scriptural messages imprinted on two blocks of sandstone which he and others believe are the tables of the Law flung down from the mountain top by Moses. He achieves impressive local reputation by passing on the revelations of these hieroglyphs. Grinnell, an envious neighbor whose family has feuded with the Purdees for many years, convinces the community that the alleged runes are no more than the erosions of weather and the depredations of worms. Purdee undergoes sickening disillusionment, withdraws into deep depression, and broods uncommunicatively for days. His internal agonies are interrupted by Grinnell's claim to his lands. It turns out, ironically, that Grinnell's house and farm are on Purdee's ground. With revenge at hand he is reminded of the season by a glimpse of the beguiling Grinnell child and sheep huddling in the door of a rude stable. Christ-like, he forgives his persistent persecutor. Through this magnanimity Purdee's shaken faith is restored. Once again he begins to descry a familiar letter, a developing word, and finally the phrase "Peace on earth, good will to men" carved in the rocks.

The trend and upshot of this story are not forced as in the others. Purdee's regenerative act is solidly motivated in his strong religious nature. The Nativity tableau merely prompts him to behave according to his principles; it does not precipitously reverse a lifetime of malice (as in previous cases). Miss Murfree's desire to tell two stories at a time occludes a profounder view of Purdee's ordeal. As she approaches intimate commitment with his ruminations, the exigencies of the feud break in and she veers off on another tack, the emphasis reverting to action rather than characterization. Although the two threads have a common denominator that in the end connects them, the psychology of Purdee's revivification gets short shrift and the story suffers a sense of integral disunity.

Miss Murfree endows the Tennessee mountains with height and mystery of universal stature through these implications of Biblical miracle and revelation. Purdee's belief—shared by many others—that the Old Testament prophets roamed these mountains and that the Lord spoke to Moses in the Great Smokies invests them with awe more primal than that inspired by ephemeral "harnts." Shelley's "Ozymandias" comes to mind when Miss Murfree sets man's brief contumacious moment against nature's impervious, limitless dominion.

She occasionally discharges ponderous sarcasms to belittle native affectations (referring to one man as "the advanced thinker" and never dignifying him with a name), but in general her witticisms are less pointedly directed from one class to the weaknesses of another class. Through the spontaneous affection of the Grinnell and Purdee children she testifies that they have "not the sense enough to know anything about hereditary enemies," that society perpetuates the very prejudices it so piously deprecates. Adroitly too she links the themes of feud and faith: "With the ramrod of his gun he sought to follow the fine tracings of the letters writ by the finger of the Lord on the stone tables."

She tries to resuscitate this fine combination of animus and conversion in "His Christmas Miracle" (1911), a retelling of the grasshopper-ant fable. She succeeds in establishing a firm basis for thrifty Jubal Kennedy's change of heart toward the improvident, lovable Bedell family, so well in fact that the replica of the nativity scene is wholly inutile. Kennedy, a thoroughgoing philistine, cannot realize he has witnessed two miracles—the Bedells and their house spared utter destruction when it slides over the precipice; his own selfless heroism in their behalf—and is still hankering for an abrogation of natural law as the story ends. To be sure that the implied doctrine is not lost, Miss Murfree declares sententiously that "The kingdom o' Christ is a spiritual kingdom"; and faith, not works, is the key to the miracle of existence.

Politics vies with religion as a claimant of the mountaineers' attention. Elections give them an unassailably egoistic moment of glory during which their favor is sought and their opinions solicited. "The Casting Vote" (1893) derives its drama from a deadlocked election and a perfidious brother. Confined to these elements, this account could have been an effective one of local attitudes and passions. Unfortunately, Miss Murfree disregards every restriction of the short story and instead creates what amounts to a skimpy novel. Action preceding and following the crisis is everlasting, and numerous other thematic considerations crowd the main issue. The story starts out to be a Christian parable on the texts of honor thy brother and turn the other cheek. Soon it deviates into a tangle of familiar bypaths.

Justus Hoxon is an all-sacrificing, all-suffering Christ, as the anagram of *just* and *Jesus* in his first name would indicate. He has surrendered his own ambitions in order to bring up his brother Walter and is now electioneering for him. In remuneration, Walter steals and marries his sweetheart Theodosia, a vain, vacillating mountain-flower without the usual martyr complex. Walter loses the election when the deciding voter hears of his unprincipled behavior. The couple returns to the mountains; he becomes a slothful drunkard, she a dowdy crone. Justus dismisses thoughts of revenge, takes a job as night watchman in a city factory, and spends his time conning the sky for another sight of the comet that blazed at him on election night. Miss Murfree appears to place immense symbolic weight on this fleeting body but, as in the novel *His Vanished Star*, the reader finds it difficult to decode its relation with the major theme beyond the vague implication that God's eye is twinkling down on good Justus. The sky is an open scroll from which, she says, "all men of receptive soul . . . have read there of the mystery of the infinite, of the order and symmetry of the plan of creation, of the proof of the existence of a God." We are now far afield from the original thesis that Walter, somewhat like Hollis in "Taking the Blue Ribbon," wins the cheapest prize while losing his marvelous brother and the election. There is certain satisfaction in the poetic quality of retributive justice: goodness is rewarded, and evil is permitted to punish itself. Justus prospers serenely in his new environment while Walter and Theodosia come to pieces quickly in material squalor that matches their moral flabbiness.

Miss Murfree's proneness to see landscape with the eyes of a painter is beautifully exhibited. "The scene was like some great painting . . . so elaborate and perfect in the coloring of the curves of purple, and amethyst, and blue mountains afar off." But there is a point where her romantic propensity gives way to the realistic: "where the rail fence drew the line of demarkation, Art seemed to fail." Nature is paradisic; man, his hovels and chattel, a blot on perfection. Discreetly she adds a human figure or two against this delicately vistaed Hudson River-school backdrop, blending when it is the mountain-flower girl, discordant when it is the utilitarian backwoodsman. Thus, despite the patent estheticism of her concept, the final effect is one of mystic intercommunication between nature and natives and author and reader. In this instance, at least, the peevish ejaculation of the New York *Times* (February 24, 1895)—"picture, picture, always picture"—is misdirected.

Miss Murfree is supposed to have written this eighty-page story in one evening, which may explain some of its weaknesses and baldly repetitive designs.

Two stories revolve around the accepted vocation of bootlegging in the mountains. The earlier one, "The Moonshiners of Hoho-Hebee Falls" (1893) is long on plot and short on motive, local color with a generous sprinkling of sermon. It is indeed two stories: Leander Yerby's relations with Mrs. Sudley, his foster mother; his Uncle Nehemiah's altercation with the moonshiners. The only bond between the two is the boy's presence in both. The story is peopled by a cluster of types, except Mrs. Sudley, who rules her household with continuous melancholy, no arguments or objurgations, and sometimes a hymn tune; and Nehemiah, a sanctimonious fraud, the most guileful and false-faced mountaineer yet encountered in Miss Murfree's gallery, who descants endlessly against sin while ruthlessly maneuvering for his own profit. Although mostly drawn from without, the inhibited woman and the doltish hypocrite are achieved portraits. More than in other stories, individuals are characterized by what other individuals say about them.

In several places the shadow of Hawthorne's method falls across this story. When Nehemiah writes his informing letter to the revenue agents, a moth comes whisking in, moves up and down the sheet befouling itself with ink, circles again and again about the candle, passes through the flame, then falls quivering on the page. The moth is Nehemiah portending the failure of his own adventure. He circles around the dangerous flame (the furnace) of the moonshiners and collapses when they capture him. The furnace in the still below the falls is utilized in the same manner as the one in "Ethan Brand." The flare from its open door points up details of place, actions, and expressions vital to the evolution of the story. A prefiguration of the raid may be seen when the firelight is obscured by the moonlight, signalizing the ascendancy of heaven over hell, good over evil. And Hilary Tarbetts stands off from the other mountaineers by virtue of his white, ascetic face and cleaner accent, "like some rustic pietist, with strange theories and unhappy speculations and unsettled mind." Like Brand, he has been absent from his native heath a long season.

"The Moonshiners" seems to have been written as yet another substantiation of the Christian tenets that the rogues of the world eventually get their comeuppance and the meek inherit the earth. "His Unquiet Ghost," published eighteen years later, treats the same constituents of moonshine and revenue agents with far less solemnity. To foil the agents, Walter Wyatt agrees to pretend he is dead until they leave the area. Eavesdropping at a forge, he hears himself reviled by several men he had counted as friends. Disillusioned, he goes to the cemetery where his body is supposed to be buried. There he sees his purportedly faithless sweetheart grieving distraughtly. Thinking him dead, she confesses her love for him. These antithetical scenes—comic at the forge, pathetic at the grave—comprise an amusing strophic movement in this leisurely, poker-face folk tale. Wyatt is downgraded and exalted, he gets bad and good views of himself, he undergoes dejection and jubilation in alternate doses. But Miss Murfree's heavyhanded dispensation of moral precepts countermands much of the humor in Wyatt's Faustian interludes. In a coda dreary with explicit preaching, she pounds the theme of Wyatt's reformation, wrought by the power of true love, while admitting that it caused no permanent change in his prankish temperament.

Hoax gives primary momentum to two other stories published about this time. "Wolf's Head" (1910) is a provincial corruption of the classic dryad myth. It manifests the ingenuity of a young woman in helping her lover escape the law and entrapping him for herself. This straight-line narrative has ingredients garnered from earlier works, a hoary denouement, a jovial spirit throughout, and a laconic O. Henry ending. The cast of characters is standard. The loquacious grandfather—now a stock figure—carries the burden of introducing the situation. Point of view shifts thereafter to an urban sportsman who plays surrogate for the author. Bloated polysyllabics offend when they come directly from Miss Murfree; for instance, the moon's "peculiar untranslated intendment which differentiates its luminosity." In other cases, it entertains. The city man hears the story about the fugitive "what war growed up in a tree" and muses about "the dryadic suggestions of a dendroidal captivity."

"A Chilhowee Lily" (1912), another anecdote, involves stronger factors of city-country contrast than had appeared for some years. However, it is only a feeble refrain on the hopeless yearning of the country girl for the city man, with just two notable effects: (1) Evanescent Loralinda Byars, the mountain-flower, is correlated feature for feature with the Chilhowee lily in opening, middle, and closing paragraphs to create a sturdy, if obvious, envelope structure; (2) The conflicting romantic-realistic impulses of local color are strikingly and succinctly demonstrated. After displaying a mountain cabin under "the annihilating magnificence of the moon," Miss Murfree trends to the other extreme:

> By daylight the dreary little hut had no longer poetic or picturesque suggestion. Bereft of the sheen and shimmer of the moonlight its aspect had collapsed like a dream into the dullest realities. The door-yard was muddy and littered; here the razor-back hogs rooted unrebuked; the rail fence had fallen on one side, and it would seem that only their attachment to home prevented them from wandering forth to be lost in the wilderness; the clap-boards of the shiny roof were oozing and steaming with dampness, and showed all awry and uneven; the clay and stick chimney, hopelessly out of plumb, leaned far from the wall.

In dealing with native superstitions Miss Murfree catches the feeling of awesome mystery engendered by the overpowering mountains, the darkness of forests, and the primitive remoteness of the mountaineers. Without straying from rational interpretation, but not always providing one, she succeeds in permeating her stories with a legitimate sense of the weird. "The Phantoms of the Foot-Bridge" (1893) is in the best tradition of murky ghost stories. It proceeds on a plane of hint and repetition, of expectation working toward fulfillment. Every scene of importance has its presage in symbol or miniature. Millicent's apparition is preceded by three haunts that heighten probability and whet anticipation; her mystical appearance with a lighted candle prefaces the tragic shooting of Emory Keenan in the deserted hotel; her cap prefigures death by association for Keenan or John Dundas; the screech owl, a harbinger of death, recurs ominously. Miss Murfree's technical skills, almost completely ignored in criticisms of her work, show here to fine advantage.

John Dundas is an imposing physical specimen out of dandified romantic fiction, with Byronic appeal of silence and sadness for the lovely, simple mountain maid. His carefully shaven face, his immaculate cuffs, his black cloak with bright-blue lining, and his ring and gloves are derisively labeled feminine by rough-cut Keenan, who would no more wear gloves than a petticoat. His clumsy red finger and Dundas' delicate hand illustrate by synecdoche the vast separation of town and mountain. Nevertheless, the theme is negligible and none of the characters displays distinguishing marks except the superficial Dickensian feature of a jaunty soldier's cap on Millicent's pretty golden head. Miss Murfree's penchant for explanation fills the final page with unneeded details of aftermath.

In "The Mystery of Witch-Face Mountain" (1895), a fully plotted novelette with no deviation in its narrative momentum, the activities of two juries—the coroner's, reviewing the murder of the city stranger, and the jury of view investigating possibilities of building a road—induce essential unity; for the murder and the discovery of oil form a central strand upon which every element hangs. The mystery is revealed as anti-climactic afterthought and the story straggles on to a redundant conclusion, an infirmity Miss Murfree cannot seem to overcome. Barring that and the gratuitous pedagogy, this is one of her least congested, smoothest flowing stories.

The parallel with Hawthorne's "The Great Stone Face" is unavoidable even though the face in "The Mystery" is formed by accidental juxtaposition of several natural phenomena and appears only when the oil content in a nearby stream is ignited. There is no inspirational intent as in Hawthorne; instead the face has an aspect of snarling mockery, and the mountaineers expect bad luck any day it is visible. Allegorical nomenclature is present in Constant Hite, perfect pun for a mountain dweller, and in Nick Peters, the bandit with whose devilry the murder may be associated. And right out of "Young Goodman Brown" are the conjectures about witches in the woods and the series of ambiguous rhetorical questions regarding the nature of the miraculous fire.

Miss Murfree leans speciously on classical names, frequently straining to elevate her mountain heroes and heroines by inconceivable analogies with Greek deities. Minerva Slade is twice blessed in that she is specifically compared with Hebe (as Millicent had been with Diana). Although Narcissa Hanway does gaze once into "the lustrous dark surface of a tiny pool" and blenches from her own image, her qualities owe less to mythological than to horticultural allusion. Her "flower-like face" is invoked at least three times.

The machinery of law and the natives' attitude toward law form a strong motif here, but the contrast of cultures surpasses it. The initial note is struck when the nameless city stranger realizes "that sense of distance in mind and spirit which is the true isolation of the foreigner, and which even an identity of tongue and kindred cannot annul." The other alien, Alan Selwyn, is an ineffectual valley man flawed by tuberculosis, the stigma of city existence. His secrecy is resented by the mountaineers, and his clothes are considered "fantastic toggery." Neither man survives the mountain experience; Hite, Narcissa, and her brother endure. After Selwyn's death, jealous Hite perceives that Narcissa's grief is not for a departed lover but "a sympathy akin to his own and to her brother's." Mountain vitality and solidarity are upheld. Hite will probably marry Narcissa in time.

Superstition, hoax, and the wily Indian share equal interest in Miss Murfree's last published mountain story, "The Herder of Storm Mountain" (1920). In language largely crisp and simple (leaving out "holophrastic" and "intervenient") she unfolds a story not unlike "Over on the T'other Mounting," bedecked with Cherokee lore she had acquired in the intervening years. It is an effortless pleasantry, with one jarring facet: the constable's outspoken disgust over Lem Forsey's insistence on making a legal and burdensome matter out of a mere Indian casualty. For his departure from local mores, Lem is dismissed as "teched in the head."

"Una of the Hill Country" (1912), a lightweight satire on male vanity and female discretion in playing up to it, is a feminist dig at a man's bleeding ego with little observable value except as a local-color daguerreotype set in a frame of culture contrast. Town-country tension is subordinated to ridicule of the mountebank mountaineer. Valeria Clee, an explicit mountain-flower (to paraphrase Gertrude Stein, a wild rose is a wild rose is a wild rose), renews the action and theme which Miss Murfree had rehearsed at full novel length five years previously in *The Wind-fall*. Valeria is plucked out of her mountain surroundings and established as consort to a lion in a traveling circus. Her "ethereal figure, poetic type of beauty" captivate audiences everywhere, but she is not taken in by "the glitter and gauds of her tinsel world." Not one of these allures "could withstand the simple goodness of the unsophisticated girl." They retreat before "the power of her fireside traditions of right thinking and true living which she had learned in her humble mountain home." In such naïve terms Miss Murfree projects the assumption that simplicity is purity and ignorance innocence—an anti-intellectual, pseudo-pastoral pose of part-time peasants. Unique manifestations such as the barbecue-barn dance, snatches of folk ditties, and the infirm grandparents lend solidity to the story; but anomalous references to Endymion and Hercules restore the air of artificiality.

Last of the mountain short stories engaged in comparison of values is "Them Old Moth-Eaten Lovyers," published in *Century* (May, 1913) but never collected. A controlled effort far superior to many in her volumes, this tale sings the heartwarming Darby-and-Joan ballad of a lovable old couple who savor moments of glory during a visit in town, have their first quarrel in forty-five years of marriage, then reconcile in the intimate atmosphere of their lifelong mountain home. Somewhat like the two sisters in Jewett's "The Dulham Ladies," Editha and Ben Casey have lived inbred lives together (only one separation since childhood) and now seem like fatuous valetudinarians to all but themselves. Editha, in fact, is one of the most fetching old ladies in Miss Murfree's fiction, having none of the customary crone attributes.

Miss Murfree maintains a tone of light jollity while presenting the comedy of retrospective youth sympathetically but evading the inherent sentimentality in the homely theme of indestructible love between two elderly people. She goes back to the hickory logs in the deep fireplace and the scarlet peppers swinging from the ceiling, and to dialect popping with vivid idioms ("plumb jokified," a "hirpling old codger"). She balances scenes of sacred and profane love, of past and new generations, of speakeasy and log cabin with a restraint uncommon in her earlier local-color writing. And she unites all elements with a trite but apposite enveloping symbol of Cupid in the first and last passages.

CHAPTER 5

Mountain Microcosm

BETWEEN 1885 AND 1897 Miss Murfree published six mountain novels for adults. After a decade during which she channeled her talents into accounts of the colonial frontier, Indians, and the Civil War, she returned to the original stream with *The Windfall*. In 1912 the last of this category, *The Ordeal*, appeared. Thus, over more than a quarter-century of fluctuating literary fashions, she added substantial panels to her expanding canvas of life in the sequestered highlands of Tennessee.

Written concurrently with the short stories, especially in the first period, the novels share coequally in the slow organic growth of the Settlemint, Lost Creek, Big Injun Mounting, and Harrison's Cove into a consummate microcosm. Throughout these novels the names of topographical salients and population centers recur; familiar cognomens crop up in segment after segment; faces, dress, talk, and interests vary minimally. The same experiences are re-examined: of country-city dissension, of the flower-faced girl's hapless love, of the frenetic religionist, of the moonshiner, the fugitive, and the 'harnt'. Reading all of these over a short span engenders monotony, but monotony defensible on the score of realism. In so removed and circumscribed a region, immured from change for generations, thought and action seldom deviate from the pattern. If an overly active imagination must diversify, it must also falsify. Miss Murfree retains her integrity even if she pays the price of going to the well too often.

Her powers of narration, necessarily haltered in the short story, are given full sway in the novel. Despite the admitted lenity of that form, the reader nevertheless feels a lack of discipline on her part. Movement lags and ancillary plots sap the vigor of the main action. Explanation of this laxity may lie in her utter indifference to predetermination: she simply sat down and wrote. Sometimes she had a central idea in mind although now and again it eluded her. She often quoted Sydney's "Fool, said my Muse to me, look in thy heart, and write."[1] As for characterization, the novel provides ample room for circumspect study of a developing personality, but she is content in most cases to stop this side of revelation. Her brother spoke perceptively on this: "Her pictures of people are of types, not individuals; and where it is thought an individual has been drawn, it is because that person possesses, in a large degree, the peculiarities of his class."[2] Miss Murfree's flair was epic, not dissective.

I The Prophet of the Great Smoky Mountains

Miss Murfree's first and finest novel of mountain life elicited unstinted praise from reviewers in the South. The Wilmington *Morning Star* coupled her name with Hawthorne's and declared that "She is by all odds the best novelist the South has produced." The Nashville *Banner* opined that "No finer story has been produced since *Lorna Doone*." The *Sunday School Times* found it a relief from the Howells-James brand of realism that doted on "unimportant deeds of uninteresting people." *The Prophet of the Great Smoky Mountains* (1885) was well received in England, and Northern critics without exception admired the fresh, virile force she brought to her hitherto unexposed world. In his debut as conductor of "Editor's Study" in *Harper's,* Howells restated his aversion to old-fashioned romantic novels in general and to Dickens Gothic in particular, scoring Miss Murfree for her lapses into "the bad school we were all brought up in."[3]

The title is in a sense a misnomer, for Hiram Kelsey, the prophet, does not dominate the book. Basically, this is the history of Rick Tyler's tussle with the law and his unsuccessful suit of Dorinda Cayce. The account of the mountain preacher's losing his faith and redeeming himself in death crosses the main narrative line frequently. However, Kelsey remains an intermittent if intense figure. Incident is uppermost, promotion of the absorbing theme—an individual's troubled quest for spiritual truth— sporadic and secondary. Miss Murfree relates it to the Tyler theme of mountain justice through a series of intersecting feuds: Dorinda and sheriff Micajah Green, the Cayce men and Green, Tyler and blacksmith Gid Fletcher, the sheriff's deputy and Kelsey, Fletcher and Kelsey. Nonetheless, the impression of two distinct strands persists.

Camp meetings were commonly held in Miss Murfree's home county; and, while on vacation in the mountains, she and her sister attended at least one revival service. Thus, her knowledge of circuit riders, with their Calvin and Knox theology of hell-fire and damnation, was not founded entirely on hearsay. In Kelsey she presents a demon-haunted man in the throes of spiritual division: his "trusting heart contended with his doubting mind." The parallel with Dimmesdale in *The Scarlet Letter* is irresistible.

Kelsey is riddled with guilt for having inadvertently caused the deaths of his wife and child. Although he knows he "had no mind ter religion," he allows himself to be talked into preaching. His powerful exhortations and his deep, instinctive reading of human nature earn him the reputation of a prophet and give him uncanny influence among the natives. He contemptuously waives this attribution of miraculous powers but continues to prophesy. After five years of auspicious pulpiteering, during which Satan hunts him "like a partridge," his morbid conscience compels him to affirm his pride, vanity, instability, and susceptibility to temptation. He revolts at the sham and upbraids God—in whom he believes—because he believes there is no God. For him there is no way out of this paradox except to confess his loss of faith to his congregation.

Kelsey's presence and voice permeate the region. The sight of him riding a horse and the sound of him reading the Bible along Big Smoky confer the quality of legend and link him with the mysterious "bein's" on the mountain. He is indistinguishable from other mountaineers in appearance except for the sparks of inspiration and frenzy in his eyes. The first intimation of his introspective guilt is his statement to Dorinda that he was praying for himself. Thereafter we watch the split within him widen as he glorifies his meekness and rejoices in his deliberate martyrdom. He carries on a protracted interior dialogue with himself as flesh and as spirit until the galvanic expiation scene. In a tone of poignant despair, he cries out, "My frien's, I stan' not hyar ter preach ter-day, but fur confession. . . . I hev los' my faith." He implores God to speak to him out of the whirlwind, but the only sounds that ensue are the beating of hooves. Sheriff Green dismounts and arrests him for alleged complicity in Tyler's escape. At the trial, Kelsey uses the Bible for imprecation against his enemies, a diametric change from his former use of it. He has lost his faith in Scripture, but he retains his faith in man. In the end, he sacrifices his life to save Sheriff Green's.

Miss Murfree equates Kelsey insupportably with Christ in a number of instances. As Christ expelled the moneychangers from the Temple, Kelsey ousts the fractious deputy from the meeting-house by the scruff of his neck. Although Kelsey is known to "hev drawed his shootin'-irons on folks agin 'n' agin," he turns

the other cheek when Fletcher strikes him. "The Lord hev for-
saken me!" he exclaims, after Jake Tobin refuses him church
funds for bail. Kelsey fulfills the Christian specification that a
man must die to be born again. Christlike, the prophet relinquishes his life for his adversary in the most questionable episode
in the book. Generally berated as "melodramatic nobility," Kelsey's supreme act of atonement incited Mr. Murfree's only recorded objection to his daughter's compositions and drew this
percipient comment from Howells:

> We have some fear, also, that Dickens, with his Victor Hugoish
> martyr of a Sidney Carton, was not wholly absent when the last
> end of Miss Murfree's *Prophet* was imagined, though probably
> enough he was not present to the author's consciousness. It is not
> in such romantic wise that men really die for men; the real sacri-
> fices, indeed, have been offered for races, not for persons; it is
> not after this manner that even a saint gives his life to save his
> enemy's. If Kelsey's substitution of himself for Micajah Green,
> whom the Cayces meant to kill, was insanely voluntary, it is not
> interesting, for no act of lunacy is so, except pathologically; if it
> was voluntary, it was romantic, which is worse than uninterest-
> ing; if it was accidental, it was insignificant.[4]

In the same critique Howells asserts that Kelsey "remains
misty rather than mystical," an opinion with which it is easy to
concur. Kelsey is permitted too few bouts of self-revelation to
strip away the layers of substance obscuring his essence, and
his actions sometimes miscast him as a moral opportunist. Miss
Murfree handles the reins too stiffly, guiding us to his duality
with blunt references to the conversations he holds with "the
monitor within." Abruptly she takes over herself to indict him
for ignorance and vacillation, thrusting her own notions between
him and his dilemma, between him and the reader. The final
ambiguity—whether it is religion or insanity which transfigures
him—assuredly opens extra avenues for interpretation. It also
brings to light Miss Murfree's evasion of an honest motivation
for so honest an apostate. All things weighed, this crudely elo-
quent, ravaged infidel is the most memorable character Miss
Murfree created; he is inchoate but undeniably striking.

Dorinda Cayce is a diamond in the rough, with beauty and
youthful vigor which sustain her after disappointment in love.
Uninformed and idealistic, she believes that Mount Horeb is in
the Smokies and that the Lord spoke to Moses there. She sympathizes intuitively with Kelsey because his sorrows are not

mundane but spiritual, such matters as pierced the hearts of
Elijah and Elisha. Fascinated by the romance, ethereality, and
piety of these old prophets, she identifies them with Kelsey and
sublimates the love she denies Tyler when he refuses to vindi-
cate Kelsey of any connection with his escape. One of the most
effective scenes in the book is the decisive encounter of the
lovers. The tenderness of the first half is skillfully offset by the
violence of the second, and the whole is wrapped within repetition of the word *good*. Dorinda founders in an eddy of her own
making: her hard commitment to the man she loves, Rick, against
her sense of duty to the man she reveres, Kelsey. After Rick fails
to appear at the rendezvous she set, she never forgives him. Miss
Murfree wastes no sentiment on this mountain-flower of the
sturdy variety—her goodness is not blessed. Like Cynthia Ware,
Dorinda is doomed to drift the rest of her life down a Lost
Creek of untenable illusions.

Rick Tyler has the straight yellow hair, the brown jeans suit,
and the slow, contemplative nature of the customary young male
mountaineer. He conforms to the code in his obstinacy toward
Dorinda's touching, impractical plea, relegating her to woman's
proper stratum in mountain hierarchy regardless of the cost to
himself. Miss Murfree states that he is "subacutely" pricked by
jealousy. That is as far as penetration goes.

The Cayce men are more impressive, particularly Groundhog,
father of a stalwart tribe of sons as rough, passionate, and un-
demonstrative as himself. He voices his elemental sense of
justice in a brief speech which turns out to be chronicle, character sketch, ethical system, and social manifesto, an epitome of
Tennessee mountain ethos:

> Me an' mine take no word off'n nobody. My grad'dad an' his three
> brothers, one hundred an' fourteen year ago, kem hyar from the
> old North State an' settled in the Big Smoky. They an' thar sons
> rooted up the wilderness. They crapped. They fit the beasties;
> they fit the Injun; they fit the British; an' this last little war o'
> ourn they fit each other. Thar hev never been a coward 'mongst
> 'em. Thar hev never been a key turned on one of 'em, or a door
> shet. They hev respected the law fur what it war wuth, an' they
> hev stood up fur thar rights agin it. They answer fur thar word,
> an' others hev ter answer.

In the mode of *Macbeth* and *Moby Dick*, an unlikely prophecy
is made and consummated. Kelsey predicts that the Cayces will
repent their planned murder of the sheriff, that Groundhog's

mind will die before his body and he will go down in sorrow to the grave, and that some of his sons will languish behind bars. Only the jail sentences do not materialize. Groundhog does fall into mental decrepitude; Pete Cayce patches up old feuds and becomes despondently meek; the Cayces regret their hideous mistake (not for wanting to murder Green but for drowning the wrong man). Thus the religious theme is brought to a neat, formal close.

Several other characters rise above routine treatment. Gid Fletcher, the coarse-grained "heavy," is a conglomeration of baffled avarice, revenge, and malice, with a drive to excel. Nevertheless, he has a certain sensitivity about people's motives and their reactions to his aberrant behavior. Mrs. Cayce is an octogenarian crone in spectacles, frilled cap, homespun dress of fifty years vintage, and turkey-feather fan. An extensive and colorful talker popping with localisms, homely wisdom, and strong opinions, she shrills repeatedly at the sheriff, "Don't take the bar'l," until it becomes a comic Dickensian tag-line. Also transplanted from Dickens are the two senile grandfathers in the Scruggs household. Eccentrics, they are not exaggerated out of reason. One jerks convulsively with every word and motion; one chirps "like a superannuated cricket"; both demand instant and exclusive attention. The scene in which they reminisce heatedly about Andrew Jackson and Henry Clay—the paralytic breaks down maudlinly and is carried bodily to his bed, weeping—is another of Miss Murfree's deft cameos. Brother Jake Tobin is the converse in spirituality to Kelsey. Burly, grizzled, inclined to fatness (he "sets mo' store on chicken fixin's than on grace"), he casts his eyes upward after every phrase in his sermon, smites the table emphatically, rolls out thunderous denunciations, and perspires freely into his red bandanna handkerchief. He discreetly gauges the effect of his ecstatic outbursts upon God and upon the impressionable congregation. The church meeting at which he plays the righteous antagonist to Kelsey affords the best confrontation of sincere and hypocritical evangelism to be found in any of Miss Murfree's books.

The attitude of the mountaineers toward formal law is thoroughly exposed through the hazards encountered by Tyler after he is unjustly indicted as accessory to a murder. The natives have something like contempt for the letter of the law except, of course, if it is in their favor. They do not interfere with its workings; neither do they aid in its effectuation. Kelsey excoriates Fletcher for selling out Tyler to the sheriff: "Thar ain't another man of the Big Smoky ez would stir himself to gin over ter the gallus or the pen'tiary the frien' ez trested him." He adds: "Ef the law tuk him, that's a differ," therein enunciating the code of clan and place. Groundhog Cayce justifies himself on purely anarchic grounds: "Wall, now, who made that law? I never; an' I ain't a-goin' ter abide by it, nuther." One of his sons adduces higher sanction: "The Bible 'lows ez every man air a law unto hisself," and declines to take sides about Rick's culpability. "I ain't a jedge, an' thar ain't enough o' me fur a jury." Laissez-faire is the rule; humanism, the ethic. In this country of primary passions, law is remote; man is vibrant.

The dominating themes of justice and religion converge in an upward thrust of drama at the church meeting. As Kelsey delivers his intolerable confession, the sheriff strides down the aisle. The jingling of his spurs lowers contemplation from the heavenly whirlwind to the heels of a man's boots. Law supersedes. Degradation follows the arrest of the prophet. The crowd believes Kelsey's loss of faith to be a negligible legal complication, and the spiritual significance of his crisis goes unnoticed. The personal devil that hounded him in apocalyptic seizures is incarnated as an insolent deputy. Micajah Green lays the warrant imposingly upon the Bible, signaling the ascendancy of man-made over God-made word. With this gesture, Kelsey dwindles from Great Blasphemer to ignoble culprit. The triumph of temporality is absolute.

On the whole, Miss Murfree uses symbol to subtler purpose here than in the bulk of her later work. However, the analogy of Kelsey and Christ must be accounted a failure in view of the prophet's ultimate inadequacy. So too the glowing crimson rose that sheds its petals, fades, and then dies as it becomes apparent to Dorinda that Rick will not come. Competent structurally as well as ideationally, it is nonetheless hackneyed. Classical allusions implying majesty and timelessness in the diffident natives are prevalent and not always congruous. Association with Biblical persons and legend is more in keeping with the religious tenor of the novel. At least fifteen mountaineers carry Scriptural names, references to the apostles and prophets abound, and semblances to Canaan, the Valley of the Shadow, and Moses' rock transform the Great Smokies into a latter-day Holy Land. The interlacing lines and curves of God's writing are seen in the trees, and Kelsey reads infinity in the misted peaks. Pollen falls on the open Bible as Kelsey reads it while riding through the forest, and once the shadow of a bird glides across the pages to suggest the dichotomy of the life-death struggle within the preacher's breast. Dorinda's celestial quality is expressed by an inadvertent halo, a circumstance met before and repeated often in stories hereafter with ingenious variations.

Rick Tyler is the subject of two compatible analogues. He holds out his wrists for the skeins of wool Dorinda is winding, emblematic of the steel manacles he has recently discarded and the softer shackles of marriage he is ready to assume. Imprisoned in the forge, he reflects upon the rabbit who, like himself, "got in an' couldn't git out," and upon the hounds in unshakeable pursuit, like the sheriff and his posse. Miss Murfree presents several provisional scenes which artfully presage significant events in the offing. Perhaps least conspicuous and most potent in support of the heart versus head motif is the meeting of Dorinda and the Squire—she, young, fresh, and uncomplicated, consulting only her emotions; he, old, prosy, and prolix, consulting always the book—a clear demonstration of Miss Murfree's sympathy in the eternal controversy between instinct and rationality.

Description of landscape is so frequent and so distracting that the reader is afflicted with a weary sense of *déjà vu*. Miss Murfree injects mountain vignettes into the midst of crucial action, between sentences in a conversation, into the thoughts and vision of characters—usually in terms they would not understand (Icarus in the Great Smokies) or in shapes and hues they would not observe (mezzotint under glass)—superimposing her own eye for beauty upon their long-surfeited familiarity with the panorama.[5] Yet she turns the glories of nature to more than pictorial function by giving them moral and symbolic substance.

The suspended silence and awful immensity of the mountains impress every inhabitant with the certitude of an overpowering presence. Kelsey embraces nature as an expression of God's transcendent design. He marvels at the mountains—there the ark rested, the cross was planted, the transfiguration occurred, the Sermon was spoken—and he determines to preach the name of God. Man is made to seem insignificant against "those mighty and majestic domes." Rick experiences "a frenzy of rage" as he realizes his transiency in the perennial cycle of seasons, an effect Miss Murfree achieves tacitly by setting human figures momentarily in tableau against the immemorial landscape. Yet man can find comfort or accord within the universal forces. In the woods, Amos James is refreshed in spirit, and the meaning of the world is clarified. Dorinda's joyless mood is reflected point for point in the black boughs, empty nests, and sterile outcroppings of rock.

The moon also responds to human moods. During Cayce's expostulation of revenge against Green, the moon picks out the blade of a long knife and the barrel of a rifle. When emotions subside, the moon drops down behind the summit, leaving "a melancholy waning suffusion of light." The moon acts as moral commentator by shedding beneficent or baleful light upon certain characters, and at nightfall it dilates the feelings of mystery and somnolence that overtake human beings.

The appeal of *The Prophet* to its generation undoubtedly lay in the vivid novelty of its mountain vistas, the picturesqueness of the natives, and the precision of detail concerning their way of life. Miss Murfree provides these in profusion with fondness and animation. The vernacular is zesty without being grotesque: "survigrus," "airish," "spang on the minute." Folk similes and ditties make for additional color. Inviolable hospitality and deference for elders, babies, and preachers abide untroubled beside hyperbolic threats and casual acceptance of violence. The mountain microcosm is sufficient unto itself here. Barring Dorinda's brief call on the town justice, city-country contrast is confined to Miss Murfree's rather snide personal interjections of "civilized" or "in civilization." Thus a score of local phenomena stand out on their own inimitable merits.

The church meeting with its electrifying discourses and cowed suppliants is a masterpiece of its kind and the loftiest moment of the book. The gander-pulling is amazingly specific in view of the fact that Miss Murfree probably obtained most of her impressions from a man who once gave her a lift, and possibly a look at Longstreet's account. She misses none of the pungency and sadism that prevailed at these affairs. The gathering at the Settlement to hear the electioneering is remarkably representative and vital as a cross-section of the mountain community. The general store is a strange junction of hand looms, beeswax, feathers, honey, and dried fruit. The Cayce still in the cavern, with its sinister furnace surrounded by slouching figures and elongated shadows, is typical, as is the revenue agents' raid on it. As one approaches the Cayce home, the hounds, the beehives, the henhouse, and the rain barrel prepare him for the interior of dark brown logs and yellow clay daubing, the peltry, pop-corn, and peppers swaying from the rafters, and the unconscious ballet of Dorinda at the reel. For good measure Miss Murfree describes a meal of bacon and snap beans, corn dodgers, fried chicken, honey on apple pie, all washed down with buttermilk and brush whisky.

She was to duplicate these scenes and people, and to add others intrinsic to the microcosm, but never again was she to attain so fortuitous a balance of components or so expert an amalgamation as she did in *The Prophet of the Great Smoky Mountains.*

II In the Clouds

An anonymous reviewer for the St. Louis *Post-Dispatch* (February 12, 1887) gave Miss Murfree some excellent counsel which she failed to heed: "If we may venture to offer a piece of advice to so brilliant a writer it will be this: She knows—all writers can feel—when inspiration fails them, and the work becomes a task. In all future novels let her stop right here at this point and Charles Egbert Craddock may yet become one of the great names of the age." Whether because of her peculiar approach to deadlines, the press of serial publication, or the exigencies of her domestic life at the time of writing *In the Clouds* (1886), this novel runs on long after it should have stopped and contains too many reversions to earlier works. Characters, incidents, themes, and moods of "Drifting Down Lost Creek," "The 'Harnt' That Walks Chilhowee," "Over on the T'other Mounting," and *The Prophet of the Great Smoky Mountains* are reproduced with only microscopic changes. Yet *In the Clouds* is fuller and more satisfying in many respects than *The Prophet.* Miss Murfree takes in the city as well as the country and, although this tends to deflect her into marginal areas, gives the book a contentious base which in the end bodies forth its major meaning. Scenes germane to both environments are presented in greater detail and are more carefully integrated with their narrative line. Characterization is sturdier, Miss Murfree allowing more exposure by speech and action and by remarks of other characters. Interrelationships among characters achieve greater depth. And her cross-view of society—from the lowliest mountaineer to the aristocrat Kinsard—is the most ambitious she ever attempts.

The plot itself rambles along several footpaths: the diverging stories of Mink Lorey and Alethea Sayles, Robert Harshaw and Judge Gwinnan, Mrs. Purvine and Jerry Price, the idiot and the moonshiners. Often, like Robert Frost in the yellow wood, Miss Murfree seems in a quandary about which route to follow. Still, she strongly coordinates all of these stories until Mink is sentenced. Thereafter the plot dissipates into a series of melodramatic acts which resolves all complications and impels every track into final alignment. As always, Miss Murfree excels in the single scene to the detriment of the longer sequence. The discovery of the dead juror is the most histrionic. The incantation to Tobias Winkeye, Sam Marvin's stealing corn from his own field, and the overnight wrangle of the jury are more firmly grounded in the soil of the region. Most effective is the prolonged tension which grips Harshaw, lying in bed in the roof room of Marvin's cabin ringed by hulking moonshiners who debate aloud on whether to kill him or not—a masterful manipulation of serio-comic suspense. Frequent coincidence unfortunately mars the plausibility of the story (too many people meet in unlikely places at the right time), but Miss Murfree redresses the triteness of this device by providing premonitory scenes which restore the air of realism in such instances as Rood's heart failure (he had brought his hand to his breast during the revival meeting) and Kinsard's throwing down his glove to Harshaw (an intimation of Judge Gwinnan's youthful duel).

The country-city antithesis devolves squarely upon Alethea as it did upon Cynthia Ware in "Drifting Down Lost Creek." Alethea makes the same kind of trek to town, becoming progressively less the goddess of nature as she proceeds. She touches nadir when she slumps forlorn and bedraggled on the doorstep of the jailhouse and regains her beauty and confidence only after she has settled at the familiar fireplace of Aunt Purvine's cabin. Miss Murfree leaves no doubt about her aim: she asserts "the sharp contrast between the townspeople—especially the lawyers within the bar, in their dapper store clothes, and that alert expression habitual with men who think for a living—and the stolid, ruminative mountain folks, with unshorn beards and unkempt heads, habited in jeans, and lounging about in slouching gestures."

Later she reviews the vices of civilization—commercial action, love of money, expedients and makeshifts under the law—and their deleterious effects upon country consciousness. Alethea proclaims the moral logic of Wild-Cat Hollow when she regrets that she brought trouble to Mink by advising him to do what was right. The Judge retorts gently: "The moral law is to do what seems right, no matter what happens." Thus the paramount theme emerges as a contest between the law of the wild and the law of the civilized. Miss Murfree feels nostalgic about the passing of folk culture in favor of book culture, but she does not distort on that account. Absolute ethical principles preside over those of friendship and kinship. The untamed view of life is subdued as Mink dies and as the *man* in Judge Gwinnan dies. The casual gives way to the ordered. Mink's transfer to the city prison symbolizes cancellation of the free spirit's last hope.

On the first page Thunderhead looms as "the cumbrous image of an ethereal thing," a solidified ideality. A Platonic inquiry into reality and illusion seems imminent in pragmatic mountain terms. Miss Murfree extends this impression through reports of inexplicable occurrences on the mountain, the "harnt," and Alethea's ardent religionism. However, the philosophic aspect gradually surrenders to a succession of demonstrations that things are not usually what they seem. Mink's death is therefore open to the simple interpretation that in the eyes of the mountaineers he *seemed* to be the "harnt," or to the profounder one that we know so little of our *real* selves. Are our images like Thunderhead? Are we clouds to the mind?

Miss Murfree's concept of fate is tied up with the ironies and paradoxes of illusion. Perversely, Alethea's behavior has brought distress upon both Mink and herself. Thinking to do right, she has made everything wrong. Attempts of human beings to alter the given direction of events is shown to be futile, as Mrs. Jessup also learns. Determinism, with an existential undertone, prevails. While man has a certain amount of free will to decide his immediate actions, he inevitably falls into the larger, prearranged pattern of his life. Mink's and Alethea's actions are the best examples here. Whether impulsive or deliberate, they are always in keeping with the approaching eventuation. Mink must die, and Alethea must weep.

A substantial number of obverse pairs energize the two main lines of action: Mink and Alethea, Mink and Ben Doaks, Alethea and Elvira Crosby, Harshaw and Gwinnan, to name the most prominent. In these cases there is an unprincipled person and one robustly moral. Miss Murfree takes no definite thematic stand: the good are not particularly rewarded, nor do the reprehensible duly suffer. With realistic tact, she leaves the ethical issues fluent. Justice of a conventionally approved sort is meted out to Mink and Harshaw. The others meet less positive conclusion: a stalemate between themselves and the world they have to live in.

Mink is an incorrigible prankster of the Brom Bones variety, handsome, vain, jealous, irresponsible, and "plastic morally." He repents often and easily in the face of Alethea's pleas but is sincere in his desire to indemnify Old Man Griff after destroying his mill. Mink has play-acted many a time and has now risen to true contrition. It is not unreasonable to believe that he is capable of the real thing. His final lunge to save the life of his hated presumed rival, Gwinnan, is not so completely inconceivable as most critics have deemed it. He is precisely the kind of scapegrace that would attract purifist Alethea Sayles.

"She is as poetic as Britomart," exclaimed Miss Murfree upon seeing a beautiful mountain girl driving a dun-colored heifer, and forthwith noted every feature.[6] More than a Cretan goddess, Alethea reminds us of Whittier's Maud Muller, particularly in her encounters with Judge Gwinnan. She is the determined mountain-flower type with a great sheaf of yellow hair that resembles a halo. She goes about exercising her savior complex on animals and the little idiot who are proxies for her frustrated love of Mink. Her fanatic vision has a militant essence comparable to Kelsey's. Although in earlier days she might have perished as a martyr, here she is Joan of Arc without a cause. At best, she turns out a questionable saint. She suffers guilt when her righteousness backfires, bringing Mink to grief; and she regrets her rectitude. With the mixed morality of mountain-folk she informs on Sam Marvin, whose activity had long been familiar to her, because doing so now will help Mink. Her sedulous conscience can "compromise with nothing less than the right," but her sense of right is hopelessly entangled with her feelings for Mink. A succubus that slays what it aspires to, Alethea preserves the memory of Mink as an ideal, not what he really was. The title of the novel takes significance from this ultimate illusion.

Two men with more than merely local characteristics are Judge Gwinnan and Robert Harshaw. Gwinnan radiates evidence of at least a triple identity: the judge devoted and incorruptible, the man proud and punctilious, the beast aroused by Mink's attack on his person. When he requests that no action be taken in regard to this attack—a decision the judge in him would never countenance—the man in him supervenes. Unable later to withstand a challenge to his probity, he resigns from the position which represents life to him and retires to obscurity. Harshaw is a beaming portrait of an egoistic, opportunistic country lawyer with an eye on public office. Courageous, obstinate, and insincere, he calculates every word and gesture for its value in enhancing his ambition. He sings long and loudly at the revival meeting, takes part in rural merrymaking, and connives toward his own surprise party. He respects truth not for its own sake but because he has learned that it has an "inherent capacity for prevailing." Despite his sleazy philosophy, Harshaw evokes sympathy. It seems too bad that a man of so many talents should misuse them so blatantly.

Children emerge as personalities in their own right; they are no longer glimpsed dimly around doorways or at the fence. 'Gustus Tom, Eudora, Ebenezer the tyrannical baby, Leonidas, Serena Marvin, and others have their moments in the drama; in fact Tom is a prime mover in revealing Peter Rood's misdeed. Tad Simpkins, the idiot boy, is a page out of Dickens. The brutishness of his existence, his simple uncomprehending goodness, his scrabbling for food at the pigpen, his mysterious disappearance and happy renascence have the imprint of this master.

Half a dozen others qualify in the same category. There is Mrs. Sayles, who utters the tartest remark made by any of Miss Murfree's crones: "It never s'prised me none ez arter the Lord made man he turned in an' made woman, the fust job bein' sech a failure." Old Man Griff, a destroyed, decrepit figure who constantly clasps his hands and moans over the torments of hell, is pathos *in extremis*. Beames, the cowman, continually interrupts jury deliberations to pule about the condition of his cattle. Kinsard, the impetuous dandy and dilettante, lives high and speaks brightly. A romantic supporter of valor and revolution, he exaggerates all enthusiasms and principles. He does nothing, feels nothing, and believes nothing unbecoming a gentleman. However, the Dickensian most fit and attractive in this novel is Mrs. Dely Purvine.

Aunt Purvine is an independent widow whose home has glass in the windows, a set of steps perilous to everyone entering, a company bedroom, walls pasted over with garish railway posters, and a valued clock possibly without works inside. She has a broad moon-face, spectacles, a clay pipe, and no teeth. Her talk is acerb and lustrous. She has acquired a reputation as a "vagrantin'" woman by virtue of two or three trips to town. For all of her vaunted cosmopolitanism, she is amazed that ready-made sunbonnets are sold in stores. Yet she has instinctive acumen and diplomacy far surpassing her training. Proud and frivolous, she nevertheless ensnares more of the reader's affection than any other character in the book.

Frank Waldo rates *In the Clouds* the most authentic depiction of the Great Smokies by Miss Murfree so far. Before this book, she attributed Cumberland mountain scenes to this wilder region. After her trip to Marysville in 1885, she moves out of the apple-jack area into that of brush whisky. Waldo admires her knowledge of mountain ranching but finds fault with her descriptions of landscape. In his opinion, she correctly portrays the feeling of awe that valley people have for mountain heights. However, this feeling decreases with nearer approach to the great mountains. Miss Murfree feels this awe so deeply that she cannot divest it when she enters the realm of the true mountaineer.[7]

No one can deny her knack for illuminating stretches of mountains with trumpet and red cardinal blossoms, jewel weeds, lilac Christmas flowers, Chilhowee lilies, pokeberries, ferns, laurel, and ivy. Yet her propensity for prettiness leads her to discover in this rugged Tennessee mountain terrain "A crystalline vibration, a tinkling tremor, a voice smiting the air, so delicately attuned to all sylvan rhythms, with an accent so fine, so faint,— surely, some oread a-singing!" Again, the moon looks "coyly in, as if she sought Endymion"—in a niche where a fugitive from justice is hiding. Too often she verges into this effete, pseudo-pastoral mode; but she fortunately offsets it by demonstrating nature's objection to illicit use of her bounty. Instead of blending into the rhythms of the swaying cornfield, the furtive Marvins are surrealistically "grotesque, distorted, gigantic" as they harvest, a moral comment on their iniquities.

If anything, local color is more emphatically professed in *In the Clouds* than in *The Prophet*. The forge, the sawmill, and the store are functional as news stations and as centers of community intercourse. The shooting match for beef, the nocturnal drinking bout in the deep woods, the visit to Tobias Winkeye's hideout, and the haggling over the sale of an ox are genre pictures executed with rarest skill. The hysteria that clutches the sinners at the revival camp meeting as Brother Jethro Sims exhorts them with hellfire, to the lurid accompaniment of a thunderstorm, eclipses in over-all effect the confession and arrest of Kelsey. Away from the mountains, we see a typical influx of mountaineers to the courthouse yard, a protracted courtroom proceeding, a mob at the jail intent on freeing a prisoner, a session of the state legislature, the inside of a country doctor's house and of a country lawyer's office.

Miss Murfree's familiarity with minute points of law is made clear throughout her exposition of the trial, in the quibble regarding a thirteenth juror, and in the legality of imprisoning a jury. She employs metaphors of the senses in all her descriptions, the visual predominating, with the aural rising in importance. From her musical background she extracts numerous similitudes to fugue, metred song, crescendo, basso-profundo, falsetto, and psalms of nature keyed to undertone.

Her symbols grow in quantity and operative power. She is partial to man and animal parallels here, the least satisfactory being her insistent unshaded play on Mink's resemblance to the little beast from whom he derives his nickname. She creates a dark, disturbing paraphrase when the idiot Tad screams at his racoon in the rafters, "Kem down hyar, ye idjit! Kem down hyar, ye damned fool!" Later the racoon stares into Alethea's face from the loom, just as Tad himself will stare at her from the moonlit graveyard. After Mink wins the racoon at cards, it is treed by the moonshiner's dogs. They are joined by Tige, the Sayles's dog who had been friendly with the racoon in the house. Miss Murfree may well intend to convey Alethea's bitterness against the forces of injustice threatening Mink's freedom, now augmented by persons once intimate with him. The cry of the pack, wanting blood, infects all. Another notable analogue is contained in Alethea's rescue of the lamb that has broken its leg in a sinkhole. She has a "dizzying realization of insecurity" as the ground under her gives way and she barely scrambles to safety—a representation of her desire to save Mink and the uncertainty of her moral stance in regard to her methods of doing so.

Without the rankling drawback of its duplications, *In the Clouds* must be reckoned among the best of Miss Murfree's local-color novels.

III   The Despot of Broomsedge Cove

Conversely, *The Despot of Broomsedge Cove* (1888) is one of the worst of the mountain novels. It is overly long, yet not long enough to discharge its artistic obligations. It is arrantly imitative of preceding stories, deficient in characterization, superficial in theme, with no stirring motivation or problems profound enough to engage the mind or heart. Between the novel and the reader intervenes a distance as definite as that between actor and spectator in a theater. Story is pre-eminent but not primal. Possibly the only improvement over past efforts lies in its more comfortable localization. Miss Murfree shows a surer hand in putting mountaineers through their ordinary rounds.

One newspaper critic noted "a decided family likeness" between *The Prophet* and *The Despot*. In fact, it can claim blood relationship with every mountain story Miss Murfree has already written. Teck Jepson interrupts a baptism precisely as Sheriff Green arrests Kelsey; the prohibited horse race echoes the gander-pulling episode; electioneering is prominent; Marcella Strobe undertakes two missions in Celia Shaw fashion; a card game is played by the forge fire—the list may continue extensively in respect to action and techniques.

Individual scenes, though most serve the central narrative in their way, are distended unreasonably. Information is given and repeated endlessly without particularly enhancing other aspects of the situation. Miss Murfree is simply longwinded. Her only conspicuous success in making digression seem natural occurs in the opening chapter. Thereafter she fills the interminable pauses in action and conversation with inconsequent and vexatious chunks of landscape or decorous cogitation. Examples of such scenes too full for their purpose are the interview of Marcella and Teck in Chapter III, Marcella and Longwood in Chapter XII, and the encounter at the forge in Chapter IV. Other scenes intended as drama are merely spectacle, violence expended without conviction: Rathburn choking Baintree, Baintree shooting Rathburn, numerous chapters concluding on a melodramatic cliff-hanging note. Less depends upon coincidence, but the story advances too glibly by way of necessary facts blurted out in the presence of the wrong people.

Miss Murfree has her eye fixed so keenly on plot that no major characters develop beyond their service to the story, and minor characters are caricatures to varying degrees. The concept of the duple self reappears in Eli Strobe and in Rathburn. However, it is narrowly psychosomatic, felt only when each is seriously wounded. Teck Jepson mistakes imagination for religious inspiration and arrogates divine judgment to himself. Bible-bemused rather than God-intoxicated, he ignores every humane consideration of reason or compassion. He reiterates imperiously, "I done it fur right an' justice." Marcella Strobe, a combination of haloed mountain-flower and hard-eyed realist, has two passions: to restore her father to sanity and his public office, and to determine which of her several suitors to take as husband. Impervious to abstract standards of morality, she gets her father reinstated and makes the right natural selection as a mate—Teck the insider instead of Rathburn the outsider. Teck has neither the fervor nor the dilemma of Kelsey; Marcella, neither the force nor the depth of Dorinda. Teck is as sure of himself as Kelsey is unsure; Marcella, as mundane as Dorinda is idealistic.

Rathburn is a nonentity as a person and positively impotent as Teck's city rival for Marcella's love. Andy Longwood, Teck's country rival, is languid, sissified, cowardly, and spiteful—the very stamp of a snivelling lover. Two pairs of typed mountaineers distinguish themselves slightly from the others: Parson Donnard, who drives a hard bargain in salvation, and his wastrel, hypocritical, leering son Jube; and Joe Bassett and Gideon Dake, who act as a Greek chorus scrutinizing and explicating events, presenting the community view on ethical and legal matters.

Miss Murfree has by now dropped the phrase "these people." Her sense of superiority over the mountaineers—conscious or not —is nevertheless transparent. Two instances of farce reduce natives to apish level. The first unfolds on a ledge overlooking the forge, where Parson Donnard behaves preposterously and is used as a butt by his rascally son. In the second, less broad in tone but quite as derisive, Teck tries seriously to be arrested while the deputy tries seriously to dissuade him. His is the ludicrous situation of a man trying to break *into* jail.

The author's presence is made painfully explicit through the strained humor of epigram in this less than social-comedy setting, through exclamations and homiletics imposed with the air of a disapproving theologian, and through pedestrian paragraphs clarifying the outcome of complications. Perhaps the loudest manifestation of Miss Murfree's point of view, however, is her complete silence about rape, perversion, and incest. Love is for youth a prelude of innocuous bliss or of transitory misunderstandings before marriage. The latter state is never blemished by any gesture of passion or mention of procreation. Deviations from this immaculate conception of sex are to be expected in such enclosed and remote communities, but neither in this book nor anywhere in her work does Miss Murfree acknowledge their existence.

An excellent pictorial technique, which before she has confined mostly to moonshiners' dens, comes into finer perspective in *The Despot*. As Teck walks into Strobe's home, "The feeble focus of the candle dully glowed in the centre of the table, sending out a subdued glimmer upon the faces that surrounded it amidst the encompassing obscurity. A vague glimpse was had of the smoke-blackened ceiling just above, with a rich dash of color where a cluster of strings of red peppers hung. The walls darkly merged into shadows; the fire was a smouldering, tawny-tinted coal. . . ." Sanders' forge is "a shadowy, cavernous place, suffused with a dusky red glow that barely served to show the anvil, the black hood, the sombre suggestions of wall and roof, and the figures of two startled men . . . a fluctuating, feeble glimmer upon their faces." These scenes and at least half a dozen others (Rathburn waking, the posse in the barn) express her appreciation of the power of chiaroscuro to give place deeper dimensions, to accentuate mood, to imply conflict or polarity in human sensitivity, and to indicate moral options. She has been linked with Caravaggio and Lo Spagnoletto in her ability to heighten the effects of ordinary nature through graphic inter-penetration of light and shade. Indeed, one should add the names of Rembrandt and Leonardo, for in this artistry she is truly supreme.

It is a hard search to find a consolidating motif in this ag-glomeration of narrative threads. Rathburn's book cunning and town values establish the country-city contrast as an important factor, and the ending of the novel on this note suggests that it was high in Miss Murfree's mind in the presentation. Yet it is lost sight of in the melange of Marcella's affairs and Teck's arbitrary posturing. Man as a shifting vapor is opposed to the solemn fixity of the mountains, but this proposition is effectively neutralized by as many references to the affinity of man and nature in its resuscitative ministry to the human spirit. The help-lessness of man in the clutch of fate and his capacity to influence none but the most trivial of his experiences are broached only sporadically. To take a cue from the title of the book, it may be supposed that Teck's unwarranted assumption of the role of monitor over human conduct is the author's major concern. How far may a man go in dispensing ultimate judgments about right and wrong? Teck deranges the lives of several people—Baintree is hounded, Rathburn almost killed, Marcella saddened, Strobe maddened, Sanders and Longwood discomfited, the community riled to the point of eruption. Despite all this evildoing, headstrong Teck comes off not only unscathed but ahead of the game. Such an eventuation is out of joint with her usual diagram of retribution. *The Despot of Broomsedge Cove* is plainly one of the stories in which Miss Murfree simply misplaced her guiding idea.

IV   In the "Stranger People's" Country

The pygmy legend was a source of unfailing fascination and speculation for inhabitants of the mountains. Tiny graves of stone slabs had been discovered near Chattanooga and on some of the Murfree acres. As Chapter II of *The Despot* opens, Teck Jepson ruminates about "those dim traditional pygmy dwellers in Tennessee, far back in the fabulous perspectives of time, still vaguely known in rural regions as the 'little people.'" This slender statement Miss Murfree amplifies into her best novel since *The Prophet of the Great Smoky Mountains*. Thematically weaker than *The Prophet* but superior to it in construction, *In the "Stranger People's" Country* (1891) is wisely briefer than *In the Clouds* and offers at least two memorable characters. The materials of the novel, except for the Little People legend, are all extant in earlier stories.

The first paragraph inaugurates the chief theme: the mystery of the Little People. They are said by some to be a prehistoric, extinct diminutive race; by others, to be Aztec children of uniform age and size buried apart from their kin for unexplainable reasons; and by still others, to be the infant remains of American Indians. Their graves are the objects of native superstition and scientific curiosity. The first scene of ranging importance is the infair, which introduces the subplot: the love rivalry for Letitia ("Litt") Pettingill. At this otherwise gay festival Fee Guthrie jealously attacks Leonard Rhodes, precipitating a strong accompaniment to the principal movement. The two lines become plausibly interlaced through the fact that the graves are on Fee's property and the visiting archaeologist, Shattuck, attracts Litt's affections. Fee's difficulties with Litt occupy the first third of the book; the pygmy matter is distinctly incidental. Gradually it is brought up even, then alternately extended and suspended. Minor incidents fill out the interstices, adding body and color to the major actions: Rhodes's electioneering, Steve Yates's disappearance, Leetle Mose's domestic upheavals, Buck Cheever's outlawry, Fee's religious perplexities. Plot and subplot, together with the Yates and Cheever threads, are conjoined and plaited securely in the end without the forced and coincidental devices customary to Miss Murfree's final chapters.

She achieves nicer continuity and integration here than in any of her other novels; yet, as before, her greatest strength is apparent in the individual scenes. A good number of these could be pointed out, but three come foremost to mind. The infair—reminiscent of her own "Dancin' Party at Harrison's Cove" and of Thomas Hardy's rustic celebrations—exhibits felicitously local people, parlance, viands, attitudes, and customs, especially "the unique diversion" known as Dancin' Tucker, a variation of the broom dance which almost ends in tragedy for gregarious Rhodes. The shooting in the rustler's hideout is a barely glimpsed whirlwind of action only one paragraph long, but Fee's unrecking heroism and the gory slaughter come through with devastating force—an apogee of Wild West derring-do intensified by its very brevity. Brief too is the passionate exchange between Adelaide Yates and Litt, the latter flaunting all her hopeless, determined desire for Shattuck, and Adelaide measuring with calm amazement her incredible naïveté. The scene throbs with undercurrent pressures which thrust momentarily to the surface usually unvented feminine feelings about love. Quickly over, it sets up reverberations of the internal turmoil which last long after the external clash has died away.

Another virtue of this scene is that the submerged self is divulged by the characters, not exposed by a detached narrator. This method is more generally in use than before, although Miss Murfree deems it necessary on one occasion to lead us to Rhodes's "tart internal colloquy with his inner consciousness." The reactions and remarks of Mrs. Pettingill about Cheever help substantially to round him out, just as his report to Steve Yates adds aspects to Litt and Leetle Mose. The best realized personalities are Felix Guthrie and his gaunt stepmother.

Fee has the huge proportions, graceful ease, and the square, bronzed inexpressive good looks that movie mythmakers have associated with the frontier marshal. He packs a pistol and knife at his belt and is known for the vehemence of his temper. He has been conditioned from childhood to the efficacy of force and trusts no other response. Troubled by his reputation for ferocity in the mountains, he marvels at the Lord's capacity to accept persecution. He yearns for a better world, but when he hears a "thin-lipped, turnip-hearted preacher" expound the doctrine of turning the other cheek, Fee exclaims: "That ain't my policy, an' 'tain't my practice." He would like to alter his ways to Christian behavior but cannot. So we have a man embroiled with his soul: as sincere as Kelsey, without his fervor; as negligent as Jepson, without his arrogance.

Fidelity to a promise, however, is an immutable principle for Fee. He will not desert his stepmother, whom he abhors, because he gave his word to his dying father. Over and above this promise is a fundamental human sympathy. He declares flatly that he would never turn Mrs. Guthrie out even if it were the only condition under which Litt would marry him. He does not have it within him to "gredge a shelter ter a 'oman ez be old, an' frien'less, an' pore, an' not kind, an' hev earned nuthin' but hate in a long life." Thus he is by turns a vicious bully, a vacillating devotee, a stalwart champion, a compassionate benefactor, a sad and hapless lover. Although he has a pathetic urge for faith in Heaven, his philosophy is empirical. So he tends to submit all problems to personal confrontation—with Rhodes, the sheriff, Mrs. Guthrie, Shattuck, Litt. Since Fee has no recourse outside his physical prowess, it comes as no wonder that he dies by the gun.

The gist of these anomalies is contained in his statement that "I never war cut out for a fighter." Fee recites a tale of maternal relations that has become classic in the curdled growth of modern nonheroes. Brought up by an "everlastin' wildcat o' a step-mam" who consistently beats him, he finally retaliates by biting her arm nearly through. She thereafter admires him as a "better man" than herself, proud of the courage her own savagery has fostered in him. Mrs. Guthrie has luxuriant gray hair, parchment-like face, unsmiling expression, and the barb-tongue of a crone. Her treatment of Rhodes at first meeting is shameful until he shamelessly flatters her, but almost instantly she returns to vituperation. When Fee is wounded, she attends him reverentially, "snarling and fierce and tender." With hideous happiness she spurs him on to spill blood in revenge for his slain cow.

Miss Murfree achieves her first really apt classical analogy in Mrs. Guthrie. After launching Fee on a pitiless mission, she exults "with the satisfaction of a Bellona, as she towered above them all, her stern, lined, dark old face so repellently triumphant that both her visitors felt a sense of recoil." This simile is not superficial, as so many of the author's previous ascriptions of mythological stature are. Mrs. Guthrie is veritably a goddess of holocaust. Her vindictiveness and blood-lust have established the potential which comes to fruition here. Correspondence with Bellona elevates and broadens her.

The remaining characters differ only in degree from their prototypes. Leetle Mose is the uttermost of infantile tyrants, "a supreme fetich" who demands "as unrequited an idolatry as ever was lavished on the great god Dagon." Asleep or awake, he dominates every minute of every adult's time within reach of his fist or sound of his voice. He shatters every existing record of spoiled brats for self-centered obduracy. No one will dispute the weary verdict that he is "the meanes' baby in the kentry." Mrs. Pettingill is a Dickensian figure, less disturbed by an apparent murder in her home than by the fate of her carefully prepared refreshments. So passionate is she about her culinary skills that her husband has been "fed till he foundered." To the normal drawl of the mountaineers she affixes a singular, propitiatory wheeze while pressing succulencies upon all and sundry. Mrs. Millroy, wife of a fugitive, just misses tragic dignity. Her dumb suffering is uninformed with either intelligence or protest. Lacking the animal rage of Mrs. Guthrie, she inspires pity rather than terror.

Buck Cheever—moonshiner, cattle rustler, horse thief, highwayman—is a hooked-nosed, steely-eyed desperado with a certain magnetism and no density. Rhodes is the standard euphoric, sycophantic rural politician. Letitia Pettingill falls short of the mountain-flower in beauty and of the shrew in asperity but comprises enough of the qualities of both to qualify as either. Knowing her sure attraction for Fee, she dabbles callously with his emotions. She loses her heart bootlessly to a city man and—like her sister-heroines in "The Romance of Sunrise Rock" and in "The Star in the Valley"—gains nothing from the departed swain except an occasional, wistful recollection. Shattuck, the city-bred scientist, is the obverse of Rhodes in honesty and purpose and a cardboard cutout at best.

Miss Murfree uses Shattuck as her advocate in action and thought. His point of view is inextricable from her own, and she endues him with the "capacity to enter into the feelings of the mountaineers, to meet them, despite the heights of his learning and his social position, without effort and without affectation." She believed this capacity to be part and parcel of her own makeup, as well as "his ever-ready sympathy with all sorts and conditions of people." So Shattuck is properly shocked by some mountain attitudes (indifference to Fee's attack on Rhodes). He insists, as she would, in calling for a bona fide medical doctor instead of the "yerb" doctor, and he suggests recourse to law over the assault. These can be readily understood, for Shattuck responds as an urban intellectual. When, however, the semi-literate sheriff looks into his prisoner's face and sees "tokens which in his ignorance he fancied were characteristic of the *facies hippocratica*," the author's pawn must be dismissed as an impostor.

Miss Murfree's view of nature is likewise refracted. Too often she trills over "infinite gradations" and "multitudinous shades" in bland disregard of the fact that natives do not see what her own excited eyes are picking out of the landscape. It is to her credit that three times in this book—more than in any other—she brings herself to admit this truth. Cheever looks at the shifting panorama: "It was too familiar to him, too stereotyped upon his senses, to produce responsive impressions, and he was familiar with few others, and knew no contrasts." Guthrie stares at her ineffable sky and notices only weather signs. Rhodes simply ignores all the radiance.

Her habit of interlining pauses with effusive description continues—one long scenic passage unfolds between the time Fee's hand closes over Shattuck's arm and Fee responds to a provocative remark. Yet it may be said that she transgresses less than before. Nature in this novel is palpable but it does not overwhelm humanity.

Miss Murfree is versatile as always in her methods. The moon dexterously reflects the moods of Fee and Litt as they discuss Rhodes, turning from red to gold, obscuring momently, then from gold to pallid. When Litt draws Fee to defeat again, the moon is barely perceptible. Chiaroscuro is most effectively employed in tracing the revolving relationships of the sinister wraiths in Crazy Zeb's cell. Miss Murfree's fondness for the silhouette also comes to the fore. Against the resplendent glow of the sunset, Cheever sees a group of men crouched around a smouldering fire. In this double shadow-play he describes a man who is actually not there, prevision of Fee's sudden appearance in the hideout. Here Miss Murfree arranges light in such a manner as to project the scene from the merely eerie into the occult. When she shows Fee's "whole massive figure, from the great slouch hat to his jingling spurs, clearly imposed upon the fair morning sky," or mounted men "like equestrian statues . . . in high-relief against the broad fields of the western sky above the mountain-tops," she imputes exceptionality to the human being, conferring larger-than-life grandeur and impressivity upon his spirit.

One other tendency, noticeable before but now emerging with greater frequency and impact, is to impart to natural objects the glaze of jewels on copper or porcelain surfaces. Northern ranges "wore a crystalline, amethystine splendor, with a fine green sky above them that had an opaque hardness of color, which gradually merged into amber." A stretch of barley shifts "from an argentine glister to green, and from green again to elusive silver glintings." A stream is first crystal, then jade-like, finally the brownish yellow of a topaz. And Miss Murfree turns this technique to symbolic advantage when Shattuck strolls down to the river near the Pettingill house and discovers Litt in surroundings approximating the Garden of Eden. One touch—the "glassy green waves"—indicates the flaw in the idyll, the coming disruption in Litt's life.

Fee's death is somewhat gratuitous except as it serves the principal moral of the book: who lives by the sword must die by the sword. This situation is a transposition of Teck Jepson's destiny in *The Despot* and more in accord with Miss Murfree's wonted dispersal of punishment and reward. Fee, an unbeliever, takes justice in his own hands. It is meet that he should be repudiated and lose everything, including his life.

The customary themes of common humanity and city-country contrast are powerfully evinced in the person of Shattuck, who forgets "that traits of character are as the solid wood, indigenous; and that cultivation is, after all, only surface polish and veneer." In any case, the city gets far the better of it here. However—as proclaimed in her title, first page, and last sentence—Miss Murfree is engrossed in consideration of the long design of life and death evoked by study of historical relics. Man has his day, writes his record on shards of pottery, dies, and leaves them for other men to read and interpret in later ages. "These tokens should balk oblivion," she maintains. Contrarily, they underscore the conviction that life is a fever and a fret while death is the final solution, the quiet place from which to contemplate human folly. Once again Miss Murfree certifies the eternal cycle of nature ("Every year the laurel blooms anew") and, willy-nilly, remands man to dust. Guthrie struts his hour and succumbs; Letitia strives and expires blindly. "Meanwhile the Little People sleep well."

V His Vanished Star

His Vanished Star (1894) has some of the virtues and most of the faults of Miss Murfree's preceding novels about the mountains. Description is too frequent, intervention by the narrator too prevalent, characterization too flat, incident and plot line too familiar. On the other hand, it offers spiny dialect, insight into place and people, and three viable personalities. The title is unsatisfactorily lateral to the emphasis of the book. One would expect it to refer to Kenniston and his faded dream of building a mountain resort; ultimately, it turns upon Larrabee and his specious comet. Although Larrabee is idealistically motivated, the discrepancy between his shallow character and his mystical proclivities begets an agent too frail to carry the burden of the theme. Miss Murfree demonstrates sureness of technique in disposing her substantive elements, but there is a thinness approaching transparency in her moral and philosophic content. She depends upon scene and story almost entirely, developing characters in high enough relief to function appropriately in the situation while leaving their profounder selves indiscernible.

As in *The Despot of Broomsedge Cove*, two major motifs are intertwined by common participants, each movement brought to a certain point, dropped, resumed, and resolved. Kenniston's construction project and the love rivalries of Espey and Larrabee are tied to the lesser threads of Taft's moonshining and the mystery of the subterranean sounds. Stress first falls on Kenniston, then on Espey, then anticlimactically on Larrabee's star and on Old Haight's pointless search for eighty-seven silver dollars. Attention oscillates, and power is divided. Long before the end, the reader is conscious of disunity of action and the absence of a positive protagonist. Kenniston, Captain Tems, Taft, Espey, and Larrabee are not large enough to fit the role. With her habitual passion for good housekeeping, Miss Murfree directs every string into a perfect weave in the last chapter.

Of the consequential characters Kenneth Kenniston, the city architect, and Jack Espey and Jasper Larrabee, the young mountaineers, fail to ring soundly. None is distinguishable from his forerunners in the mountain stories. Like Judge Gwinnan in *In the Clouds*, Larrabee is supposed to suffer from psychic fragmentation. Again this state is vouchsafed by Miss Murfree, not manifested by Larrabee. Rodolphus Ross, the clamorous, brutal, detestable deputy; Old Haight, the pertinacious, demented old miner; and sullen, sodden, serially drunk Dan Sykes (to the very name) are Dickens caricatures. Only three—Captain Luther Tems, Lorenzo Taft, and Cornelia Taft—have the merit of comparative depth.

Captain Tems, nicknamed Lucy in his handsomer younger days, is a lean man, tough-fibred physically and morally. He has a prickly sense of humor which he uses to establish domination over others, and he draws upon Scripture to support himself in controversy. Inflexibly honest, he comes to grips with temptation when he discovers that the cornerstone of his property has been moved to his benefit and to Kenniston's disadvantage. After an agonizing interval of uncertainty, he decides to remain silent. In his moment of moral descent a storm as baroque as the one in *King Lear* breaks over his head. Having compromised his integrity for the first time, and wretchedly aware of having destroyed his son's faith in him, this imperious patriarch thenceforth takes out his guilt on his family with gratuitous cruelties. In his battle with Kenniston, Tems loses far more than the legal point—he is stripped of his once unshakeable belief in himself.

Lorenzo Taft, a moonshiner who keeps a moribund country store as a blind, has the marks of a natural force on his rapacious, eagle-beaked face. A fearless, ruthless schemer with a florid, friendly manner, he does not hesitate to dynamite a mineshaft knowing there are at least three people in it. He is extravagantly wise, valorous, and self-seeking—an irresistible and unpredictable mixture of qualities. His daughter Cornelia is "prim, pale, and precise," a preternaturally bright child with formal face and remarkable instincts. Solemn, perceptive, self-sufficient, secretive, full of local saws and adult sarcasms, she impassively rearranges the course of her own small world and that of the grown-ups around her.

In several of the foregoing stories Miss Murfree remarks passingly on the attractive presence that one or another of her mountaineers would make on the stage. With the insistent romanticism of her outside view she often looks at the scene as one might a drama being enacted on a raised, enframed platform, slightly removed, somewhat unreal, unfolding without relation to human will, as though manipulated by a supernal playwright. On occasion her actors become conscious that they are playing roles inconsistent with their own idea of themselves, or sometimes they realize that others are playing influential roles in a drama building up around themselves. There is an increase of such implications in this novel to the extent that the cumulative effect may be termed a theater trope. Kenniston notes the incursion of Tems on "the elaborate stage of his own future"; Espey could "have graced the romantic stage, as he stood"; Larrabee reviews his incredible experiences as a "whole drama"; and Taft deliberately invents a situation and assumes a role into which he fits so convincingly that "even the most discerning might have descried no discrepancy" between the man himself and the role. By relating the theater trope to her concept of fate, Miss Murfree fortifies her presentation of life as a preordained number of acts already written, and woe to the actor who tinkers with the lines. Taft tries by sheer force of personality to alter the direction of events and brings catastrophe upon himself.

The commanding theme of *His Vanished Star* is not broached in the title but lies in the recurrent contrast of city and country cultures represented mainly in Kenniston the energetic, tourist-minded urbanite and in Tems the resentful, unprogressive back-woodsman. Neither wins, for Kenniston withdraws frustrated and Tems befouls his probity. Perhaps the fact that a young bear causes the hotel fire indicates nature's preference in this dispute. Larrabee's star, a late-comer in the resolution of this novel, disappears without divulging its mysterious message. The connection between Larrabee and the star is extremely vague. Sometimes it suggests the theme of Emerson's "Days"—in the universal failure of our illusions we glimpse God but settle for Mammon; sometimes the theme of Whitman's "When I Heard the Learn'd Astronomer"—Larrabee's native ingenuousness permits him to see the star while Kenniston's sophistication prevents him; sometimes the theme of Poe's "Sonnet to Science" or Keats's "Lamia"—the inimicability of science and romance, for "What mystic lens might serve to reveal the amaranthine wreath and the nearing pinion?" Whichever of these Miss Murfree may have intended, the parable comes lamely as an afterthought and to a character too dull to decipher its meaning. *His Vanished Star* creaks from an overload of purposes.

VI The Juggler

Unable to choose between the Zolaesque realism and the cos-tumed romanticism that were vying for first place in the field of the American novel during the late 1890's, Miss Murfree went the way of melodrama in *The Juggler* (1897). She concocts a purely romantic exchange of identity for Lucien Royce, who assumes a dead man's clothes and thereafter resides in the back country under a pseudonym. Then she offers for his behavior excessive explanation which is never anything but incredible. She exploits the romantic cliché of a beautiful girl whom Royce adores from a distance and cannot approach in his present guise. Then she dispatches him in the most grisly and grotesque scene to be found in her entire work. This is one of the few instances when Miss Murfree does not attempt to tell more than one story—Royce's false situation and his futile endeavor to transcend it. Incompatibility develops, however, in her manner of telling it. The New York *Times* (December 4, 1897) thought it "soul-harrowing" and likened it to Pepys's "Saw a man hanged, and went home right merrily to breakfast." From beginning to end, the plot is merely fantastic.

The characters are watercolor sketches, not people, against a background that calls for oil painting. Equipped with commercial morality, Royce might well be twentieth-century masochistic man obsessed by guilt and driven by bad dreams except that Miss Murfree plies him too obviously as an instrument of contrast to the usual country swains, elders, preachers, and sheriffs. Of these only Mrs. Sims rises above the page, a portly Dickens drawing, shrewd, sloppy, loquacious, and—surprisingly for a mountain wife—an inept cook who blithely blames the witches when her johnny-cakes burn.

The New Helvetia Springs Hotel reappears in fuller bearing than heretofore as the center to which the natives are attracted. Sitting on benches along the wall after they have sold their peaches or venison, they watch the waltzes or the tenpins with lethargic curiosity and pronounce the hotel a place of "freaks and frivolities." A secluded resort catering to Southern aristocrats, New Helvetia is a replica of Beersheba Springs, with its turreted roofs, rustic footbridge, silver rills, carts and horses for riding, band music, lawn tennis, billiards, bowling, dancing, amateur theatricals, masquerades, card games, and piano. Mostly it serves to confirm the difference between chiffon and calico, white flannels and brown jeans.

Here Miss Murfree brings into sharpest contravention the values of country and city, pitting a mountain-flower against a cultured charmer and a number of mountaineers against Royce. The mores of the Sims cabin, the church meeting, and the lime burner's kiln are chasmally distant from the New Helvetia's books, teas, and masked balls. For a short period Royce seems to have shucked off the artificiality of his former circuit of office, club, boating, tally-ho drives, germans, and musicales, believing himself happy in this adopted mode of primitive simplicity. Awareness of the horrible alienation he has imposed upon himself comes like a blow not long after he glimpses Gertrude Fordyce, the city beauty with sea-shell pink cheeks and irresistible elegance. He winces perceptibly next time he sees Euphemia Sims, the mountain belle he has determined to marry. "The coarse florid calico, the misshapen little brogans, . . . her drawling voice, the lapses of her ignorant speech, her utter lack of all the graces of training and culture" are more than he can pretend to disregard. He resolves to get out of his predicament at any cost. Although Royce's self-enforced exile is highly unlikely, Miss Murfree formulates out of it her most inclusive city-country contrast. First, Royce comes into intimate and extended contact with more than the customary number of mountaineers; second, the New Helvetia supplies more urban foils than customarily appear in the mountain stories. Interrelationships are deeper and of longer duration. Moreover, the hotel is in effect a protected island in a rough sea, encouraging perpetuation of foreign snobberies which might be temporarily relinquished by an individual divorced from his group.

Out of Royce's failure to assimilate, Miss Murfree adduces more strongly than ever the lesson that it is prudent to stay in one's own class and not aspire to ascend or descend. The efforts of Euphemia Sims and Absalom Tynes to acquire learning are as ludicrous as Royce's assumption of country ways which never goes beyond his ragged costume. Royce is shown to be out of kilter through two exhibitions of his legerdemain: when he entertains the uncouth natives, he fails and is pelted with stern accusations; when he entertains the sophisticated summer visitors, he succeeds brilliantly and is awarded wild acclamations. "Never the twain shall meet" is clearly enunciated. He cannot breach the ignorance that divides him from his first audience, while the second is of his own intellectual and social level. In trying to relegate himself downward and then to raise himself up again, he perishes. Euphemia and Gertrude, who remain safely in their respective castes, live and prosper, fundamentally unperturbed by his annihilation. Each of the classes extends advantages to its own. No one may strive for both without damage to his soul.

In the first and last scenes Royce puts on a show of his juggling skills. These exhibitions in a sense span the gamut of his conflicting desires. More specifically, they define the theater trope which regulates his feelings and actions from the moment he disowns his ego to the day he tries to reclaim it. Fraudulence becomes his due when he dons the dead man's clothes, so flippant as to give the impression of a costume. Ironically, that is precisely what they are. As he listens to the rude eloquence of Brother Tynes at the church service, Royce imagines himself back "in the dress circle of some crowded play-house, at the triumphant moment of a masterpiece in the science of histrionism." He makes a deliberate mimicry of passion with Euphemia in order to insure his concealment, declares that "I must needs always have an audience," and incontinently longs to see Gertrude at the hotel; for in his present circumstance she is upstage and inaccessible. The final scene compounds the earlier irony. Royce *seems* "some well-bred and talented youth of the best society, dressed for a rural role in private theatricals." His last gesture—permitting an assistant to stab him unwittingly to death in a wicker basket in full view of the audience—has been condemned as overly gory and as unnecessary to the resolution. There is ground for both criticisms. However, the ending is perfectly articulated with Royce's theatrical temperament. This macabre self-immolation, a shocking, bravura splurge, is his last and most sensational act.

Miss Murfree's inescapable text is that life is a play of shadows best watched from the security of the balcony. Her closing lines recall those of her favorite—Thackeray in *Vanity Fair*—to the very exclamation points: "Ah! Vanitas Vanitatum! Come, children, let us shut up the box and the puppets, for our play is played out." *The Juggler* ends: "Hey! Presto! The juggler has successfully exploited his last feat." Poor Royce—victim of uncontrollable drift, falsely suspected of crime, self-made pariah, betrayed by love of an unworthy woman—read his lines correctly and pulled the curtain down on himself at the proper cue. Neither he nor Miss Murfree dared to emend fate's dramaturgy.

VII The Windfall

After a recess of ten years during which she centered on the colonists and Indians of Tennessee, Miss Murfree returned to the mountains for her seventh novel, *The Windfall* (1907). The impetus came from a street fair she saw in Murfreesboro. The danger of the high diver thrilled her, and she was impressed by reading a few days later of his death while diving in a nearby town. The immediacy of her experience is not, however, transferred to the story. In it she mixes indiscriminately ingredients of local color, melodrama, social dilemma, young love, and the glamor of show business, trying rather desperately to catch and hold attention but ending with ambiguity of intent. The vapid conclusion may be blamed on the publisher, one of the rare times Miss Murfree bowed to outside opinion. Usually she listened courteously to suggestions, seemed to acquiesce, but on returning home would send a polite note saying that she really couldn't consent to the proposed change.[8]

Little matter, for *The Windfall* is a flabby rewrite of *The Juggler*, using the rusted apparatus of an unexpected legacy to rescue itself from a plot which is more spastic than dramatic. She describes landscape in the old, exhaustive, ecstatic manner brimming with superlatives. (The St. Louis *Globe-Democrat* on May 18, 1907, twitted, "Too much mountain, not enough of man.") Elsewhere one detects an aura of fatigue. The minuteness of detail of the early stories is missing. The interior of a log cabin is presented impressionistically, as a stranger might see it in a quick, inclusive glance; and Colbury could be any small town in many another region. Language with the bark on it is scarce. Jaded by previous excess, Miss Murfree simply cannot resurrect the fervor of the past.

The characters are as factitious as the plot. None of the protagonists develop materially. The familiar natives are limned in a cluster, set in a seemly frame, and left to exert an immobile effect. All dress and speak to their purpose in the action, having scant motivation of their own. The hotel clerk who talks in strings of staccato phrases is a throwback to Alfred Jingle of *Pickwick Papers*. Shadrach Pinnott is made of the same flesh as Ishmael Bush in *The Prairie*. They share Old Testament names and hard patriarchal traits. They resist encroachment on what they consider inalienable rights, defy taxation, move westward when cramped for self-expression, live by the rule of the rifle, detest officers of the law, deny vested interests in property, and squat in sullen defiance of society.

The central figure is Hilary Lloyd, part owner of a traveling circus stranded in the Great Smoky Mountains. By arousing the jealousy of two men, he unites the motifs of local color and social contrast: Binley, a fugitive mountaineer, believes Lloyd to be in love with Clotilda Pinnott, a mountain-flower; Jardine, an insufferable city prig, knows him to be in love with Lucia Laniston, a vivacious, fairly lightheaded visitor at the New Helvetia Springs Hotel. Both lines advance sluggishly, the mountain aspect disappearing for long intervals; nothing of dramatic import happens until Chapter XI, when Binley threatens to shoot Clotilda. This episode is rung in to reawaken interest, for Miss Murfree's transcendent concern in *The Windfall* is a quadrilateral comparison of values rather than the lives and loves of the mountaineers.

Miss Murfree's city-country conflict usually involves an outsider in contention with an insider for the love of a mountain-flower, but in *The Windfall* she expands and complicates the issues. Two outsiders (Lloyd and Jardine) compete for the love of another outsider (Lucia) against a rural background. The outsider-insider struggle (Lloyd and Binley) exists only in the inflamed imagination of Binley. To that extent the mountain locale is incidental to the action. Miss Murfree presents a conceptual pattern of four layers: (1) the mountaineers, "heavy, jeans-clad worthies with their sunbonneted helpmeets"; (2) the townsfolk, "sedate, blackcoated, elderly merchants" of Colbury; (3) the Southern city, "special smartness" of "fawn-tinted suit" and russet shoes; (4) the Northern city, Lloyd and the cynical, slangy personnel of the street fair.

The emphasis falls upon the upper-class standards of Southern society, exemplified primarily by Lucia and her Aunt Dora. When the latter believes that Lloyd's heritage consists of a run-down plantation in a Louisiana bayou, she adjures Lucia, "Of course you couldn't consider so ignorant a person, with so frightful an accent and choice of phrases." Lucia agrees, telling Lloyd, "We are of different worlds." When it transpires that he is worth millions and is distantly connected with a first family, Aunt Dora reviles herself for making such "a terrible mistake." "Money makes such a difference," she assures Lucia. In the end Lucia finds it in her heart to accept Lloyd, who makes the transition from mountebank to model of taste in marvelously short order. The validity of this theme is rendered questionable by Lloyd's windfall. Would Lucia have regretted her decision if he had not struck it rich? Is social commitment to be valued over individual instinct? Miss Murfree seems finally to follow the social code of her day and place, supporting the dogma that marriage outside one's own stratum is heretical and foolish.

Point of view issues from Lloyd and the New Helvetia guests, Miss Murfree sounding most clearly through the snob Aunt Dora. The reader's distance from the mountaineers is greater than in any of the other mountain stories. Natives are looked at, not entered into. "What a wild country—what wild people," says Ruth Laniston. And the author pours acidulous Thackerayan homilies over their unprotected heads. Thus, much of the contrast is superficial; it hinges on clothes and language, and fails to penetrate incisively either rural mores or aristocratic manners. Yet this represents an interesting return to her earliest phase of writing—satire of social strategies.

Once more Miss Murfree applies the theater trope with eminent effect. Lloyd, who is innately histrionic, sees the magnificent ranges as backdrops to his seedy show. "Gee—what a flat!" he exclaims. He lives constantly in this illusion of the world as a stage. Watching Clotilda dance in the orchard, unconscious of his presence, he is entranced as if she were indeed "a feature of some Thespian exhibition." It transports him almost out of reality for, like Yeats, he cannot distinguish the dancer from the dance, the fact from its simulation. And vice versa, theater crosses over into life when he realizes that Clotilda is too simple-hearted to know stage fright, "a product of civilisation, the evil of self-consciousness." Again Clotilda practices her "histrionic intuitions" to save Lloyd from attack by Binley. He diagnoses her intent and dissembles in his own right. Life *qua* drama also controls the situation in the cave when Lucia recognizes Binley under his disguise and Lloyd laughs at her: "I'll get you to write me a play!—you are a prodigy at plots—I can see that!" Here, with several lives in the balance, actuality is more dramatic than drama, truth stranger than fiction. Miss Murfree is at her best when she sends her players teetering along the tightrope between reality and make-believe.

VIII   The Ordeal

The last mountain novel, published after a lapse of five more years, is without doubt the poorest. The vein and the verve are completely worked out. The Boston *Transcript* (February 1, 1913) wasted no words: "It is an enormous pity that after so many years *The Prophet of the Great Smoky Mountains* should have so unworthy a successor." "Bricks without straw," muttered the *Outlook* (December 7, 1912). *The Ordeal* (1912) bares the last writhings of the momentum that swept Miss Murfree to the fore of the local-color vogue. It is a flimsy contraption of narrative stencils in which melodrama piles upon sentimentality until the whole edifice collapses under the soggy coincidence of a man seeking an etymological gloss and finding a kidnapped boy. There is little detectable merit in scene, characterization, invention of incident, social revelation, or theme.

For once, no haloed mountain-flower girl appears. There are moonshiners, but they are strictly cartoons. All the major activators are sojourners in the mountains and have severely limited connection with the natives. Miss Murfree suggests lightly that people have more than one facet, that they might behave in ambivalent and unpredictable ways, but no one does. Lillian Royston, a shallow pragmatist who trades on her physical attractions, experiences several interior monologues carefully managed and externalized by the author, all very grammatical and proper even in moments of highest anxiety. Julian Bayne, a Rollo boy grown to man's estate, undergoes two or three of the same, so well-bred and flaccid they may be interchanged with hers. Archie Royston, an upper-class facsimile of the infantile tyrant, wreaks a cloying Bret Harte influence upon the "indurated hearts" of murderers and a taciturn Indian-witch widow.

Upon the sedulously self-controlled Bayne, Miss Murfree thrusts her own fascination with philology. He carries on a sustained discussion of idiosyncrasies in mountain speech, their ancestry in Old English and their equivalents in French, Italian and Spanish, Spenserian usages, et cetera. This material is made to serve point of view by demonstrating the elemental detachment of the vacationers from the natives, and it sparks the denouement as a factor in the recovery of Archie. Autobiography also figures in Miss Murfree's handling of the technicalities of law, more strongly in her presentation of the mountain hotel—with its piazzas, bandstand, observatory, and rooms so similar to those at Beersheba Springs, and the summer bungalow—with piano, library, rugs, gun rack, and other creature comforts to be found at Crag-Wilde, the Murfree place in the Cumberland Mountains.

No overriding theme develops. Fate exerts its usual capricious omnipotence in bringing about its desired ends. After a series of barely possible concurrences, Archie is retrieved and Bayne succumbs with rather poor grace to the charms of Lillian Royston. Perhaps Miss Murfree meant to convey her principal objective in this ringing exhortation to Lillian: "Be yourself. . . .

Rely on your own judgment, consult your own intuitions, rest on your own sense of right and justice and conscience, and you cannot err!" The luminosity of Emerson's self-reliance loses some of its glow, however, when projected by so parsimonious a spirit as Julian Bayne.

The mountain microcosm that Miss Murfree constructs in these novels consists of a hard core of realism wrapped in a shimmering membrane of romance and sentimentality. It may be, as she said to Richard Watson Gilder, that "there is not a vast difference between idealism and realism,"[9] but the invisible difference finally brought her down. She knew the place and the people of her chosen domain well enough to portray them without trappings, but her disposition was to caricature and to invent. In her last works she became an emaciated parody of herself.

In these novels, as in the short stories, scene and style possess her attention more insistently than do the complexities of human character or the enshrouded communication between souls in grief or joy, hate or unconcern. As a novelist, Miss Murfree lacks the depth, judgment, and architectonic instinct necessary for prime achievement. As a local colorist, she stands with the most competent in the genre.

CHAPTER 6

War Over Tennessee

AS THE INEVITABLE EMBROILMENT of the Civil War approached, sentiment in East Tennessee was mainly opposed to secession. When the fighting broke out, a shift of sympathy could be detected toward the Confederacy. Nevertheless, many men joined the Union ranks. The area was of great strategic importance, producing its quota of casualties and its heroes in generals Morgan, Forrest, Bragg, and Rosecrans. Too young at the start of the war to appreciate much more than the uniforms and the rodomontade, Mary Murfree watched the war swirl past her at Grantland and surround her in Nashville. Impressions deepened as she grew into adolescence. When the shooting stopped, she returned to Grantland and saw the devastation at first hand. Ten years later, as a woman who remembers the old but has matured in the new, she reflected her feelings in a chronicle of the Reconstruction days which had to wait almost a decade for publication.

Now and again in the mountain stories a reference to the war breaks through the surface, but it is always brief and has no bearing on the development or outcome. In all, Miss Murfree wrote two novels and three short stories which have direct relation to the war. Three decades intervene between the two novels, a gap of ten years between the first and second stories. The subject obviously hovered in her mind only to yield precedence to successive waves of local-color fiction and historical novels about remoter epochs. The conditions which had brought on the war were, of course, hardly remedied by it; and passions still ran high in respect to carpetbag government in the South. Never a controversialist—she made minimal mention of the Negro—she assured Messrs. Hurd & Houghton that in her first novel "no sectional feeling is manifested nor indication of any political bias."[1]

I Where the Battle Was Fought

Where the Battle Was Fought was written at least eight years before it was published in 1884; shortly after *In the Tennessee Mountains* had attracted considerable public acclaim. Rejected

by Lippincott and by Houghton, it was drastically revised, submitted to Osgood & Company, and accepted. Despite unquali-
fied triumph as a writer of local-color stories, Miss Murfree
declared that "in my opinion [*Where the Battle Was Fought*]
contains by far the best work that I have as yet done."[2] Time
has not upheld her conviction.

A writer's involvement with his first novel is notoriously ardent
and autobiographical. This factor may account for Miss Murfree's firmness about the superior quality of *The Battle*. It is
woven with the most intimate filaments of her existence—memories of the house where she was born and lived in the first
seven years of her life, and to which she returned until it was
demolished. The *mise en scène* of this novel is a ruined mansion
in an old battlefield around Fort Despair, near the town of
Chattalla. The house—with its cannonaded cupola, blackened
fissures, and relics of ante-bellum days—is an imaginative re-
creation of Grantland after the Battle of Stone's River during
which the Confederates suffered ten thousand dead or wounded
and were compelled to fall back. The strafed roofing was used
for army shelters; the heavy timbers, for a powder magazine.
Only two brick offices in the yard survived; all cattle, implements, fences, orchards, and books were pillaged. The fields
were strewn with minie balls, rusted bayonets, discarded military equipment, and were pockmarked with deep empty graves.
Fort Despair is Fort Rosecrans, and Chattalla is Murfreesboro.
Miss Murfree rode across these fields and examined the redoubts.
She also read French engineering texts in order to describe the
fortifications accurately.

More significant than any of these particulars is the atmosphere that envelops the setting. From the first sentence, which
strikes an ominous, ghostly note, and continuously to the last
page, a mood of portentous gravity looms over the battlefield
and infects every character's thoughts. The oft-repeated phrases
"haunted thickets," "empty graves," and "unquiet ghosts" take
on a rhythm of incantation, lauding the presence of a vital secret
among these shards of the dead past. The insistent refrain of the
title heightens the Gothic effect and returns us to the grim center as surely as Hardy does with Egdon Heath in *The Return
of the Native*. Baskerville believes that Miss Murfree's "superb
landscape-painting has never been used more suggestively and
impressively."[3] More often, she has been rebuked for hyper-
intensity and repetitiveness. Her method of cohering super-

natural innuendo with tangible commonplace details rouses expectancy to a degree neither could evoke alone.

Other autobiographical elements are visible in her familiarity with legal jargon, courtroom procedures, lawyers' prerogatives, and the suspension of the law of limitations upon which the main plot of this novel devolves;[4] in the children's tutoring at home; in the Bandusia Springs resort; in her joke about General Vayne's heavy handwriting; and in the disposition of Marcia Vayne, who balances effervescent girlishness with a "mature appreciation of the seriousness of life" and traumatic childhood memories of shrieking shells, fleeing non-combatants, and grisly obituary lists. Moreover, Marcia is consummately delighted with "her little ill-feathered shafts of wit." Yet, among the main characters, she is the least of Miss Murfree's deputies. Mrs. Kirby, John Estwicke, and Maurice Brennett more frequently speak the author's mind.

The vague, vaporous battlefield, expelling glimmers of light and echoes of death, induing all of life with a phosphorescence of fear, must be considered the dominating personage, as the mountains are in so many of the local-color stories. Its influence penetrates even the viscid consciousness of the idiot Graffy Beale. People fall into three broad categories: Thackerayan aristocrats with names out of romantic convention—Fortescue, St. Pierre, Estwicke; Dickensian commoners who run to monosyllabics—Beale, Tait, Toole; and an intermediate, unsavory group whose surnames grate—Jartree, Brennett, Keevor. At this early date Miss Murfree perceives the multiplicity of human feelings and motives. She reports "subacute" awareness, "doubleness" of personality, and "double-sided" reactions; and she elects to tell the reader about these herself before letting their effects emerge in speech or action. Naïvely, she announces their existence as though they were exceptional. She skirts the edge of the psyche, looks down, and decides not to leap. Excluding a small handful of instances, she maintains this practice throughout her career.

Miss Murfree adopts Thackeray's technique of setting pairs of contrasting characters into motion, thereby exposing each other's qualities and propelling the action through their interactions. The principal sets are General Vayne and John Estwicke, Marcia Vayne and Antoinette St. Pierre, Austin Travis and Maurice Brennett. Of these Vayne and Estwicke are most efficacious, differing crucially in matters of age and youth, loyalty to past

and present, filial and passionate love, relative and absolute
morality, hyperbole and bluntness, extroversion and self-consciousness. There are other pairs as irrevocably mismated as
these, but many of the antipodal figures confute one another
only temporarily, such as Colonel Percy and Vayne, or Horace
Percy and Estwicke.

Estwicke is the deepest achievement. A Southern-born captain
in the Union Army stationed in Tennessee, his seeds of contention sprout as much from his murky temperament as from his
anomalous position. He is aggressive and reserved, impulsive
and punctilious, gregarious and introspective. A man who has
no questions to ask of heaven or earth, he has a talent for sarcasm but is also capable of mocking himself. His impetuous acts
of pride are followed by long bouts of self-condemnation and
moral flagellation. In a scene which predates the twentieth-
century psychoanalytical séance, he recites a calamitous tale of
father-son relationship. This revelation of his true family name—
changed by his grandfather to spare him the onus of his father's
ruinous obsession with gambling—is a bitter catharsis of parental
rejection, of resentment, pugnacity, guilt, remorse, self-crimina-
tion, and lost identity. The compulsiveness with which he de-
claims his humiliating masquerade excites the reader's sympathy
for his harried, suppressed life.

Estwicke's adversary, General Vayne, is not entirely external.
He undergoes dark nights of the soul over which the author
draws a curtain, permitting only glimpses of a man in crisis pac-
ing endlessly back and forth. Chiefly, he is meant to be the
typical Southern gentleman who has come upon bare days. His
dignity is incongruous with his broken-down estate, and he is
earnest this side of being ludicrous. He talks in capital letters
and logy aphorisms, flaunting his anachronistic ideals in the
midst of the dreary collapse. Seen through his "moral magnify-
ing glass," everything Southern is grandiose and irreproachable.
He announces that "God created first Tennessee, and with what
was left over made the rest of the world."

Out of the discord between Vayne and Estwicke emanates the
sturdiest theme of the novel—the struggle between forces of the
South and the North for ascendancy of the past over the present.
Vayne illustrates failure of the old South through loss of his arm,
his material privations, his hollow magniloquence, and his quix-
otic dreams about a dead era. Estwicke's vigor and apparent
lack of sensitivity are modified by his being "a home-made

Yankee," providing subtler reactions to the old mores by one familiar with their operations and objectives. Marcia springs the controversy into the open when she exclaims that, in comparison to Estwicke, her father's kind of soldier "has gone out of fashion." Miss Murfree's purpose begins to show through when Vayne apologizes publicly for his attack on Kendricks—a restrained farce which jogs the whole foolish scaffold of gallant rules under which the old South lived. The possibility of reconciliation is admitted when Estwicke risks his life on the exploding pier for Beale and Tait. Thereupon a native opines that "there might be some fine fellows among those Yankees at the barracks."

In the outcome, Miss Murfree predicts the emergence of a new South, one born out of coalition with the strength and vision of the North (Estwicke) that triumphs over the old traditions (Vayne) and infuses the new generation (Marcia) with a germ of hope for the future. Although momentarily acquiescent to the dictates of the old order, Marcia eventually declares herself consonant with the new way, accepting Estwicke despite her father's objections. Criticism in this political and social allegory is mild, leveled indulgently from within, but the satire of Southern manners is unmistakable. The attractions and advantages of progress are noted, and the Northern stand is favored without blatant rejection of hallowed Southern institutions.

Marcia Vayne is not a predictable stereotype, nor does she contain any hidden fires, as does her friend Antoinette St. Pierre. Languid and seemingly ineffectual, Miss St. Pierre displays startling ferocity toward her enemies. Miss Kirby is a light-minded, matchmaking gossip, forever stimulated and disappointed by the vagaries of young lovers. Through her, the author promulges the frailty and frippery of upper-class protocol in the South, and her own acute perception of feminine psychology. Written around the same period of her satirical essays, *The Battle* bristles with drawing room witticisms delivered by the narrator independent of the characters.

Maurice Brennett is interestingly drawn in two shades. There is a hint of doubleness in the hard lines of his lips, which mark the glacial control he has established over his turbulent nature. Described as "harder and sharper than the hardest and sharpest," he nevertheless exhibits sentimental interest in music and lyric drama. A rapacious schemer intent only on getting rich, he malevolently affects everyone with whom he consorts. There are two chinks in his armor of vice: (1) although a cunning tactician "with a head for expedients" who takes every advantage of stupidity and cupidity, he remains unconcerned about the longer strategy and fails to plan enough steps ahead; (2) he is consumed with diabolic pride—"Other men expect events to come to pass. I *make* things happen."

Within Miss Murfree's deterministic order of existence, where man is empowered to shift one or two bits of the mosaic but not to alter the fundamental design, Brennett moves purblind and inadequate. Despite his grand avowals of free will, his fate is to become "the chosen instrument" of justice and self-defeat in a situation he had intended to manage for his own profit. He is amazed at fate when it works to his benefit, but he cannot conceive that it may also work against him. His elaborate mechanism falls to pieces when, by another inadvertency of fate, Keevor chances to see Tom Toole in a barroom in Chattalla. Brennett is cleverly adumbrated by Casey, the sleazy gambler whose downfall comes less through clumsiness than the inexorable machinations of fate. Both men cheat, both are apprehended, both escape the full consequences of their crimes.

Miss Murfree's inclination to equate life and the theater finds metaphoric expression in such phrases as the "heart-drama . . . on the human stage," as well as her stage-conscious sketches of John Estwicke. However, her most expert presentation comes in the scene in which Edward Keevor, an actor, experiences a transfer fantasy. As part of Brennett's ruse to rob Antoinette St. Pierre, Keevor impersonates Estwicke's dead father. In time, Keevor becomes possessed by the role he is playing and believes he *is* John Fortescue. His speech, though overlong and histrionic, befits his temperament, and is moving. "I am dead!" he cries, "I have lost my identity." In the frequent use of the theater trope, here and in later works, Miss Murfree comes close to anticipating the modern preoccupation with schizoid personality.

The motif of common humanity which Brennett reluctantly concedes is further strengthened by alliance with the theater trope. He is furious over the realization that "these louts" have within them "complex elements of hidden sensitiveness . . . which make up life in worthier spheres" and can thereby hamper his program. Miss Murfree makes it clear that, whether in the gaudiest metropolis or in the dingiest village in the world, "the great fundamental facts of humanity" preside. All men and women are brothers and sisters under the skin. "Crowded upon this narrow stage were roaring farces, and sentimental melo-dramas, and elements of high tragedy." This conviction, more-over, constitutes another justification of the close attention local colorists pay to their seemingly inconsequential places and people.

The lower fringe of the populace is ably summarized in Tom Toole, a rustic ferryman whose dress, language, ignorance, loyalty, and helplessness forecast Miss Murfree's capacity for local color. Tom, by permissible pun, is a tool of the plot. Not-withstanding his illiteracy, he reads the newspaper item which leads to reversal of the dramatic trend. Pickie Tait, dirty, tat-tered, tow-headed, is the classic amoral ragamuffin of the fron-tier. Allergic to the restraints of civilization, he uninhibitedly lies, steals, and blows up the pier. Together, Toole and Tait point up the contrast between country and town values which extends through the several echelons of society represented. Graffy Beale, the "idjit," enjoys protection and immunity by virtue of local superstition that anyone bereft of his brains is marked by God for some special, unrevealed purpose. Miss Mur-free romantically grants him unsounded depths of affinity. He is adored by children, shiftless Negroes, and yellow dogs; he has an instinctual gift of music; the moon and the mists enter into conspiracy with his moods and movements.

Nature and man are shown in other phases of relationship. A snowstorm beautifies Chattalla, rendering smooth and luminous what man has managed to disfigure, confirming Cowper's dic-tum that "God made the country, and man made the town." Man, absenting himself from the original element, turns gross and sordid. Estwicke senses an "oration in the air" but is devoid of the thrill he knows he should be feeling: "my nerves won't respond. I don't hear it." And a note which grows voluminously in the mountain stories—man's insignificance in the face of na-ture—is struck unequivocally. Man's presence is slight, discord-ant, "an alien incongruity foisted upon the scene."

"Mary's moon" asserts itself prominently in this first of her novels. It is employed with nice versatility: as a stage light to pick out prime physical details or emotions suffusing a face; to sustain the mood of mystery and death or the illusions of young love; as the symbolic eye of God falling affably upon His good creatures and direly upon the bad; as a moral factor evoking lilies in a wasted garden. Three other techniques which develop in later stories also appear. Two stem from Miss Murfree's penchant for making nature follow art: the earthworks have the vitrified look of Japanese cloisonné, giving off a sheen of green enamel; the Tennessee terrain is feminized *en fête champêtre*, a pastoral pose that "predicates upon nature a parasol." The third technique derives from Scott and her own dramatic flair. Tableaux recur—equestrian figures against the sky; battlements in stark outlines; the jutting, grotesque pier—magnified and emitting supernatural implications.

The card game in Meredith's room at the Marston hotel is one of many in Miss Murfree's stories. Although she studied the rules of several games and played an interminable number of poker hands with her family, it is alleged that none of her presentations shows any acumen. This point is minor when one considers her purpose, which is to engage the participants in a shadow play of life wherein conflicts are acted out and the essential character of each player emerges. In this game, the lengthiest outside of "A-Playin' of Old Sledge," the man beneath the flesh is brought to the surface. Tom West, a callow sycophant, passes out at a very early stage; Meredith becomes the voice of reason; Casey cheats; Estwicke defers magnificently; and Brennett watches every move keenly and objectively. This mimicry defines the basic role of each man in the novel.

Miss Murfree's diction and descriptions, while excessive, are on the whole less exotic and congested than in the local-color stories. Polysyllabic monsters and periphrases rove unchecked, Biblical and classical references abound, as do Latin, French, and Italian expressions. Blind allusions are snidely inserted; for example, the horse pricking on the plain, and the precious byplay on Percy and the horse Hotspur. Conversation is stilted and conspicuously clever; too often a quip is elongated until it terminates in a neat envelope form. Peremptory interruptions by the author are frequent and annoying.

A lovely lyrical interlude, recalling the chapter "Diversion Played on a Penny-Whistle" in *The Ordeal of Richard Feverel*, overtakes Antoinette and Meredith in the midst of their efforts to save her property. A protracted, stylized apostrophe, it presumes a never-ending idyll of love in a replica of the Garden of Eden. It is somewhat regrettable that Miss Murfree turns it to satirical use, for the language is exalted and the tone could have been sustained without palling. Indeed, tart social satire and verbal ironies dominate those segments of the book not permeated by the spirit of the battlefield. Miss Murfree's subliminal sense of superiority over lower-caste natives escapes in gratuitous jibes which have no bearing on development of character or action. There is no provocation for the contempt she heaps upon Tom Toole, "an illiterate country lout, with no knowledge of the science of optics." This attitude, evidently unsuspected by her, was to prevent full identification with the indigenous people and customs she treated so vividly in later years.

As to construction, Miss Murfree sins in the matter of proportion. She overshoots the mark in some of the exciting episodes, rings in complications of questionable worth to the necessary outcome, and does not always succeed in coordinating them with the main lines of action. The bogey of coincidence obtrudes in three important instances. All this is not to say that the narrative is clumsily evolved. The two main plots—the love story of Marcia and Estwicke, the legal intrigue over Antoinette's inheritance—move along with gratifying velocity, joined and bolstered by several complementary subplots.

The title of the novel comes finally to signify far broader fields than where the military battle was fought. Among other battles waged are those of Marcia and Vayne to sustain body and soul, between old and new values, between Estwicke and Vayne, between Estwicke and young Percy, Brennett and Antoinette, Brennett and Keevor, Pickie Tait and orthodoxy, Beale and Toole, Estwicke and Keevor against their submerged identities; and between justice and mawkishness in the Jartree case.

Where the Battle Was Fought demonstrates at the earliest stage that Miss Murfree's own struggle would have to be against unreined volubility, opulent plotting, and expansive characterization. A reviewer in the New York *Tribune* for September 14, 1884, said benignly: "Exuberance, however, is a venial fault, and practice will soon teach Mr. Craddock a wise economy of his material." His optimism was miscast. Miss Murfree's exuberance flourished like the proverbial green bay tree. Economy was foreign to her nature.

II   The Storm Centre

By 1905 the kind of local color written by Miss Murfree had been dislodged by a sterner regionalism. Incapable of adjusting to the harsher mode, despite the promptings of Walter Hines Page, she turned back to the milieu of her first novel—the Civil

War in Tennessee. In *The Storm Centre* she coalesces her memories of life at Old Grantland and in Nashville during her girlhood, spicing them with fanciful and sometimes fantastic
figments of romantic adventure. With all its faults this novel is
a maturer accomplishment in respect to structural and thematic
components. The plot is simpler, the conflict of values more
complex.

Fluellen Baynell, a captain in the Union Army, is taken sick
and lives during his convalescence in the home of Judge Roscoe,
a friend of his father, in occupied Roanoke City. This home is
the figurative storm center of the title. In the midst of war, confusion, hatred, and mixed loyalties, it serves as a place of comparative peace and refuge. All the effective action swirls around
it, all the vital elements develop in one of its three levels: the
cellar, where the horse is illegally secreted; the middle floor,
where day-to-day domestic activities unfold; the attic, where the
Confederate son of the house hides. By these alternations of
urgency and constraint Miss Murfree keeps her kinetic metaphor
alive. This house, too, holds in abeyance the seething desire of
Baynell to marry the Judge's resident niece, Leonora.

The Storm Centre is an elaborate charade in which every
character represents an attitude of the time and place. East
Tennessee voted more than two to one against secession, and a
considerable number of its citizens retained their sympathies
for the Union even after declaration of war. There seems to have
been no concerted resentment against the occupying forces, although here and there sentiments like those of the deeper South
could be heard. Thus Miss Murfree had a lavish spectrum of
feelings to examine, from the severe to the moderate Northerner,
from the tolerant to the intransigent Southerner, and the equivo-
cal shades of those caught between the two antagonists. As
exemplifications of these phases, her characters succeed; as people, they lack viability.

The main tussle ensues between Baynell and Leonora. The
captain, a martinet with his men, is proud and dismal as a lover.
He has an exacting temperament which will not permit him to
lie even to save face for his beloved. He reports the presence of
the horse in the cellar and disapproves of conversation about
even the most trivial military moves. He fleetingly considers "the
vast subject of the abstract values of right and wrong, the ultimate decrees of conscience, whether in matters of great or mi-

nute importance," but he invariably reverts to the irrefragable ethic based on his official position.

Leonora Gwynn is a beautiful widow with a look of dreary lassitude who goes about in frumpish black clothes. She can be understood only in relation to her husband Rufus, a gambling, drinking brute who beat her viciously and ran through her fortune in convulsive dissipation. A symbol of the old wasteful violent culture, he is killed by a horse he is thrashing. Leonora represents the South reduced by a degenerate code to a point of sodden quiescence, "forever dominated by the sense of disaster, and despair, and flight; forever looking backward, forever hearkening to the troublous past—exhausted, listless, hopeless, every impulse of volition stunned." She vegetates dourly in the storm center, refusing Baynell's proposals until he appears a persecuted martyr at his court-martial. Abruptly she recognizes his golden attributes of constancy, honor, and judgment—all of which he had demonstrated over and over again in close proximity—discards her widow's weeds, and accepts him. The psychology of her transposition is unconvincing. Do women marry men for their "vibrations of chivalric ethics"? In any case, she escapes the fetid atmosphere of the old false gallantries into the bracing fresh air of the present without the tragedy of Faulkner's Emily. Baynell and Leonora are unresponsive, papier-maché creatures. Their union is improperly motivated and, at best, unexciting.

Judge Roscoe seems a slightly modified portrait of Miss Murfree's father. The Judge is a nervous, agreeable man who has provided sons for the army and jeopardized his wealth for the cause, yet he does not feel bound "to hate individually every fellow-creature who has opposite convictions." A voice of the reasoning, intellectual South, he is balanced by his son Julius, a mettlesome warrior with none of the psychotic vices of Rufus Gwynn. Mildred Fisher embodies still another mutation of response to the invaders. A traditional belle, she serves as counterpart of Julius to the extent that both carry on in the old way, despite new circumstances; they are too young, too impetuous, too shallow to comprehend the irrevocability of the change. She "receives Yankees" gaily but reminds them that her father and five brothers in the Confederate vanguard are also waiting to "receive" them. She projects a dichotomy of blood and banter, of magnolias and mayhem—the old South with its great heart beating above the sound of its great hurt. She is the typological opposite of Leonora. Mildred marries impulsively and with flair, a splash of bright red across the grey wreath of war and desolation.

Two Union officers, Colonel Ashley and Lieutenant Seymour, embrace the philosophy of when in Rome live with the Romans. They enjoy the hospitality and the women like gentlemen, affecting solicitude and overlooking polite taunts. They are objects of disdain to punctilious, aloof Captain Baynell. Far more implicated are the two faithful, ambivalent Roscoe servants caught between the old regime and the new dispensation. With freedom a suit too new to wear, they attest the dilemma of many Negroes of the time, uncertain of which course to choose—love or liberty. Uncle Ephraim is garrulous and querulous, shrewd and useful in a crisis. Called "the double-faced Janus," he agrees instantly with Union suggestions that he leave his servitude; nonetheless, he stays on to help his masters out of difficulty. Aunt Chaney, spuriously gruff and utterly devoted to Leonora, also elects to remain. Queried as to which side she favors, she answers, "bofe sides . . . 'cordin' ter de politics ob dem we is talkin' to!" Their native guile is shown to be more effective in times of trouble than that of their white superiors. In no other book does Miss Murfree so seriously consider the plight of the Negro during the breakup of his world.

Upon this primary strife of North-South and past-present reconciled through the marriage of Leonora and Baynell, Miss Murfree superimposes the grander theme of mutual understanding which would wipe out man's inhumanity to man. There is not enough knowledge of the horror and pathos in other lives. We need only note it to stop hating and fighting. Baynell reads to Leonora a passage containing this message. She reacts cynically, feeling that no one in the world can plumb the recesses of *her* sorrow. Glimpsing Baynell's torment, she turns compassionate. Curiously, nature appears insensitive to man's vicissitudes. Miss Murfree sets Baynell's unwarranted trial in significant juxtaposition to a view of the landscape, an available, neglected paradise within which man plays out his twisted, meaningless existence.

Characters are chiefly created by Miss Murfree's own depositions, and secondly through opinions uttered by their peers. An example of this method is Ashley's remark about Baynell: "He is about as stiff, and unresponsive, and prejudiced, and priggish a bundle of animal fibre as ever called himself human." To which

Leonora adds: "He seems unguarded, and impulsive, and ardent." Of course, Baynell is all of these in turn. The Negroes are unfortunate parodies, clowning for "de white folks," committing malapropisms, and quivering with superstitions. Miss Murfree's potential for exposing character through interior monologue is displayed when Leonora reconstructs her relations with Rufus, accomplished not by maudlin recital to Baynell but flooding back into her mind as she sits crocheting near him by the fire. She picks up threads of her work and her thoughts in perfect unison. A deft touch is Baynell's brief interruption and her rhythmical resumption, lending a sense of reality and immediacy to her unspoken reverie.

Miss Murfree's proficiency as a local colorist returns in good stead here. Close attention is given to details of place—interiors and exteriors, the hotel, the people in the streets, the arrival and departure of a river steamer, the war-ruined areas. The garret in which Julius hides, with its conglomeration of broken furniture, relics, dust and silence, typifies the old South in which he symbolically finds refuge. Styles in women's attire and music popular in this period are precisely rendered, as are military drills and the conduct of a court-martial. Realism prevails in these descriptions, indeed a naturalistic note creeps in; for Miss Murfree does not shy away from violence, passion, or ugliness. Mildred watches in sick dismay the blood coming in jets from the mouth of a wounded soldier whose fingers are dripping red from the hole in his stomach. Julius, Baynell, and Leonora are also depicted in the throes of injury. As Poe makes a fetish of eyes and teeth, Miss Murfree makes a fetish of Leonora's hair in its full beauty and horror. Lovely on most occasions, intermittently the reader sees gory hanks of it sticking to the balusters as her husband drags her down the stairs.

The gloom of war impends, without attaining the persistence or density of the mood in *Where the Battle Was Fought*. The tearless cries of the children are pathetic, and mute fear is reflected in their daunted eyes and paling cheeks. A man is taken out to be shot, kneeling on his coffin—"And is nobody, *nobody* sorry?" The grimness and heartlessness of war are often invoked, but the storm center constantly alleviates the despondent, disastrous effects.

The omniscient author is stanchly in charge, manifesting her old faults of idealizing landscape; injecting unacknowledged quotations or paraphrases from Shakespeare, Swift, Burns, and

Sheridan; whitewashing masculine dialogue; and flashing Latinate polysyllables. However, the style is generally easier, the
descriptions shorter and more clearly focused. The moon shines
its wonted number of times, mostly as decor or spotlight, less
often as symbol or instigator of mood. The Old Maid card is an
augury of Baynell's long interlude of destitute hope, and the card
game trope is woven into Miss Murfree's concept of fate. The
deaf and dumb child, although derived from a wedding ceremony of two mutes which the author once saw in Memphis,
seems a transfiguration of her own handicap. Little Lucille is
never made to feel her deficiency, surmounts her obstacle by
excelling in studies and painting remarkably for her age—a reversion to Mary Murfree's Popocatepetl-spelling days.

The novel opens with brisk introductions to scene, characters,
and imminent action. Thereafter, it proceeds in a single line
with only two divergences: Julius' adventure of escape and
Mildred's inadvertent excursion behind the lines, the first of
which eventually applies to the central plot. Even Leonora's
flashback is progressive, although Miss Murfree herself inter-
poses additional horripilating details which she could very well
have inducted into Leonora's natural outflowing account. Complication is limited to the major roles and involves such elemental
ingredients as war, love, law, flight, and human ingenuity in
a pinch.

The climax at the court-martial strains credulity. It is hard to
believe that a captain with impeccable ethics, often publicly
practiced, and with a hitherto unblemished record would be
sentenced to death on so flimsy a network of circumstantial evidence and the unsupported testimony of a deaf-mute child. Nor
can one accept the coincidence that among the members of the
court should sit a noted aurist who can exchange sign language
flawlessly with Lucille. Other confluences of this sort defy probability: that Baynell's father's college chum should live in proper
proximity to the captain's headquarters; that Julius should adopt
the alias of John Wray, Jr., of Manchester, England, exactly
duplicating the name and home of the blockade runner who appears at the same time at the same hotel; that Mildred's horse
should carry her right into her brothers' bailiwick. The defects
are those of incident rather than construction, and for once Miss
Murfree refrains from wholesale gathering of loose ends in the
conclusion.

The Storm Centre is indubitably a regression to *Where the*

Battle Was Fought. Although less brooding and less dynamic, it exhibits wider awareness and appreciation of the issues implicit in the conflict—the North-South animosities, the collapse and changing ideals of the South, the slaves' dilemma, the cost of the war in terms of personal integrity as well as lives and property. With more arresting people to propel its themes, this could have been a significant novel for it has greater sturdiness, simplicity, and insight than its predecessor.

III   *Three War Stories*

Miss Murfree published three short stories in which the Civil War plays a substantial part. The war itself is secondary but its consequences are far-reaching in the lives of those it touches. The principal action in each takes place in the Tennessee mountains. Since these stories were written relatively late in Miss Murfree's career, one may expect many devices already encountered in the mountain stories. So it is. Characters, themes, and setting are thoroughly familiar. The outcome in every case recalls an earlier work.

The first part of "The Bushwhackers" (1899) calls up Crane's *The Red Badge of Courage.* Hilary Knox is strikingly like Henry Fleming in his boy's view of war as a parade of flags and fifes, burnished arms, fiery horses, gallant companions, and as an opportunity to flaunt one's bravery. He receives from Jack Bixby —a man in his own outfit—a wound so severe as to necessitate amputation. After Hilary's discharge the story goes rapidly to pieces in a swirl of bathos. He helps Bixby, now leader of a gang of bushwhackers, to escape from an abandoned summer resort because he realizes that it is Christmas Eve. Hilary returns home to find his sweetheart, who had rejected him, now ready to marry. He learns to write with his left hand, moves to a valley town, and is elected clerk of the circuit court. This is a ragged mass of incident with no unity except Hilary; it is several stories in one, including war heroism, loss of romantic illusions, a deviated love affair, persistence of ambition, and the flowering of a career.

Bixby is the devil to Hilary's saint in a morality play about absolute, aggressive evil lunging unprovoked against passive goodness. Bixby is intrinsically malicious and jealous, intent without reason to destroy Hilary. He keeps up an outward semblance of friendship while undermining Hilary with his superiors. Hilary is revolted by Bixby's devious wiles but takes no hand to ward them off. "Strangely softened" by the scene which reminds him of the Star of Bethlehem and the Nativity, he aids his inveterate adversary in keeping with the Biblical principle of peace on earth, goodwill toward men. By the rule of poetic justice, Hilary rises to a comfortable position in the world.

During the Civil War the hotel and cottages at Beersheba Springs were used for refuge by many families, and also as recuperation centers for Southern soldiers. Miss Murfree evokes the devastation of war through her depiction of the hotel in a time of desertion—a melancholy spectacle of wrenched doors, shattered windows, dusty rooms, and cobwebbed piazzas overlaid by an aura of weeds, lizards, and silence. Briefly she reflects the controversy of allegiances in Tennessee. Hilary's mother spiritedly opines that he will be "fur the Union, too, like everybody in the mountings ez hed good sense," whereas he responds to the impulse to repel the invaders.

Miss Murfree's acute feeling for the behavior of adolescents becomes evident in Hilary's parting and return to Delia, the mountain girl appalled by, then reconciled to, his missing arm.

"The Raid of the Guerilla" (1909), which occurs in the same vicinity, is a take-off on the story told about the wife of a proprietor of Beersheba Springs Hotel who gave packages of coffee to Forrest's soldiers as they crossed over the mountain after their prodigious raid on Murfreesboro. The Civil War touch is supererogatory, for this is in effect another sad tale of the mountain girl who waits and yearns for a lover who will never return. The local color is strongest in the dialect, less minute in delineation of scenery, and thinner in portrayal of character. All presentations are more casual than in the early mountain chronicles, where they were at least vivid, if verbose. Miss Murfree has ceased to be elaborate, out of sheer weariness with the subject; and she has also ceased to appeal.

In this single-line story of two connected episodes, all of her stock situations and stereotypes reappear. Ethelinda Brusie is the astonishingly lovely mountain-flower with white face and "yaller" hair, wooed briefly and won by Captain Ackert, the valiant outsider. There are the usual gabbling grandpappy, the crone granny, the prematurely aged mother by the fireside, the tow-headed youngsters, a one-armed blacksmith, his half-witted helper, a miller, and a squire-judge. Not one of these displays the slightest depth. Precedent events are revealed through a lumbering flashback of details long familiar to everyone in the Brusie household. Ethelinda, a Union sympathizer, has aided the escape of some Northern troops. She confesses this to Ackert, a Southern commander, in order to save the life of a suspect. Taken by her nobility, Ackert sees her as one of the saints in the Bible—"an' plumb beautiful besides." Out of this episode evolves the theme of undifferentiated humanitarianism: "Perhaps the revelation of the sanctities of a sweet humanity for a holy sake, blessing and blessed, had illumined his path, had lifted his eyes, had wrought a change in his moral atmosphere spiritually suffusive, potent, revivifying, complete." The sentimental upshot is instant love. However, Miss Murfree stabs it with a glinting irony of fate. Ackert is killed in battle, and Ethelinda languishes unknowing.

This formula story, concocted for neutralist readers of pulp fiction, implies an undercurrent of love between the opposing factions, a sort of hands-across-the-conflict theme. It is a far cry from Miss Murfree's estimable work. The New York *Times* (July 29, 1899) made it an occasion for rattling sarcasm: "There is no available record as to the number of times the moon has crossed the Tennessee mountains since Charles Egbert Craddock first made it perform that transit in 1884. This luna record, moreover, is possibly held by *The Prophet of the Great Smoky Mountains* although *The Raid of the Guerilla* is a close second."

It is said that Miss Murfree wrote "The Lost Guidon" (1911) in one night, and perhaps that should suffice as criticism. A patent morality too baldly specific about the symbolic correlation between the lost guidon and Casper Girard's lost honor, it nevertheless scores some effective points as an allegory of flesh and spirit. Girard, a sergeant whose company has been wiped out, continues waving the guidon after the battle; he is convinced that it will inspire the dead to rise and rally against the enemy. A chaplain retrieves the pennant after Girard collapses from exhaustion and discards it in a crevice to prevent him from overtasking himself again. At a reunion of the regiment years later in New Helvetia Springs, the chaplain observes Girard's moral downtrend and recalls the incident of the guidon. Shamed, Girard reverts to his better self. The young sergeant's "Guide right!" is restored as the grown man's shibboleth.

As the author works it out, the reformation is not as simple-minded as it sounds. The felicitous debate between pragmatic surgeon and transcendental chaplain brings to light essential antithetical values: the flag itself and its spiritual connotations, Girard's physical collapse and the decline of his principles, the concealed guidon and his immersed virtue. Unfortunately she pounds too hard at the interpretation, thus impairing the subtlety of its development.

Colonel Duval and his overweening daughter provide a base for social distinctions, the card game trope illustrates Girard's fall from grace, and Miss Murfree exonerates the New York *Times* with her jejune pun, "Isn't the moon heavenly?" In her short stories about the Civil War she had nothing new to say.

A Season for History

LOCAL-COLOR WRITING remained in favor with the American public until the mid-1890's. Thereafter it rapidly surrendered to a type of historical romance founded on the popularity of Blackmore's *Lorna Doone* and perpetuated by Stevenson, Stanley Weyman, and Anthony Hope. In the United States the first widely known practitioners were Lew Wallace, F. Marion Crawford, S. Weir Mitchell, and Charles Major. *When Knighthood Was in Flower* (1898) closed a door that had been opened by "The Luck of Roaring Camp" (1868).

Miss Murfree was capable of romanticizing a real situation this side of authenticity, as her mountain stories amply prove. This new crossed-swords and clothes-horse type of extravaganza, however, was more than she could conscientiously advocate. With the exception of *Where the Battle Was Fought* she had published only stories of the Tennessee mountains for adults and children from 1878 to 1897. In that year Macmillan invited her to write a book for its Stories From American History Series, to which Grace King, George Eggleston, Frank Stockton, and Gilbert Parker had contributed volumes on Florida, Southern soldiers, buccaneers, and Canadian explorers. She fell upon the suggestion with avidity, for here was local color taking on the patina of history. She wrote practically nothing in the next two years, bending all her efforts to research. She read every account of pioneer Tennessee available in the state libraries and book stores, traced records of the French and Indian War period as far off as the British Museum, and saturated herself in local Indian language and lore. In 1899 *The Story of Old Fort Loudon* appeared. Within the next seven years she produced two other historical novels and seven short stories.

While she wished—as all writers do—to be vastly read and admired, Miss Murfree did not have a best-seller mentality. In these annals of early settlers and Indian wars in colonial Tennessee, she deliberately eschews the flamboyance of popular historical romance. She pictures no sublime heroes swooping down to save by a hairsbreadth immaculately gowned damsels in dire straits. The urge for authenticity which drove her to read law assiduously and play interminable card games impelled her to scrupulous investigation of the mores and minutiae of the period. Her disposition to record the vanishing culture of the Tennessee mountaineer beset by industrial change extended backward into the age when Indian existence underwent a similar kind of incursion by the white man. With the consciousness of class differences which informs her mountain, Civil War, and Mississippi stories, she observes the ineluctable conflict between these two societies and points up racial differences which inspired greater vehemence in the struggle. Her concept of fate prohibits any admission of genuine human progress from the historical point of view, and her standard theme of common humanity is both substantiated and extenuated. Her sense of the meaning of history gradually becomes distinct through thematic implications, treatment of character, and veneration of artifacts. In a small way, she had indicated this concept in In the "Stranger People's" Country, His Vanished Star, and "The Riddle of the Rocks."

I The Story of Old Fort Loudon

In The Story of Old Fort Loudon (1899) Odalie MacLeod expresses the American dream of unlimited, ebullient expansion along a line of beckoning frontiers. In this land of primeval beauty and hope the soul might rise without restriction to heights not yet achieved by man. For two reasons this attitude fails to assume scope or importance in this novel: first, it gets little attention in competition with exciting incident; second, it is severely confined to Odalie and eventually dwindles to just another opportunity for a female to rearrange her possessions around the house. The military commanders, for example, look backward to a life separate from this new world. They see their present station as a penetration of enemy territory and a holding action, not as a triumph of civilization or of the human spirit.

Miss Murfree's qualitative comparison of red man and white and the nagging question of the latter's moral right to the aborigine's soil further complicate the issue of progressive development in human nature. In their relations with the Indians, the settlers exhibit three contradictory facets: they are clearly more advanced, they are corruptive influences, they are less intelligent. On the whole, the balance falls in favor of the white man. Native superiority of ingenuity is exhibited by Oconostota who consistently outwits Captain Stuart. However, there are values in the civilized mode without which the Indian seems doomed to extinction. Atta-Kulla-Kulla avows that the Indian does not yet know how to utilize the advantages of the white man's state of development. Left to their own devices, the Cherokees revert to riot, grotesqueness, and discomfort. They no sooner take over Fort Loudon than it becomes a warren of garbage, filth, and flies.

Miss Murfree grants the Indian "subtle intelligence and a natural benignity," but her bias unfurls when Captain Stuart thinks of Atta-Kulla-Kulla as "truly remarkable . . . without education, of course, and without even the opportunity of observing those of a higher culture and exercising sentiments esteemed of value and grace in a civilized appraisement." The white man's preëminence is nevertheless tainted and sometimes made to appear no advance at all. Odalie feels that the Indian would be more trustworthy if he had not been taught otherwise by white man's example. Stuart reminds Demeré that not long ago torture —by thumbscrew, iron boot, and fire—was one of our own methods of punishment or coercion. And in one of her numerous editorial interjections, Miss Murfree sardonically regards the Cherokees' hypocrisy and "vaunting clamor of conscience" as "almost civilized." The white settler, then, does not represent an unequivocal improvement over his red predecessor in the long spiral of history.

Add to the above evidence her concept of fate—that life abounds with "fatally uncovenanted" events which no one can foresee and which order one's course, will or nill—and the shape of her historical perception becomes determinable. Since man is haply in the hands of Providence, his ability to rise freely above himself is rigidly constrained. Only infinitesimal changes within the arbitrary patterns are permissible. And since she also accepts Rousseau's principle of common humanity—that mankind shares generally the same thoughts and feelings through all times and all places—no exalted theory of man's unabated drive upward can be drawn from this book. In fact, there is little humanism but much antiquarianism in her historical sense. She sees history as an immense bonehouse of tradition, of mementoes which preserve a romantic record of "the mysterious, mythical" past. She reveres vestiges, remains, fragments, relic paintings, sarcophagi, and mummies for the marvelous stories of lost populations which they evoke, the pride of place they engender. She has a curator's rather than a philosopher's view of the historic process.

Geography, therefore, plays a leading role in all of Miss Murfree's historical fiction. The passage of time imbrued the rivers, forests, and mountains of Tennessee with myriad impressions of departed civilizations which she zealously sought to extract. In *Fort Loudon* her representations of locality are as graphic as those in her best local-color stories. Indeed, the book opens with a chromatic vista of the Cumberland range at sunset. The Great Smokies, Hoho-Hebee, Chilhowee, and Eskaqua become part of the larger prospect as the story spreads. The primordial plenty in this unspoiled region of fish and game, honey, fruits, and nuts creates a paradisaic atmosphere that still prevails a century and more later. The vivid description of buffalo bulls fighting at a salt lick, with a crouched panther as chief spectator, returns the wilderness to an era predating man. Indian legends of mineral wealth in copper, lead, and gold are evidenced in ancient mines and by outlandish tools. The Cherokees' village and council house, as well as their costumes, speech, and daily routines, are meticulously depicted.

The settlers have come for varying reasons: love of adventure and change, hatred of law and order, the sovereign opportunity for a new life in a new country without the thralls of a social system. Male apparel consists of coonskin cap, fringed buckskin shirt, deerskin leggings, knee breeches, and long stockings. The ladies cling as long as possible to their "civilized" garments, then weave clothes of rougher, more practical stuff. Life in a remote and lonely settlement, where fishing and hunting are the staple occupations, is relieved by cards and dominoes, singing, dances, pantomimes, gossip, jokes, and anecdotes. A pioneer house-raising brings together all the diverse elements. The adjacent garrison provides its modicum of entertainment through market drills, dress parades, fencing bouts, and a resplendent Christmas ball. The officers' mess hall is lovingly re-created to the last hanging wampum.

Fort Loudon, "stanch, grim, massive," is central to the action here as Fort Despair is in *Where the Battle Was Fought*. It too constitutes a vibrant personality which is eventually debauched. There is this difference, however. Enamored of her facility for research and carried away by her findings, Miss Murfree indulges in pedagogy far beyond the needs of fiction. Her informed talk of terrepleine, counterscarp, glacis, barbette, gabion, and other features of fortification adds little to the conception of Fort Loudon's function. On the contrary, it kindles irritation when encountered among heaps of superfluous detail regarding other matters. The author's infatuation with facts leads her to record faithfully and tediously every relevant item about the people, place, time, and events—to the detriment of both history (which should of course be particularized in such instances but not to the extent of overshadowing humanity itself) and the imagination (which should not be stifled by absolute compliance to the actual).

Miss Murfree turned to history when her creative impulse was waning. Unfortunately, she tried to make of research a substitute for the mythopoeic faculty. She wished to awaken interest and enlarge sympathy in the authentic Tennessee past, but her method produced neither good history nor good fiction. She went to extraordinary lengths to establish the correct name of Fort Loudon's commandant. The treaties of the Cherokees with French and English, and the treacheries on both sides are dealt with exhaustively. The words and phrases of the Indians are parenthetically translated. But the worst of her novelistic malpractice is manifested in nine crowded pages of footnotes following the text. In these she cites a plethora of authorities on Indian and regional data with the finicking precision of a doctoral dissertation, as though the validity of a novel depends upon documentary support. She could not accept the freedom accorded an artist as opposed to an archaeologist; consequently, her book suffers from its instructive tone. It has never been well received.

Miss Murfree revives the incidents in 1758-1760 surrounding the fall of Fort Loudon and the perfidious massacre that followed. The story follows two lines sporadically—the chronicle of the pioneers, which peters out toward the end, and the siege and capitulation of the Fort. This split in thematic allegiance allows neither to effect a satisfactory integration of all the components. Unfolded with few subtleties of presentation, the narrative is almost devoid of symbol. More frequently than before she inserts little pennants of prevision in the style of "Little did they realize. . . ." The last half dozen pages drearily summarize the career of each of the prominent figures to as late as 1813. Those who are not dead live happily ever after. In this account of their finest hours, however, we find no really forceful drama, emotional conflicts, moral engagement, or significant historical implications.

The main personages lack volume. They demonstrate attributes rather than sensibilities, perform rather than behave, but are suitably equipped and prepared for their assignments in the plot. As one thinks back, it is dispiriting to find that neither the MacLeod family nor the captains Stuart and Demeré remain uppermost in the mind. More memorable are such incidental individuals as O'Flynn the florid young corporal, Gilfillan the gigantic scalpless hunter, Monsieur Galette the red-eyed ear-ringed trader, the singing African Negro cook, and a cat—each with Dickensian credentials, each testifying to Miss Murfree's skill at the gouache technique of quick, thin, enticing strokes. The cat is her most extended animal portrait, displaying as much personality as any of the human beings. Slightly past kittenhood, she assumes every prerogative of an only child, raises hob with military decorum, raids the cook's traditionally inviolate domain, and accepts love on sufferance—all accomplished by Miss Murfree with a deliciously comical touch.

Both captains are indefectibly brave and loyal; otherwise, they are diametrically opposite. Stuart is bluffly funny, Demeré as sober as a code book; Demeré takes an affronted, averse attitude in crisis, Stuart is cool and offhand. Thus, in sport or in danger, their complementary temperaments provide a range of possibilities and meaning. Odalie, Fifine, and Mrs. Halsing seem prototypes of Miss Murfree's later mountaineers—the lovely mountain-flower, the infantile tyrant, the sharp-tongued crone. Oconostota is in the confirmed mold of wily, sinister Indian chiefs. Atta-Kulla-Kulla, the one Indian with more than two dimensions, turns unbelievably in favor of Stuart's cause.

She pauses regularly to honor the landscape but her language throughout this book, expository as well as descriptive, is never so clotted as in the earlier mountain stories. She favors the un-inflated diction of document, and an air of scholarly restraint hangs over her prose. Allusions are not obtrusive and come mostly from the Bible and classic mythology. A motley of com-mingled accents emerges in French through Odalie, in Irish dialect through O'Flynn, and in carefully researched Cherokee phrases. Interesting experiments like "unfriend" and "un-shake-off-ably" have a modern pulsation, and there is a minimum of horrendous Latinisms.

The pedantic tone which rises from persistent interjection of historic and philological particulars is exacerbated by a number of analogous practices. Miss Murfree shatters perspective by presenting Stuart as he "has been described by a contemporary historian." She constantly clucks over the ignorance of absolutely unschooled Indians, in one case because a Cherokee "had never heard of Babel, poor soul," and again because the myth of Jason and Medea at Colchis is a closed book to Willinawaugh. She becomes caustic about the intellectuality of pioneers, taking Daniel Boone to task for committing three misspellings in a single inscription—"slaughtering his 'bar' and the alphabet with equal calm and aplomb." She scolds at characters for neglect or shortsightedness, prophesying dark consequences for their folly. And always the pen is mightier than the sword, knowledge keener than a knife, most plainly when Hamish concedes that Odalie's *Vocabulaire Française* was more efficacious than his rifle in saving their lives. Although removed by more than a century from these protagonists, Miss Murfree could no more banish her sense of cultural superiority over them than she could over the analphabetic mountaineers.

Several familiar rhetorical devices are aptly employed. The theater trope, though minor here, has two telling moments: when Odalie carries on the perilous pretense that all the MacLeods are French, and when Hamish impersonates a woman to escape from the fort. The mountains are glorified by association with Olympus. The moon lights up vital proceedings, spreads sympathy for the beleaguered white man, and reflects the changing moods of men and affairs. Frontier beauties are allied with flowers as firmly as are their later mountain counterparts: Odalie is "a splendid tulip," Belinda Rush "a white rose," and lesser maidens "little daisies or violets."

Miss Murfree's most successful symbolic stratagem involves the portentous lady's silk riding mask which hangs on the wall of the officers' mess hall. At the outset, the atmosphere is gay with promise of a bright new existence and the mask is "dainty, fresh . . . suggesting a fair and distant face and eyes that looked forth on scenes more suave." After the siege and surrender of the fort, this "flimsy memento" shows "no suggestion in its vacant, sightless orbs of the brightness of vanished eyes, with no faint trace of the fair face that it had once sheltered." Demeré flings it into the fire. The saga of sadness after jollity begins; the friendly mask of the false Indians is also discarded.

A point Miss Murfree makes more powerfully in subsequent pioneer stories is that the kinship of color is stronger than any political treaty. Despite whatever animosities between white men of differing nationalities and whatever alliances exist between white nations and Indians, in moments of extremity white sides with white, Indian with Indian. Alexander MacLeod gazes at a Cherokee chieftain and notes the "deadly, racial hatred" burning in his eyes. Miss Murfree does not skirt the fact that within her frame of common humanity some segregation based on "bitter grudges and wrongs" flourishes.

II   A Spectre of Power

A Spectre of Power (1903) is an exercise in scholarship more dense in background data than *The Story of Old Fort Loudon*. Jean de Laroche's dream of empire built "on the ruins of a score of fantastic projections of old, braced and held to interdependent cohesion in a thousand details" sustains a continuous barrage of documentation and finally collapses under the sheer weight of authenticity. Once more Miss Murfree leans upon a bibliography of manuscripts and letters, incantations recorded at the Smithsonian Institution, infinitesimal details backed by precise dates, and seven pages of massed authoritative footnotes. The relationships and hierarchies of the Cherokees, their rites and regalia, their customs, courtesies, sports, and superstitions, the conclave in the council house, the anatomy of the guest and trading houses—every aspect of antiquity rung into the story is excruciatingly specified. She demonstrates again that, for her, history is a romantic reconstruction of the past on the evidence of its fascinating relics. She fails to arrange these into a meaningful scheme, allowing mere fact to overwhelm not only truth but fiction. She did not realize that—to paraphrase Jefferson—those historical novels are best which use history least.

Miss Murfree's misplacement of emphasis is regrettable, for she amasses the ingredients of an absorbing novel: a precarious situation, an unexploited terrain, interesting if not profound characters, an eternal triangle, homicidal Indians, curious cultural usages, and eccentric supernumeraries. The narrative follows Laroche's ambitions to their frustrated end, only' slightly encumbered by the love rivalry of Laroche and Push-koosh for Akaluka and the more important competition of Laroche and MacIlvesty for Lilias Lesly. Laroche's incognito is of a piece with Keevor's in *Where the Battle Was Fought* and with Royce's in *The Juggler*. Like Royce, Laroche realizes somberly that he is enacting a farce in repudiating the sane and orderly civilized world for one with which he has no true affinity. Like Hamish in *The Story of Old Fort Loudon*, he escapes in women's garb.

There are numerous other parallels to earlier stories, but more distracting is the improbability of several critical episodes. After breaking out of the guardhouse, MacIlvesty secretes himself inside an effigy of the Ancient Warrior in a cornfield in the heart of Indian country. He remains there undetected and overhears important plans discussed by Indians hovering around the figure. He is seen by an Indian girl when he emerges; nevertheless, he manages to elude capture and to help foil the plotters. It is hard to believe that he could hide so long in the scarecrow without being discovered by Indians who can *smell* buried gunpowder. Neither is it likely that he could have got out of the area alive after being spotted. While it makes for high dramatic tension, even a hothead like Lt. Everard would hardly attempt to arrest Laroche in the midst of his adoptive tribe of hostile Cherokees. Again, all the pieces fall into place in a surpassingly happy ending. MacIlvesty and Lilias are married, his family is restored to its former worthy position, Laroche reaches discursive old age in the salons and cafés of Paris, the French withdraw from Tennessee, and the Cherokees cease their harassments.

Miss Murfree perforates psychological boundaries and time-sense, destroying the illusion of a self-sufficient story by exclaiming "for aught I know" in the middle of a listing of biological specimens. Verisimilitude may be served when she informs the reader that certain barriers in the Cherokee River are "known now to modern engineers as the 'mountain obstruction,'" or when she caps the description of a buffalo-skin boat with "A queer craft we of to-day would deem it." However, the shock of sudden expulsion from the created world of the frontier nullifies any gain in immediacy.

In her accustomed way Miss Murfree does all the thinking for her characters, disclosing motives and reactions in direct declarations to the reader. Lilias is a luminously beautiful romantic in love with a chivalric notion rather than a man. She fastens upon Laroche, under his alias of Tam Wilson, because he embodies her beau ideal. When he reveals himself as a Frenchman, she glibly shifts to MacIlvesty, who has demonstrated that, though he loves her as a woman, he loves honor more. Unconscious of

MARY N. MURFREE

the irony in her stance, she tells him he is now her Tam Wilson.

Callum MacIlvesty, a poor but lofty Highlander, is non-commissioned because of his family's divestment of station for political reasons. An acquiescent lover, he is usually shown to disadvantage against the dashing, volatile Laroche. Miss Murfree infects the latter with just a suggestion of effeminacy in looks, as she does some of her manliest mountaineers. Subject to dualistic moods of bellicosity and blandness, hilarity and despondency, he is little troubled by moral dilemmas, basing his decisions as much on diplomatic as on religious or humanitarian convictions. He is elated by his easy ability to displace MacIlvesty in Lilias' affections even though he regards the affair as a ghastly simulacrum of love. His sensibility, like that of the other two lovers, is barely scratched.

Until the imminent departure of the trader's party from Ioco Town, the packmen and other minor figures are non-existent as individuals, leaving the impression that the settlement consists solely of the Lesly family, MacIlvesty, Laroche, and a few nondescript Indians. Of the last, the Choctaw chief Mingo Pushkoosh glitters pictorially in silver and feathers as might be expected of a visiting dignitary. His names signify "Prince Baby," and he evinces both the imperiousness of the first and the unbridled egoism of the second. Befittingly, he is a subtle schemer yet often childlike, passionately blurting out his secret thoughts. Akaluka, the young Cherokee widow, is dramatically presented as Eve in several instances, setting up expectation of a revival of the Lilith (Lilias) legend. Laroche is indeed loved by the dark and the fair, but this implication is not sustained. Miss Murfree nevertheless universalizes through this Indian Eve the feminine traits of vanity, perversity, and caprice.

Of the lesser white men only Herbert Taviston lingers in the memory. A comic and cowardly botanist, he owes something to Fenimore Cooper's Obediah Battius. With his pink cheeks and spruce clothes, Taviston is ludicrously out of place in this environment. He goes about with an umbrella over his head, a thermometer suspended at the height of his nose, wears a gaudy floriated dressing gown and an absurd nightcap. Like Dr. Battius, he applies Latin names to all natural specimens, emerging as a caricature of scientists attached to expeditions such as Lewis and Clark's, or, more broadly, a burlesque on the excesses of scientific rationalism.

No truly central theme develops. Predominant among the ideas

which issue from the Indian-white relationships is the previously
stated doctrine that over and beyond all political allegiances of
French and British with the Indians a stronger motivating factor
prevails in "racial hatred against the white man—ineradicable,
unappeasable, now and again only pretermitted for a time in
favor of some special individual." The same holds true for white
men in ultimate distress. Blood is indubitably thicker than
treaties.

Miss Murfree seems of two minds regarding the superiority of
primitive over civilized mode. The Tennessee River lifts its voice
and thunders "primeval truths"; yet the subtle white man, child
of civilization, usually eclipses the subtle Indian, child of nature.
"Inborn subtlety is no match for the ratiocination of cultivation,"
she says. On the other hand, when Lt. Everard confronts Moy
Toy, the advantages lie with the latter. Everard appears ignorant
in contrast to the chief's legacy of antiquity, symbolism, cere-
monial, and inscrutability. Moy Toy's "learning by inheritance
and intuition" is infinitely preferable to "the modern education"
of "the highly civilized man." The "seigneurial secret of civilization that made it the lord of the world," she adds acidly, "[is]
the simple formula for the manufacture of gunpowder."

The plight of the Indian, in that era of transition when he was
alienated from his tribal habits and not yet acclimated to the
white man's, receives serious attention. The innocent Indian—
defrauded, debased, and destroyed by the unfeeling mercantile
morality of the white man—is caught between Matthew Arnold's
two worlds, the one dead, the other powerless to be born. Here
Miss Murfree's sympathies are all with the aborigines. Hers is
an early cry against their spiritual and psychological dislocation.
Skeptical of the greed and rapacity of her own kind, she has Moy
Toy ask, "Christianity is to make the red men good? Then tell
me, why has it not made the white men good?"

She derives from religion further assurance that history as a
record of human progress is purely visual and illusory. The
Cherokee, after a lifetime of professing Christianity, will openly
reject it for the faith of his fathers. No steady movement forward
is discernible. An interregnum ensues between primitive and
civilized stages of society during which degeneracy occurs. She
cites Indian ceremony and language as well as religion to illustrate the loss of vital spark. A culture in retrograde retains the
manner without the matter, the shadow without the substance.
These manifestations are important in their preservations—from

them the originals may be reconstructed. But she indicates that the older society is no longer capable of appreciating the original meanings and the new society is incapable of understanding them. So her sense of history remains one of revering remnants largely for their own sake and for the awesome power of suggestion they disseminate.

The style of expression slips back to many iniquities of the past: tautology, foreign phrases, overwrought Latinizations, and turgidity. Tone ranges from the grisly realism of hair "dabbled and dulled with brains and blood" to euphuistic multiple puns about the head (of a family) becoming so heady as to lose his head. In depictions of landscape the rhetoric is as rich as ever, and her enamelwork technique is particularly evident. Summits change from amethystine to crystalline to "splendid jeweled luminosities of the Apocalyptic jasper"; in one "unnaturally bright" scene the mountain is emerald, the sky sapphire, the river silver; woods are intense jade; another river shines "now like silver, now like steel, now showed a burnished copper glister"; all nature shimmers and gleams metallically. At other times it is replete with the poetic idealism of the Hudson River school of painting, a "roseate purpling" light hovering over serene expanses. The world is "so fresh, so misty sweet, so newly created" that she cannot resist Rousseau's dream of God's innocents in the infancy of time. In another transcendent idyll of man within nature such as Meredith devised for Richard Feverel and Lucy Desborough, and which Miss Murfree parodied in *Where the Battle Was Fought*, she places an entire assemblage in a beautiful trance amid "invisibilities of mist and shadow . . . waiting for unnumbered ages till some magic sound should break their bonds." A flock of glittering white swans reflected in the steely sheen of the river consummates the effect of enchanted fantasy.

The nerve-thrilling Dance of Death, during which the Cherokees thrice circle the house of those they intend to destroy, is one aspect of the theater trope Miss Murfree imposes over this story. With frequent references to the drama, stage whispers, pantomime, and the histrionic profession she reinforces Laroche's assumption of an imaginary identity, Tam Wilson. Despite his Frenchness, he plays the part to the hilt, taking in a whole household of otherwise canny Scots. When he confesses to Lilias, she insists on clinging to the myth of Wilson rather than acknowledging the reality of Laroche. Shocked by a fraudulent mummer, she continues to perform her own role, transferring to another man the ideal she had created out of romantic fancy. If Miss Murfree had delved more deeply into such matters than into antiquarian trivia, *A Sceptre of Power* would have been a more praiseworthy novel.

III   The Amulet

The Brooklyn *Eagle* (November 17, 1906) and the *Independent* (February 28, 1907) greeted *The Amulet*, Miss Murfree's last novel about pioneer Tennessee, with openhanded joy. The former pointed to "the art, the exquisite taste and skill" of the book while admitting the banality of the incidents; the latter extolled its elegance and scholarly precision while classing it as her best story in this genre. *The Amulet* (1906) is, in fact, a rather vapid recapitulation of her preceding historical novels and one of the thinnest of her longer works. A pendant to *The Story of Old Fort Loudon*, it contains numerous allusions to that tragic experience—Choté, Keowee Town, Tellico, Moy Toy, Oconostota, Montgomery, Grant, Captain Demeré—and traces the aftermath of the Cherokee troubles which started there and culminated in the redskins' defeat and degradation. Like the last of her local-color stories, *The Amulet* arrived after the popularity of its kind had disintegrated. Frank Norris, Upton Sinclair, and Lincoln Steffens had diverted interest from costume romance to the shame of our cities.

There is no appended section of notes in *The Amulet*. Miss Murfree incorporates all her research into the text. According to legend, the gem which gives the novel its title was a giant red crystal. She explains that Adair thinks it a gigantic carbuncle, others a garnet, and that most probably it was a red tourmaline of special depth and richness. The Indians believe it wards off miscellaneous evils and prevents missionaries from capturing their souls. The heroine strains to invest it with greater symbolic significance, but the record of its passage and effects cannot sustain her invention. It remains simply an attractive jewel about whose properties the Indians are superstitious.

Miss Murfree manipulates parallel plots of love rivalry and Indian menace, offering an episode of each alternately. The two mesh when Ensign Raymond is chosen for the mission to Choté, the Cherokee city of refuge, and Arabella Howard solicitously adjures him to return safely. When he brings her the amulet and she pledges it to the Indians, thereby declaring her attachment to Raymond, both lines of action are resolved. Though the pattern is neat, the story is at best flabby. The first half tinkles with contrived wit and tea-table intrigues incongruous to a frontier garrison. The first intimation of action does not occur until the end of Chapter IV when sonorous notes of the conch shell from the Indian village counterpoints the resonance of roll-call drums in Fort Prince George. This dialogue suggests the imminence of trouble, intensifies the sense of an ominous clash in the offing. Expectation of another massacre is built up through repeated evocations of Fort Loudon and through several critical situations: the rescue of Reverend Morton from Old Tamotlee, the corn-trading at Keowee Town, the powwow at Choté, the granary fire in the fort, and Arabella's approach to the Indians who are mourning for their amulet. But nothing ever happens. The end is happy and vacuous. All Britishers return to beloved old Kent apparently untouched by their experiences in primitive Tennessee.

To derive a sliver of solace from this plot, one must probe Miss Murfree's accompanying artistry. The novel is constructed within a frame of the Cherokee word for *moon*. It is the subject of an extensive discussion at the first meeting of Arabella and Raymond, and it is the final note in the novel after they have been married. Like a Wagnerian leitmotif, it is repeated on key occasions and constitutes vague but pervading linkage in their romance. For the Indians, the moon "is but the sun asleep." For the lovers, the moon returns with spiritual connotations, as perhaps their amulet. They keep their feelings for each other in abeyance until the close. Then the sun rises.

Another procedure used to advantage is that of prefiguration. Many occurrences are forecast by similar, usually veiled and abbreviated, instances. Such vignettes enhance plausibility and continuity, rouse the sense of recall, and deepen the meaning of subsequent action. Notable among these are connections between the boots seen under the bed by the maid and the banging on the door during the storm—a false and a real alarm; the missions to Little Tamotlee and to Choté; Captain Howard's intuition and realization concerning cannon in the Cherokee country; Tus-ka-sah confusing his name with the reality of self and the Cherokees confusing the image and the actuality of the amulet; the game of Loo, and Raymond impulsively carrying off the amulet.

Characterization is almost exclusively by physical description and direct statement of traits. Some individuals help delineate others by revelatory remarks, but that is the extent of clues to motivation. Arabella, Raymond, and Mervyn are stock figures in a love triangle. Arabella, reputed to be clever and a force for good, remains a flippant coquette and never lives up to the claims Miss Murfree makes for her. Raymond is dark, poor, honest, brave—all white. Mervyn is blond, rich, a snob, and a sneak—all black. Mrs. Annandale, a Jane Austen duenna constantly plotting social strategies, is Mrs. Bennet transported to the Indian frontier. Captain Howard is a mechanism, and the Indians merely show off costumes and ceremonies. On the secondary level Reverend Morton is a Dickens eccentric complete with identifying tag line; Robin Dorn, a Scott drummer boy. Lieutenant Jerrold has possibilities but no real opportunity to express them.

The language is lavish with Scottish, Irish, and Indian dialects, and tongue-tripping combinations return with a vengeance. The English dialogue, intended to be sparkling, is merely sophomoric. Point of view and tone derive from Miss Austen's socially focused vision and from Thackeray's cynical philosophic dicta. In this vein, a country-city contrast is drawn between the elegance of dress, manners, and cuisine of the captain's entourage, amplified by numerous allusions to the way it was in Kent, and the raw improvisations of the wilderness.

Miss Murfree frequently enunciates a favorite thesis—the origin of American Indians in the lost tribes of Israel—seeing analogies in their Semitic customs and the barbarous rites. More emphatic, however, is her restatement of the incapacity of Indians for civilization. Raymond is aware of their power, perspicacity, and subtlety; yet he theorizes that they are "a remnant of a different order of being, the conclusion of a period of human development." Inferiority in the Indian is asserted as fundamental. He cannot be molded into the discipline of the army camp, so the only Indian remedy for Captain Howard is bullets. Mrs. Annandale, less feral but no less obtuse, says to Arabella: "God made them, child, God made them. Humanly speaking, He might have done better." And, finally, without proxy Miss Murfree declares: "They were no more men—not even savages; they had entered upon that peculiar phase of their being which seems to those of different standards absolutely demoniac and demented." Her conception of history is again observable as a series of self-contained cycles no one of which necessarily enriches its neighbor or successor. Progress in human nature is not continuous but subject to advance and retrogression. Determinism rather than humanism rules her universe.

The gravest defect of perspective in these historical novels, however, is her excruciating fidelity to fact which dams the flow of story and submerges the drama of human personality. She could not accept Napoleon's definition of history as a fable agreed upon, nor could she have read with profit Emerson's views in "History": "Time dissipates to shining ether the solid angularity of fact. No anchor, no cable, no fences avail to keep a fact a fact." Demi-romantic though she was, it never came to her that in fiction based on history the fact becomes incidental when turned to figurative use. Undeviating devotion to the actualities of place and events hobbled her imagination and kept her from achieving any notable results in this sphere of literature.

IV Short Stories of the Frontier

In the space of five years Miss Murfree published all seven of her short stories about colonial Tennessee. One was collected in *The Bushwhackers* (1899); six appear in *The Frontiersmen* (1904). Five of them touch on the contentions between French and British for domination of Indian trade between 1734 and 1762, and two are anecdotes out of Indian legendry. Although written at the height of the demand for historical romance, they make no concessions to the popular taste for spiced fiction. Miss Murfree's uncontrollable urge for factual realism stifles their rich inherent qualities and gives them the flavor of chronicle.

Exhilarating incident and many varieties of humor are evident within this straitjacket of data. *The Frontiersmen* has a section of footnotes fourteen pages long in which Miss Murfree completely unleashes her penchant for microscopic scholarship. She delves into derivations of Indian expressions not already explained in parentheses in the course of the stories; describes the rules of games minutely; quotes or paraphrases historians, military officers, and missionaries of the area; comments on Indian traits and tendencies; furnishes additional information about tribal wars, British expeditions, political and commercial intrigues and treaties; and clarifies Indian religious functions, rites, myths, dynasties, genealogies, and hierarchies. And she supports her statements by reference to official documents, manuscripts, or secondary sources such as contemporary periodicals.

This ponderous apparatus, added to tone-destroying interjections of exposition in the stories themselves, puts too heavy a burden of pedagogy on the tissue of fiction. Her love of the time and the place leaves her finally between the two stools of local color and local history. The outcome is an indeterminate medley —sometimes reconstituted history, sometimes personalized folklore, sometimes amusing anecdotage—turned out by a self-conscious regional archivist with a poetic flair. The tales are frail and overlong; three of them stagger under thematic intimations too weighty for their frames.

"The Bewitched Ball-Sticks" and "The Visit of the Turbulent Grandfather" are disposable items which deal solely with Indians. Both are exotically picturesque in the local-color manner, both revolve around rivalries (love in the first, politics in the second), both are comic in tone. They recount the deceptions practiced in gaining advantage, and in each case the dupers are ironically duped. Amoyah's cunning and lighthearted insouciance catch one's sympathies, but no character has satisfactory depth. The only proposition discernible in these slight pieces is Miss Murfree's belief that, while man may manipulate some short turns in his destiny, fate decrees the inexorable direction.

"A Victor at Chungke" concerns a young Englishman whose parents had been murdered by Cherokees when he was a child. Otasite has been brought up by a chief who looks upon him as a son. A white trader encourages Otasite to re-establish his original identity. After a chungke (stone discus) contest which he wins, Otasite is accidentally killed. Out of this situation arise stronger considerations than those in the preceding tales. The tragic irony of existence and the helplessness of human beings in the hands of fate are illustrated by Otasite's thwarted plan and by his untoward death. The paradox of an English boy brought up in savage circumstances poses the relative values of heredity and environment. The ensuing conflict is embodied in Otasite, whose dress and talk is at odds with his auburn curls and "kindly English eyes," and it is personified in the opposing influences of the Indian chief and the white trader. A country-city contrast is broached when the Governor of South Carolina offers to take some Cherokee youths in his schools and make *scholars* of them, which the Cherokee chief counters by offering to take some South Carolina youths and make *men* of them. A final motif verges on the oedipal: Otasite, target of two contending "fathers" in the chief and the trader, resolves to uncover the mystery of his true father. This story starts briskly, then oscillates between drama and documentation with the result that the crucial action is vitiated.

"The Exploit of Choolah, the Chickasaw" and "The Captive of the Ada-Wehi" take place during the victorious campaign of Colonel Grant against the Cherokees in 1761. "Choolah," a fictionalized chronicle, is neither straight story nor straight history. It contains a titillating olio of elements which fail to jell properly. Miss Murfree's solemn tutoring recurrently mutes the buoyant romantic tone. Doggedly she constructs a vehicle for three ideas. First, she bolsters her conviction that there is ethnic connection between Indians and ancient Hebrews by adducing their mutual aversion to pork. Second, she iterates her faith in the congenital bond of blood by letting an English lieutenant free a Frenchman —at this time mortal military enemies—from captivity by Indians friendly to the English. Third, she projects a modification on her usual pattern of history: a Tolstoyan mosaic composed of "a thousand little jagged bits of varied incident inconsistent and irregular, and with no single element in common but the attraction of cohesion." The irony that permeates most of these pioneer stories appears prominently when Colonel Grant, who normally genuflects to the letter of military law, is constrained by an amusing coincidence to forego court-martial proceedings against the lieutenant.

"The Captive of the Ada-Wehi" is least clogged with details of history or landscape. In the absence of an obstructive author, the story moves fluidly along two channels. Replaying the fable of Androcles and the lion, one of Colonel Grant's soldiers is rescued from the Indians by a Cherokee squaw whose hungry papoose he had once fed. The ada-wehi, an Indian ghost with putative magical powers, has the peculiar status of a live man presumed to be dead. The situation is basically serious since human lives are at stake, but the underlying comedy borders on farce, and tension is relieved by dramatic irony. The argument which emerges is that of romantic self-reliance. Superstition and savagery have upheld the Cherokees for centuries. Resorting now to reason and diplomacy, they have been reduced to a point of humiliation. While Miss Murfree takes no side in this anti-intellectual issue, she has never made reason seem so befuddled or civilization so undesirable.

Comedy is the keynote of "The Linguister." Miss Murfree indulges in a variegated scale of smile-provoking devices to point up the sly feministic moral that woman knows best. The tone throughout is jocular and mocking. The heroine's name—starkly incongruous for so little a person—is Peninnah Penelope Anne Mivane. Often used in full, it provides a measure of inflection for the rest of the teasing, satirical components. Richard Mivane and his Negro manservant Caesar are divertingly offbeat, as is Xerxes Alexander Anxley, a radical religionist. John Ronackstone, a Natty Bumppo type, exposes the genteel pretensions of Mivane in the funniest scene of the story, which is almost matched by Mivane's unwitting revelation of reports gathered during his simulated deafness. Several droll moments are generated by the disharmony of high diction and low topic, and by other verbal gymnastics. Most effective, however, is the gradual deterioration of a virile, eruptive situation into one of utter farce. Rough men wanting to display their prowess in a fight are neutralized by the ingenuity of a small, weeping woman who leaves them feeling foolish and staring sheepishly at each other.

Along with this obvious titter at the absurdities of masculine pride flows a sober undercurrent of recrimination. Although women have not been socially or legally acknowledged as equal to men, they are in fact superior to them in many respects. Miss Murfree intimates that the world has been badly run by men and that, given the reins, women would lead humanity into peace and significance by routing vanity and violence from daily affairs.

Other serious themes poke their heads through the screen of buffoonery. Mivane creates a contrast between frontier and civilization with his cloth suits, powdered peruke, and social affectations; Atta-Kulla-Kulla defines the dissident propensities of white and red men; unjust expropriation of Indian rights is sarcastically denoted; the irrepressible march of emigration westward is asserted; and the pragmatic morality of ends over means is briefly debated. This is too massive an overlay for so slight a story, and the overweening freight of early local history crushes it out of all semblance to its apparently humorous intent.

CHAPTER 8

Mississippi Manners

FOR THE LAST PHASE of fiction that she essayed, Miss Murfree turned to Mississippi. There seemed no better recourse when the Tennessee vein ran dry. To Robert Underwood Johnson, editor of the *Century*, she wrote: "I know that region and people as well as I know the mountains of Tennessee. I have spent much time in Mississippi on our own plantation in former years and in visiting the homes of friends—and the River is especially familiar to me, not only the region of the 'great lands' and the lower stretch through the delta country but as high up as St. Louis, where I lived for nine years."[1] Later she took an extended ride down the river to renew her impressions of the locale. Perhaps, too, she had treasured in the back of her mind the hypothesis broached by an anonymous critic of *In the Clouds* at the height of her career as a local colorist: "Suppose, for instance, she were to let the Mississippi River run through her story, instead of having the Tennessee Mountains surround it."[2]

Ten years after that conjecture she incorporated in *The Juggler* (1897) scenes on a river boat that recall Twain's *Life on the Mississippi*. Again in *The Storm Centre* (1905), she offered vivid pictures of the river and its vicinity. In both cases they were incidental to the main matter of the novels. From 1908 to 1914, however, she produced two novels and two short stories wholly devoted to this new area. Just as the frontier novels blend local color and local history, the Mississippi novels combine local color and social analysis. In this final stage of writing, Miss Murfree reverts to her two strongest capacities, the initial assertions of her creative impulse. But two forces conspired to keep *The Fair Mississippian* and *The Story of Duciehurst* from the ranks of her best work: the erosion of her powers after more than three decades of unremitting authorship; her capitulation to the popular desire for plots with intricate contrivances and spectacular turns of fortune. This compromise is deplorable, for she demonstrates again that she could have excelled if she had followed her own direction rather than conform to the dictates of her times.

In these novels she scrutinizes a society in the throes of un-wanted change, the aristocracy intent on conserving its pre-rogatives untarnished, the *nouveaux riches* or the ambitious mid-dle class striving to rise. She examines the morality that moti-vates the upper class, peering behind its glitter into the secret ugly places. Her reports on the customs, manners, attitudes, and speech of the specific groups in her special sphere are satirical and biased. Like her incomparable models, Jane Austen and William Thackeray, her aim is to judge and to correct.

I The Fair Mississippian

The doltish reviewer of the Boston *Times* who hailed *The Fair Mississippian* (1908) as "the best story Miss Murfree has yet written" must have been ardent about ghosts, hidden documents, chivalric rescues, sudden floods, unlikely love affairs, fortuitous telepathy, subhuman marauders, and happy endings. All the shopworn devices of romance and melodrama converge in this hodgepodge of a plot that is among the least original in her entire canon. At least three incidents are reminiscent of Huck Finn on the river. Essential information is lamely supplied through lengthy recitals of past occurrences by one character to another who is presumably quite familiar with the details. Jerry Sloper's bear story is a bald pretext for introducing a gaudy bit of local color. Desmond's hearing a bell that was never struck is sheerest supernatural nonsense. The accidental discovery of a long-lost codicil right at the brink of a mortgage foreclosure is low theater. Flaws of this sort and many others mark a narra-tive which has just one redeeming feature: Miss Murfree lays out a single line of progression and hews to it nobly.

The merit of this novel lies not in its story but in the author's proficient evocation of the South's social ethos in an epoch of disintegrating values. She accomplishes her best effects by con-trasting aristocrats and river rats on one hand and, more in-cisively, established and aspiring representatives of the higher class. She utilizes both people and places to invest this inter-course with meaningful distinctions. Not since her inaugural essays in *Lippincott's* during the mid-1870's does her sense of social criticism come through with such acuity.

Great Oaks—a replica of Fair Oaks, one of the Murfree planta-tions in Mississippi—is "seigneurial." With its score of red chim-neys, wings, ells, bell tower, mills, stables, sheds, orchards, vine-yards, and clustered houses for slaves, it is "a principality indeed, the realm of the rich and powerful and learned." At the other extreme is the Knoxton shanty boat smelling of oakum, tar, and junk, with its broken-backed chairs, bunks, gewgaws, and cheap assortment of wares. These polar worlds come into collision when Honoria Faurie, proprietress of Great Oaks, boards the flatboat to purchase a bicycle for one of her sons, is assaulted and almost abducted; again, when the river pirates raid Great Oaks.

Mrs. Faurie, a regal young widow, has frivolously spent the income from her husband's estate on yachts and trips to Europe. She personifies unattainable attributes of health, wealth, and beauty to the Knoxtons, who seem transplants from Miss Murfree's mountain stories. Jed, a thickset, loutish predator, has no respect for law or the proprieties; his wife, who has a worn, reptilian look, listens coldbloodedly to his accounts of murder; Ethan is a pre-Faulknerian grimacing, capering idiot. They and their cohorts in crime constitute the lowest layer of Mississippi society. Miss Murfree avoids complicating the clear, chasmal disparities between them and the Fauries by neglecting to introduce the more mobile, buffer class of residents. Jerry Bainbridge, overseer of the plantation, is barely permitted to display the sturdy virtues of the middle class. Although he discovers the propitious codicil, he is absent during the climactic clash of the two antipodal classes at Great Oaks.

Infinitely more subtle are the differences Miss Murfree observes among members of the upper segment. The enmities are less openly manifested, and she indicates a twofold struggle of equally elemental proportions: between subdivisions of the ruling contingent, and between the standards of past and present. Again, she implements her thesis through emblematic use of two houses. Great Oaks, the epitome of *ancien régime* in the South, is significantly out of touch with the movements and influences of the times; it is embedded in alluvial lowlands forty miles from any town larger than a hamlet or a railroad way station. Its rooms are hung with family portraits and good paintings; expensive ornaments and vases complement the furniture, which is of carved rosewood and mahogany. Carpets are velvet, drapes of damask and lace; books, long undisturbed, rest behind glass. An air of serene, self-satisfied elegance envelops the place. Completely adverse to this monument of a gracious past is the blaring ostentation of Dryad-Dene—home of Colonel and Mrs. Kentopp—whose pretentious title is itself an affront to the simple dignity of Great Oaks. The crystal chandeliers at Dryad-Dene are reflected in the glossy floors, which support rich Oriental rugs and gilded chairs and sofas. Venetian glass and porcelain vases, Persian urns, and Chinese curios are scattered about. Brightly polished brass andirons and fenders and stained glass windows round out this bizarre medley. A ballroom in the third story is "another intimation of the intensely modern spirit of Dryad-Dene." The grounds are laid out in formal Italian style, and there are palms and Japanese tree-ferns.

The occupants of these houses accord with their respective possessions. Mrs. Faurie at Great Oaks retains the gusto of her forebears for heedless spending. She is delicately beautiful and always faultlessly dressed. A poor manager with no head for the future, she perseveres in a protected fantasy world which cannot visualize catastrophe to its way of life. Her three sons, products of the old school, are precious rather than precocious, pompously cosmopolitan in witticisms, apt in etiquette, and versed in all the immemorial snobberies. Her Uncle Stanlett is an ante-bellum standard-bearer of masculine chivalry which has climbed down from its horse. He personates a ghost in order to suppress evidence from the past which would have deleterious consequences on the present. As a thematic symbol, he need not have assumed a role for, psychologically, he is precisely that—a ghost from a dead era trying hopelessly to stave off an emergent truth.

At Dryad-Dene Mrs. Kentopp is as meretricious as her blond hair. At thirty-eight she is somewhat haggard but dresses and poses as the eternal coquette. Her husband affects the latest dudish fashions and greets everyone with a robust bonhomie he does not feel. Neither has fine perceptions nor the gift of selflessness. They value people only for their station, and they desire above all to be accepted as sophisticated leaders among the élite. Miss Murfree sums up the proposition squarely: "If Great Oaks were reminiscent of the past, it might seem that Dryad-Dene was a respecter only of the morrow."

Dryad-Dene is the postwar South in a hybrid state, moving toward a new day and new modes but not yet there; it is caught between two periods and striving to encompass both. None of the forest trees are immediately around the house, and the river is not visible. These portents and the many imported appurtenances proclaim the alien quality of the house and its owners. They are remote from the indigenous roots of the region. They speak in foreign accents for customs and innovations destructive to the old provincialism. In their frantic scramble toward a spot at the top, they trample down great traditions of stability and refinement.

Other characters contribute other colors to this portrait of a cultural revolution. Selena Allandyce is a strong-minded representative of the "new" woman. Aggressive, satirical, defiant of conventions, she flouts the prejudice against red hair in Southern belles and wears riding breeches to a formal tea. Her opposite number in a balanced pair is Gertrude Kelvin, who looks like a white rose and who spends the summer indoors with a novel in order to preserve her complexion. As against Selena's derby, she favors a high silk hat, all femininity. Mr. Loring is a synopsis of the emergent repulsive commercial class, aping the ways of the North and superseding the disenfranchised Southern aristocracy. Born of poor parents only a few miles from Great Oaks, he is a self-made millionaire bent on acquiring the estate and retiring there. He has little sympathy for the destitute, rates everyone on a financial basis, consciously domineers, and is never intentionally frank. More than anything else, he desires to be mistaken for one of the erstwhile princelings of Mississippi. It is indicative of his rising kind that he covets the old (Great Oaks) and is avidly sought by the new (Dryad-Dene). His bachelorhood is the stamp of his barrenness.

Most acute in unveiling the upheaval of past standards is Edward Desmond, Miss Murfree's nominal hero. A bright and handsome college graduate left penniless by an impractical father, he takes the job of tutor to Mrs. Faurie's three sons. He has a puritanical ardor for hard work and achievement, disdains money and fashions. Proudly he declares that the paltry salary cannot buy his identity nor annul his personality. His position and influence at Great Oaks slowly distend: in the beginning he is treated with respect and courtesy for his knowledge, then as a valued guest, then as one of the family, and finally as controlling element in matters of property interests or management, "from whose decree there was no appeal." Desmond is from Maryland, the outside eye leveled fondly though sternly on the fripperies that have survived in plantation society. He appreciates the good material latent in the Faurie boys but deplores their "puerile folly, superficial observation, false standards, and . . . total lack of the habit of application." So he sets about to rehabilitate them, Mrs. Faurie, Great Oaks, and in essence the foundered South. He brings a new sense of order and decorum to a decadent situation not yet responsive to the demands of a new scheme of life, cutting away the indulgence and arrogance that hinder progress.

Despite his advantages of breeding, family status, former wealth, and cultivated deportment, it is made clear to him that the chief criteria for acceptance "among frivolous people" are place and money—not talent, not integrity, not past standing. When he tells Selena and Gertrude that he is tutor instead of guest at Great Oaks, both of them—regardless of other dissimilarities—are struck by "appalled astonishment" at this deficiency of station. Desmond detects scorn in the eyes of obsequious domestics, who have small toleration for poverty outside their own rank. To make his way successfully, he has to battle on every level of prejudice.

Miss Murfree makes Desmond the sounding board for her most intense expression of attitude toward the socially privileged:

> Desmond was impressed with the fact . . . that the very rich are fearless of the ordinary operations of disaster. The aegis of great possessions overshadows them. The law is their ally, for their protection; the imputation that by their negligence, or assumptions, or bravado, or inconsiderateness it could be arrayed against them is in itself a ridiculous impossibility, a sort of grotesque parody on fact, a distortion of the powers of established order. All other menace is likewise abated in their favor. The dangers of travel are minimized for them; the distresses of sickness are mitigated; every ill that flesh is heir to is softened and alleviated and embellished till they are scarcely to be identified with the woes, savage and hideous, that rack the multitude; and death itself is so bedizened and beautiful and exalted that it ceases to be the great leveler.[3]

There is a touch of spleen in this statement of upper class immunities, as though she resented its application to a noodle like Mrs. Faurie. Miss Murfree was not unfamiliar with Desmond's condition of depleted fortune and no doubt considered that, in cases like Desmond's and her own, such license should be the natural concomitant of blood and brains.

Desmond is on the seedy side of the lightheaded aristocracy, restraining and directing them. Rescue comes for them from within their own class by one with concrete middle-class virtues, rather than from the fairly repellent woodchopper Jerry Sloper or even the acceptable supervisor Jerry Bainbridge (same class, same given name). Thus Miss Murfree sustains the superiority of the superior. If in no other manner, her bias comes through in this preference of hero, as so often it did in her unconscious dissociation from the Tennessee mountaineers.

Second in estimation after her dissection of social mores is her depiction of locale. The Vicksburg *Avalanche* (October 23, 1908) twitted her about the "startling and unexpected adjuncts" of river pirates and occasional alligators sprinkled in like pepper and salt to season the dish. However, the Nashville *Banner* (November 7, 1908) defended her "exquisite word-painting" as supplying "the dreamful charm belonging alone to the far South-land." The spontaneity of her early mountain descriptions is unquestionably gone; but, quibbling aside, Miss Murfree does create a sense of place and atmosphere which is impressive. Good examples of this are the two mansions and the shanty boat, already discussed. Obscuring these is the river. By repetitive recall of its myriad sights and sounds, the Mississippi becomes a force in the story.

Miss Murfree catches the elemental flavor of the deep ooze along its banks, "the dank, rich vernal odor of the earth, the pungent tang of herb and tree." Frequently, she peers into the Gothic murk of cypress sloughs, lifeless jungles overhung with Spanish moss, black lakes, and sluggish bayous. The river is a labyrinth shifting its channels with deliberate malice—"damn that old corkscrew"—and it takes on an aspect of inscrutable perversity, a metaphor of life itself. One day Mrs. Faurie invokes a surrealistic conceit in which the river encompasses not only life but death and history and anthropology. If the Mississippi were drained, its bottom would show in a kind of apocalyptic resurrection all the boats, the bones of people drowned in fires, collisions, swampings, and sinkings. All nations and races would be represented there, "and who knows what prehistoric people."

The vast welter of waters, extending beyond reach of vision, and its lawless invasions impinge upon the inhabitants' consciousness as an ubiquitous source of danger to rich and poor alike. Half a century earlier the river had carried away the point known as Faurie's Landing and now flows menacingly close to Great Oaks. The river is power and providence to the lowly flatboat denizens it tosses about on capricious currents and eddies. Miss Murfree equates it with fate, as though the two are in cahoots to despoil humanity, the river viciously serving the ends of destiny. The primacy of the upper class is reasserted when the Mississippi vaults the levees and comes to the very doorstep of Great Oaks. In the ensuing victory the hands of na-

ture and fate seem felicitously aligned with the Fauries. The effect is heightened by the rhythmical *knock-knock-knock* against the veranda by the raider's dead body on a dog chain, and the spirit of the river is never more oppressively present. (Miss Murfree makes one small concession to the formative powers of environment. As Desmond gazes down at the wounded outlaw on the veranda, he reflects upon the possibility that squalid social conditions may have molded him into something he was never intended to be.)

Yet the immense solemn river fails to saturate every recess of the story as does the battlefield in *Where the Battle Was Fought*. Most of the time the river is within ken but somewhat remote, "emblazoning the middle distance." At other times its mythic quality is dissipated in physiographic details. Its rugged force is lost in elevated, inept analogies, as when Miss Murfree collates it with the Stream of Time or the river Styx. Finally, she strips illusion to the bone by declarative statements about "the dominant old river" when in fact she had not made it dominate.

Miss Murfree's concept of fate is clearly divulged. It is a Calvinistic God malignly visiting "Terror, Doom, and Death" upon His wretched creatures. His scheme is one of preordination, an inexorable "chain of events, fettering the lives and fortunes of all." Man may feud with fate, but he is condemned without appeal. Prefiguration and a shade of mysticism add strength to the simplicity of this theocratic vision. The river's potential for flooding is established before its climactic surge toward Great Oaks. The raid and murders at Whippoorwill Landing preview the scene at the Faurie plantation. Mrs. Faurie's hallucinatory view of the Mississippi as a doomsday repository materializes when the river reaches for the marauder's floating corpse. And the unaccountable summons of Desmond in Honoria's hour of peril by a bell which does not actually toll is also forecast. Fate, in short, is like a well-laid plot.

Miss Murfree remains detached from characters and situations, modulating her esthetic tone to include Thackeray's skeptical social aphorisms and George Eliot's ethical truisms. The week-end at Dryad-Dene throws revealing rays on the attitudes and activities of the mottled, new high society burgeoning in the South during the period following the Civil War—its dancing, drinking, dining, hunting, talk, dress, manners, and amenities. The languid badinage that passes among members of this upper crust at the Kentopp home is self-consciously arch and wicked;

it means to be blasé but succeeds only in being gauche. With calculated spite Miss Murfree prods Loring, who aspires to aristocracy, with odious reminders of his humble background— one kind of snob bringing down another. Pious imprecations and quick forays into the mystery of the geologic universe echo the Eliot manner. Passion between lovers achieves the pitch of Desmond placing his arm around Honoria. Once a lawyer says "hell." But Miss Murfree can be thoroughly Naturalistic too, in presenting an intoxicated idiot, a bleeding man, and a bloating corpse with touches of horror and probability not unlike Erskine Caldwell in low key.

Befitting a novel of manners, the language is strewn with foreign phrases, particularly French, the affected expression of *haut monde* which the Kentopps and Loring hanker after. Classical and Biblical similitudes are regularly adduced—Honoria is Diana, Juno, and Helen of Troy; Great Oaks is Noah's Ark— as are blind quotes and paraphrases from Shakespeare, Bunyan, Dickens, Pope, and Swift. Anachronisms like "quotha" and "sooth," and periphrasis like "finny trophy," "sylvan folk," and "bibulous exercises" squirm nervously in a twentieth-century text. Too much depends on misspelling, bad grammar, and elisions for indigenous dialect. Simple idioms appear, but unique localisms are sparse.

Miss Murfree's partiality for a good "round" story prevents *The Fair Mississippian* from attaining significant depth as an analysis of manners or genuine eminence as local color. She has improved steadily in technical and symbolical methods, in matters of pattern and fulfillment, but not in perceptive excavation of human character and motivation. Her figures are prisoners of coercive plots, showing no growth and little freedom to act independently. Had she avoided the narrative trap, she might by now have developed a Jamesian mastery of psychological interrelationships within a web of social imperatives. This novel is the best index to what might have been.

II The Story of Duciehurst

In July, 1910, Miss Murfree tried to sell the serial rights of her new Mississippi novel, now nearly completed, to *Century* magazine. It was designed to follow up the "unusual success" of *The Fair Mississippian*, and she assured editor Johnson that this book "takes a much stronger hold than its predecessor . . . both on the region and the people and I think it is destined for even more popularity." She averred that it was "the logical improvement of a subsequent effort" and that the story was very carefully elaborated to the end.[4] Despite her protestations, Johnson turned it down. Issued by Macmillan in 1914, *The Story of Duciehurst* proved to be her last published book. It lives up to few of her claims. The style is simpler; the plot, melodramatic throughout, albeit better managed. The characters are transparent, casting no shadows; and Miss Murfree attains less identification or sympathy with them than ever before. Frenetic incident and sentimental tone predominate. Over all, she is the professional storyteller with no personal involvement—a surer hand but cooler heart.

Miss Murfree once more asserts the existence of multiple layers in the human personality. Paula Floyd-Rosney is "subacutely" aware of an ambivalent conflict within herself, and Colonel Kenwynton glimpses more than one persona in Hugh Treherne. However, Paula's bisection is revealed by courtesy of a detached third-person point of view; and each of Treherne's selves is treated in sequence, with no confusion of phases. After so many previous references to subacute reactions and the approach to the mysteries of identity in this novel, Miss Murfree introduces an actual psychiatrist into the plot. In respect to Treherne's sleep-talking he murmurs, "Subconscious cerebration." She speaks "the jargon of pathology" yet shies away from using its insights as tools to pry open the Pandora's box of the human psyche.

The Negroes in this novel are stage stereotypes of stupidity, overflowing with droll malapropisms and unable to adapt to the awkward arrangements of a deserted house. They are wholly manufactured products, what the worst local colorists led readers to believe were typical Negroes, comical in their abysmal limitations. Habitués of the river are more deeply realized, often by analogy to their environment. One of the river pirates has a curiously soaked aspect, as if overlaid with the slime and decay of the riverside; even his voice sounds water-logged, a sort of protracted gurgle. Josh Berridge, the outstanding swamper, suggests "some distorted bit of unclassified and worthless flotsam . . . left high and dry with other foul detritus." The water stains on his garments and his character are irremovable. Upon these representatives of the lower group Miss Murfree demonstrates her old adroitness in connecting race and place, as she did so superbly in blending mountaineers and mountains.

At the other end of the scale the aristocrats also emerge as

creatures of their place, observing their codes fastidiously, rising
or falling by their allegiance to ideals that have become impractical. Colonel Kenwynton, a man of stately carriage and
courteous manner, epitomizes the old South in speech and actions. A word portrait of Miss Murfree's father by "one who had
the freedom of a friend in that cultured home,"[5] leaves little
doubt as to the Colonel's model. His home and properties de-
teriorate all around him while he carries on obliviously, "a
species as extinct as the Plesiosaurus," making grandiloquent
sounds and gestures as the funeral bell of his generation tolls.

Edward Floyd-Rosney is Rufus Gwynn of *The Storm Centre*
brought up to date. A handsome, mordant villain, glacial in his
perfection, he indulges his own desires inordinately, flaunts all
the insignia of wealth and station without nudging the canons
of good taste, and tolerates no deviation from his opinions or
orders. He strikes his wife brutally under cover of her coat when
she resists his wish. When she finally flees from his home, he
rationalizes his own provocations, makes an insincere concilia-
tory move, then reacts furiously at her refusal to bend to his
will. After his defeat he takes to drink and ends up a murderer.
Paula is the lovely, suffering wife and mother who submits to
his spirit-breaking tyrannies until her child becomes involved.
Thereupon she rebels. She is, however, no exemplary martyr.
Superficial and sarcastic, enduring Rosney's veiled barbarities
for the sake of the comforts he provides, in the end she undergoes total transformation to his own scornful attitudes. She lies
brazenly in order to have her way with a former lover, wears
"a fashionable version of widow's weeds," and otherwise proves
that she and Rosney are two of a feather. Her moral topography,
like that of the Delta country, is low and muddy. In her uncertain social and ethical anchorage, Paula is as close a resemblance
to Becky Sharp as Miss Murfree accomplished in all her works.
Hildegarde Dean, her simple and honest counterweight—the
kind of nice girl all elderly men approve of—never arouses
enough interest to be accepted as heroine to this ultimately
vicious anti-heroine.

Miss Murfree almost breaks through her discreet screen by
attributing duplication of identity to the Ducie twins. (She
would have been shocked by the modern suggestion that there
is a definite strain of homosexual attraction between them.)
Adrian says, "When I am with Ran I feel as if I were looking
into a mirror." And Randal, in the pilot house with his murdered

brother, "looked down into his own dead face, as it were." She insinuates profounder similarities—like those of the Sicilian brothers who felt each other's physical and psychical wounds—but evades engagement with these recondite enigmas of personality. The twins also develop into incarnate symptoms of the times.

With this cast of principal players and with a suitable variety of supernumeraries, Miss Murfree constructs an allegory on the social changes that occurred in the South after the Civil War. The Ducies portray the emergent South. Both have lost their patrimony but through modern business methods are revitalizing the cotton fields. In addition, they are ambitious to regain and refurbish their old rundown plantation, Duciehurst. Rosney, a throwback to the hauteur and egotism of bygone aristocracy, interferes with their plans and eventually kills Adrian. Paula displays the fallible values of the ruthless new-rich to whom money and power are paramount, while Hildegarde, who marries Randal, is the quiet legatee of the South's better elements. Marjorie Ashley, a bouncing redhead of twelve, speaks for the spirit of the new South—a rebel not entirely free of conformity to old mores. Major Lacey, a blinded veteran with Tobias Shandy's idiosyncrasy for military reconstructions, makes only "groping progress" without his Negro manservant, exults in memories of himself as a dashing young officer, and looks forward only to the next regimental reunion. Paula's aunt and uncle, the Marjoribanks, constitute the solid core of society; they are wholesome, fair-minded, religious, paragons to their children, and untainted by upper-class follies.

Treherne decries the "strange things" that have come about because of the war: "The rich are the poor; the right are the wrong; the incompetent sit bridling in the places that the capable have builded." The truth of his plaint is illustrated by Colonel Kenwynton, who is said to talk about "honor, and patriotism, and fair-dealing in politics, and such chestnuts." His audience applauds but secretly laughs at his antiquated idealism. Miss Murfree's tone is one of regret for the passing of these norms. Her contempt for current conduct is expressed in Paula's depraved choice of Rosney (the old aristocracy of wealth) over Randal (the new aristocracy of talent and initiative).

Several homes symbolically reflect the several stages of change: Duciehurst, a ruined old-fashioned mansion, swept away by the Mississippi (stream of Time); the Colonel's plantation in moribund but restorable condition; Ingleside, the spare, decorous, linoleumed home of the Marjoribanks; and the gilded magnificence of Rosney's dwelling. Rosney calls his yacht the *Aglaia*, Greek for anything showy as opposed to useful. The highest emblematic moment in this drama of collapsed manners comes as Paula steams past the erstwhile site of Duciehurst in her yacht —the demolished majestic old era and the uncaring, onrushing mechanized new world.

Miss Murfree shows throughout a keen sensitivity to the dictates of social comportment and psychology in both high and low society. The Rosneys are pointedly aware of the penalties for individual flouting of group codes—disfavor or ostracism. Paula submits wordlessly to her entrapment, putting on a semblance of adulation toward her husband's every motion, thought, or preference. Edward makes obeisance to "the coercions of good society" by masking his displeasure strategically on some occasions. Among Negroes, Miss Murfree observes the minute punctilio and insistence upon differences in stratum between "saloon darkies" and manual laborers.

For the rest, there is little to distinguish *The Story of Duciehurst* from any run-of-the-mill thriller of its year. The plot is an attic crammed with dusty leftovers of countlessly repeated instances: a ghostly edifice, hidden treasure, a recovered document, a sunken steamboat, a loveless marriage, a mistaken-identity murder, a *deus ex machina* river. The tenor of language and incident is consistently melodramatic, but the structure is soundly engineered. Mood is conveyed through emphasis on the direful qualities of place and people: a river rogue's shack, moon over the desolate river, Duciehurst like a latter-day House of Usher, the sepia landscape, a renegade blacksmith, a half-tipsy debarred jockey, and Rosney's ugly undercurrent sadism. Autobiographic detail is recognizable in the complicated legal status of the lost quitclaim, the singing sessions around the piano, mention of the Stone's River campaign, and the similarity of Duciehurst to one of Miss Murfree's father's plantations, which was inundated during the war, and of her uncle's, which was undermined and carried off by the raging waters.

Most indicative of Miss Murfree's attitude toward the altered situation in the South are her remarks about the deliberate destruction of this symbolic mansion. She feels that the lower classes were now expelling long-pent tensions and malice against its condescending grandeur: "It had required both time and strength, as well as wanton enmity, a class hatred, one might suppose, bitter and unreasoning, the wrath of the poor against the rich." The fall of the house of Ducie was a tragedy she intimately understood.

III *Short Stories of the River*

In 1912 Miss Murfree published two Mississippi stories which also articulate her love of the old patrician frame of mind while acknowledging that new social-economic doctrines have rendered it obsolete. She reconciles her nostalgia by implementing both stories with detestable aristocrats who rouse no sympathy with their plight.

"The Phantom of Bogue Holauba" starts out as a tingling ghost yarn and ends as a tart commentary on the Southern way of life. The reader is led to believe that some rational explanation is forthcoming, but the initial direction is abruptly shifted. Thematically, the conclusion is irrelevant to the recurrent appearance of the ghost. The female protagonist delivers an ethical harangue totally out of tune with the preceding development. When Gordon and Rigdon hesitate about revealing a dead man's confession, Geraldine Norris scarifies them for shirking moral judgment, as well as social responsibility, and promptly burns the document. She berates their willingness to let "a sick theory of expiation of a dying, fever-distraught creature besmirch his repute as a man and a gentleman, make his whole life seem like a whited sepulchre." Thus Miss Murfree announces a hands-off policy on an extensive area of Southern guilt while striking a feminist blow at the inferior wisdom and humanity of dawdling, imperceptive men.

In this story the common man lashes out successfully at his upper-class tormentor. In his boyhood Keene sets adrift the boat of a poor Polish river trader who is thereby ruined. He dies during his futile search for it. When his ghost begins to wail along the banks, a series of fatal mishaps overtakes Keene's family, climaxed by his own illness and death. The diagram of social conflict and upper-class degradation becomes distinct. Keene turns sober and repents the frivolous actions of his youth, trying feebly to make restitution when it is too late. Mrs. Keene determinedly puts an attractive face on matters—for, like her red hair which suggests the use of chemicals, she is disguising the reality of a bankrupt spirit. Geraldine is defensively derisive and literally wears her poverty on her sleeve—her gown is ostentatiously darned. This is Southern nobility *après la guerre*: neither past nor present generation is capable of coming to terms with the new dispensation.

"The Crucial Moment" is a melodramatic unfoldment of murder, chase, capture, escape, and retributive justice governed by irony and rounded with pathos. Hoxer, the common man, takes inadvertent revenge on the aristocratic Jeffrey and in so doing destroys himself. Fate perversely nullifies this good man who had come up through the ranks on his own skill and industry—a splendid representative of the rising middle class who considers himself "as good as anybody and would take nothing off nobody, and cared for no old duck just because he was rich." It is tragically ironic that Hoxer visits the irascible Major only to reassert the integrity of his workmanship. He is drawn into a quarrel, kills Jeffrey in self-defense, and flees into the swamps. It is sentimentally ironic that he and his faithful pup bring about each other's death, a sad end for virtue and an abnegation of poetic justice.

Miss Murfree seems all on the side of Hoxer although unable to embrace him. He has capacity and intelligence far in excess of Jeffrey, who displays all the defects and none of the decency of the higher class. Hoxer is reduced to a frightened fugitive by forces he did not set in motion and which he tried to divert when they became evident. Significantly, his defeat is effected by nature, not by Jeffrey or his peers. It would appear that the era of equality is in sight though not yet a verity.

Of all the characters in both these stories, Hoxer is the only one with a hint of more than two dimensions. During the pursuit he becomes aware of a vivid other-self, "some foreign entity, cogently reasoning, swiftly acting. . . . This Thing that was not himself." A hitherto unsuspected personality from the depths of his instinct—a primordial, protective giant bridled by social cautions—has come dynamically to aid him toward survival. We prepare for an encounter of egos, but once again Miss Murfree forbears taking more than a timid step toward the subliminal jungle. Hoxer expires conventionally.

The river is prevalent in both stories but overspreads neither. In the first, it furnishes the properties for disaster and an horrific backdrop for the specter's exploits. In the second, it is the restorative factor; it clears the slate for another, perhaps successful, assault at encrusted values. As usual, incident elbows characterization and meaning off the field.

Juvenilia

THE FIRST NOVEL of mountain life published by Miss
Murfree was, in fact, not *The Prophet of the Great Smoky
Mountains* but *Down the Ravine*, a story for younger folk, which
ran serially in *Wide-Awake* from December, 1884, to May, 1885.
In all, she wrote for the junior group two mountain novels, her
only novel with big-city setting, and a baker's dozen of short
stories. These juveniles she turned out concurrently with adult
offerings during her first twenty years as author, and they share
most of the felicities and failings of her artistry in that period.

I *Mountain Novels and Stories*

The mountain novels and stories are shorter than their adult
counterparts. In the main they concern boys, whose nature Miss
Murfree came to understand through close association with her
younger brother. They are shown balancing over precipices,
climbing up trees and down hollows, hunting coons and treasure,
doing chores, and contending with older brothers. Mostly they
are Horatio Alger heroes in homespun, often the sole support
of the household; industrious, kind to animals, shy of wrong-
doing, ambitious for success. They undergo misfortune, persevere
stalwartly, and come through with flying colors—models for all
good boys to emulate.

Themes correlative to such upstanding virtues are applied
directly—Miss Murfree never hesitates to step into the middle of
the action to wag her finger like a Dutch aunt at her young
readers. They are enjoined to listen to their parents; for all
mothers are kind and perceptive, all fathers stern but wise.
Strength comes through hardship and sacrifice. Evil is consistently thwarted, and goodness eventually triumphs. The
principle of romantic infantilism prevails throughout—love and
innocence are instinctual in children. As yet undefiled by mundane influences, they are incapable of malice themselves and
inspire good actions in elders.

Adults fall into the same typed compartments they occupy in the mature mountain tales, but they seem sometimes rather cruel in their taunts and threats to the youngsters. As a change from the older presentations, the mother in these juveniles is not the crone, a role reserved for some other female, or even male. Mothers have had a hard row, but it has not soured their temper. They are sad and patient.

A sense of homogeneous region is established through recurrence of place names in the Cumberland and Great Smoky ranges, and Miss Murfree favors nomenclature attractive to children—Parch Corn, Persimmon Ridge, Tanglefoot Cove. Descriptions of landscape are neither so frequent nor so lengthy, for Miss Murfree correctly gauged the attention span of teenagers. She provides excellent local-color pictures of such typical sites as a salt lick, a tanyard, a general store. The folklore and superstitions of the area, drawn from stories told by her Negro nurse, are profusely dispersed in the text.

Point of view is continually disrupted by sudden, disjointed transitions; by the officious narrator's intrusion of pale parlor quips, snide asides, sober homiletics; and—most distractive—by mouth-filling diction which would give older readers pause ("saltatory," "primogeniture," "exculpate," "supersedure"). Yet the boys talk precisely like their fathers, idiomatically and anecdotally, with rich swaths of understatement and drawling humor. The intent of these stories is to amuse while instructing; the tone generally sentimental and comic.

Besides *Down the Ravine* (1885), Miss Murfree wrote another formula novel, *The Story of Keedon Bluffs* (1887), in which she surprisingly permits characters far more caustic opinions and partisanship on the subject of the Civil War than in any of her adult works. Eight of the short stories in *The Young Mountaineers* (1897) were collected from *Youth's Companion*; two others were first published in this volume. Written specifically for young people, none rises above their plane of comprehension, and none warrants individual analysis here.

II   *The City Novel*

The Champion (1902), a novel about a printer's devil, is laid in St. Louis, where she had lived for nine years, but the city is never identified. The volume is slim in size, slim in substance, remarkable only in the fact that for the first and last time in her more than forty years of authorship Miss Murfree devolves upon the world of electric lights, automobiles, and telephones. She depicts St. Louis slums with a garish realism reminiscent of Crane's *Maggie*: dirty, dingily lighted streets; tall, gloomy tenement houses limiting the sky and air; women quarrelling shrilly on street corners; frowzy customers of both sexes reeking of beer and whisky in a low saloon; a street urchin smoking the stump of a cigar garnered from the sidewalk. However, she attempts no penetration of the social, economic, or moral implications of urban living. Miss Murfree's pious intonation, designed to provoke loathing of the locale in good boys and girls, paradoxically succeeds in enhancing its allure.

CHAPTER 10

Past, Present, Future

MARY NOAILLES MURFREE enjoyed an uninterrupted writing career of almost half a century, her first essay appearing in *Lippincott's* in May, 1874, and her last in *Youth's Companion* in December, 1921. For approximately half of that span of years the name of Charles Egbert Craddock at the head of a short story or novel called up instantaneous attention from editors and pleasurable anticipation in readers. This condition sustained itself during the finest hour of local-color literature in America. She stayed at the peak of the movement from the moment the *Atlantic Monthly* published "The Dancin' Party at Harrison's Cove" (May, 1878) until Houghton Mifflin issued *The Juggler* in 1897. By rare coincidence this was the thirteenth of her twenty-five books, precisely the midpoint. The twelve volumes that followed *The Juggler* wandered into topics other than the contemporary mountaineers of Tennessee who had brought her international repute—and wandered back—but never again recaptured the magnetism of her earlier works. Nevertheless, she was fortunate in grabbing the tail of a comet and riding it majestically across the sky during her most efficacious period.

Miss Murfree, of a retiring nature, never sought public blandishment nor played the game of publishers' teas. She outlined her position unmistakably in a letter to William M. Baskervill on March 30, 1897:

> In reply I would say that it would give me pleasure to receive your call but I prefer that you should postpone it until after your sketch of my works and life shall have been published. I have never influenced nor prompted anything whatever which has been published concerning me or my writings. . . . Everything that has been published concerning me and my books has been wholly spontaneous on the part of the writer and I take a certain satisfaction in this fact. I have never given even any slight item to be included in such a sketch save the merest biographical data . . . and even this I have done only in two or three instances during the last thirteen years.[1]

She had no need for personal publicity; her stories promoted themselves. *In the Tennessee Mountains* achieved over twenty editions in an amazingly short time, and reprints of her other books—notably, *The Prophet of the Great Smoky Mountains*—were common up to the early 1900's. For two decades her byline was a consistent ornament of the *Atlantic Monthly*, the Harper magazines, and *Youth's Companion*. Eulogistic reviews of her vigorous approach to a freshly uncovered region and people dotted the periodicals and newspapers of the day. She was set on a par with Hardy, Harte, Black, Blackmore, Jewett, and Cable by enthusiastic critics; and the Birmingham (Ala.) *Herald* on May 19, 1907, proudly dubbed her "The Prophetess of the Great Smoky Mountains." The New York *Times*, which usually tweaked her about the glut of moons and mountains in her tales, solemnly acknowledged the worth of her "artistic idealism" in its estimate of *The Raid of the Guerilla*: "[Miss Murfree] has become one of the classics of American literature; her Tennessee mountains is a tangible monument to her genius" (July 29, 1899).

Signs of deterioration in her status began to rise in the mid-1890's among the pages of the very magazines that had eagerly disseminated her stories. They reached meridian when the *Critic* wondered why she was no longer as interesting as John Fox and summarily declared that she "belongs to a misunderstood past."[2] The year 1898, during which she published nothing, marks at once the downward turn of her creative gusto and her critical standing. With the following remarks about *The Young Mountaineers*, the *Nation's* reviewer thumped a doomful bell for Miss Murfree: "The scene which was set a good many years ago and elicited spontaneous applause, now receives only that perfunctory attention which we bestow upon an old friend whom we privately regard as something of a bore."[3]

But the verdict of the most influential American littérateur of her own epoch should be noted before passing on to later appraisals. William Dean Howells, who was the first to publish her mountain stories, avowed that "no critic can hereafter recur to the art of her time and not feel the importance of her contribution to it in this type"—the "pale, white-rose" heroine.[4] And contemplating her total accomplishment, he wrote: "There seems in the dust and smoke of recent literary explosions an eclipse of that fine talent, as strong as it is fine, and as native as it is rare; but I hope that when the vaporous reputations blow away, her clear light will show the stronger for its momentary obscuration.

She was the first to express a true Southern quality in fiction, and it was not the less Southern because it rendered the strange, rude, wild life of a small section of the greater section which still unhappily remains a section."[5]

When Miss Murfree died, the New York *Times* (August 2, 1922) allotted her an obituary of four lines at the bottom of page 17, sure token that she had outlived her era. The judgment of her biographer that she really had died after her fourth book (1885) seems untenably harsh: "Beyond any doubting, if Mary Noailles Murfree had died then, or had never written another line, her reputation as a novelist would be far higher than it is today."[6] It is true that she said most of what she had to say in these first books. But it is also true that she developed subtler and more effective ways of saying them. Alexander Cowie deftly sums up her current situation: "Most of Miss Murfree's novels are now nearly forgotten; she never quite developed major powers and her undeniably excellent local color and her fine discernment of psychological detail could not sustain her. She lacked the breadth and weight to carry her down the years."[7]

With the onset of the twentieth century Miss Murfree suffered several calamities as a writer, and from some of these she may never recover. Local color, her most powerful medium, succumbed to regionalism and a tougher realism. World War I spawned a generation of Americans so lost that it searched for its roots abroad and in the boiling cities. Areas cordoned off from contemporary influences were no longer looked upon as havens of nostalgia but as targets for satire or nests of psycho-neuroses. Literary styles and tastes changed conformably with technologies and attitudes. Morality and manners rushed in where angels had feared to tread. In this wholesale bouleverse-ment of values, the authors most properly attuned to past time were thrust farthest from public gaze. Miss Murfree was one of these.

To the modern reader her debits would appear to outnumber her assets. She is tradition-bound, too heavily beholden to too many masters: to George Eliot for pastorale, pedantry, and ser-monizing; to Walter Scott for gaudy story, picturesque heroes and panorama; to Charles Dickens for extravagant characters and implausible coincidence; to William Thackeray for flippant, skeptic intrusion and snobbish observations; to Jane Austen for constricted feminist perspective on society; to Bret Harte for excess of sentiment and pathos; to Nathaniel Hawthorne for Gothic symbol and ethic tone.

Displeasing too are her persistent iterations of incident and plot, whether borrowed or invented, in book after book; the interchangeability of characters from one story to another, particularly the mountain-flower maiden, the inarticulate hero, the crone, the imperious baby, the snide city girl, the unappreciative city man; and her failure to probe the psychological vitals of these protagonists despite her repeated assurance that they have "subacute" tremors. Her massive doses of panchromatic landscape, her ponderous Latinate diction, portly Johnsonian constructions, and faithful phonetic rendering of dialect discourage readers gaited to Hemingway and O'Hara. Her shallow adherence to mechanistic fate as the determinant of behavior and of poetic justice as a foreseeable outcome of action are also irksome in an age in which none of the scientific or moral invariables have survived.

Miss Murfree displays all the defects of the conventions to which she subscribed, and it is to be expected that even her considerable talents would pall over an expanse of sixteen books devoted to the sights and lives of a homogeneous people in a stagnated area. Repetition resulted and monotony followed; for no locale of that size or kind can provide physical scenes, interesting individuals, or social-moral-economic themes of sufficient variety and depth to warrant a lifetime of literary exploration. Her inclination to return to the small circle of Tennessee mountains was evidently inexhaustible, and therein lies the major contemporary objection to her works. Reading through her shelf of books brings on undeniable weariness. However, this is attributable to the recurring sameness encountered *after* the first volumes of mountain stories. Taken singly, any one of her better efforts affects the reader as a bright excursion into a fresh, new world. As chapters III, IV, and V of this study hopefully verify, Miss Murfree erected a substantial edifice and put living people in it. She had not the gift of architectonics presently admired: her short fiction does not demonstrate the knack of unmasking character in a flash of insight, and her novels often meander mindlessly. But the microcosm does emerge—the colors, sounds, costumes, customs, beliefs, occupations, institutions, allegiances; the tragedies, ironies, and humors of love and faith evolve within a solid, functional, credible framework. By transmitting the beauties and miseries of this retracted region, Miss Murfree at once reveals and preserves another unique segment of historic American sensibility. This is her bequest to the future.

One is left to speculate on her possible niche in literature had she chosen to concentrate on a realm of experience diametrically removed from the crudities of mountaineer life—the world of fashionable society, of ritualized lines of comportment, the atmosphere of women's drawing rooms and polite rapier thrusts. In her first essays, partially in the Civil War novels, and prominently in her Mississippi stories, her perspicacity in these matters testifies convincingly that this world could have been her oyster. She had the vocabulary and wit to divert the prattle of salons to satiric purpose. She had the intellect to penetrate and disclose lucidly the indivisibility of manners and morals. She had the wisdom to observe that society binds, that it can ruin its rebels, but that it can hold cultural ideals—good or bad—intact through periods of intolerable stress. She had every requisite to become a social historian on the order of Edith Wharton or Ellen Glasgow. Her most grievous misstep may have been when she turned away from the garden party and took the long path up the mountain.

In the continuing reappraisal of American writers, what seems in store for Mary Murfree? There can, of course, be no predicting the storms of change that will transfigure styles and subject matter and attitudes, the unaccountable shifts in taste and judgment that will bury some authors and resurrect others. But from the vantage of almost a century of assessment, local color seems securely established as a significant arc in the cycle of our national literature. In her re-creation of life in the Tennessee mountains Miss Murfree gave expression to a place, a people, and a moment in time which may never again see its duplication in the history of our civilization. She is one among a glorious dozen who brought light to scattered geographic and sociological enclaves inside the United States during the last quarter of the nineteenth century. Her Tennessee community is a vital cell in the assimilating organism that has developed into the American character. As a guide to this facet of our culture, her work is of everlasting value.

From the strictly literary point of view, Isabella D. Harris asserts that, after adequate study has been made of Miss Murfree's eighteen novels and some fifty short stories, "she will probably be lifted from her present place among forgotten writers to a secure position among American minor authors."[8] This view has merit to the extent that her books undergo a severe winnowing process. Five volumes would suffice to keep her reputation afloat with the best of the local-color school. Three of these would be mountain chronicles—*In the Tennessee Mountains* (containing eight of her finest short stories), *The Prophet of the Great Smoky Mountains*, and *In the "Stranger People's" Country*. The fourth would be her spectral recollection of the Civil War, *Where the Battle Was Fought*. And, since she excels in the episode rather than in extended narrative, a final volume could comprise dramatic and comic excerpts from her other mountain novels, three or four of her better stories not included in her earliest collection, interpretative scenes from her novels about pioneer Tennessee, passages of description and social contrast from her postwar Mississippi novels, and "Flirts and Their Ways," her maiden effort as a critic of manners.

If the function of the author is to consider the raw materials of human existence, assemble them cogently, infuse them with the light and intensity of his own perception of truth, and present them with viable reality, then Mary Noailles Murfree is a writer to be remembered. In the register of American local colorists, her name stands among the most eminent.

Notes and References

Chapter One

1. Biographical data for this chapter have been drawn mainly from Edd Winfield Parks, *Charles Egbert Craddock (Mary Noailles Murfree)*, (Chapel Hill, 1941); and from two unpublished Master of Arts theses, Mary S. Mooney, *An Intimate Study of Mary Noailles Murfree, Charles Egbert Craddock* (George Peabody College for Teachers, 1928), and Eleanor B. Spence, *Collected Reminiscences of Mary N. Murfree* (George Peabody College for Teachers, 1928).

2. Grantland had "about a million books" upstairs, a statement made by Mary's sister Fanny to Spence, p. 9.

3. Spence, p. 14.

4. "Where Will It End?" *Atlantic Monthly*, I (December, 1857), 144.

5. James Russell Lowell, "The Seward-Johnson Reaction," *North American Review*, CIII (October, 1866), 537.

6. In her list of popular reading during 1850-1860, Grace Warren Landrum names most of these and Chaucer, Chesterfield, Ossian, Beattie, Burns, Wordsworth, and Maria Edgeworth. "Notes on the Reading of the Old South," *American Literature*, III (March, 1931), 60-71.

7. Frederick Law Olmstead, *A Journey in the Seaboard Slave States* (New York, 1856), p. 625.

8. Spence, pp. 11-12.

9. J. B. Killebrew and J. M. Safford, *An Introduction to the Resources of Tennessee* (Nashville, 1874), p. 748.

10. A detailed description of the resort is to be found in Blanche S. Bentley's *Sketch of Beersheba Springs and Chickamauga Trace* (Chattanooga, [1928]).

11. John M. Stahl, *Growing With the West* (London & New York, 1930), p. 323.

12. See Edd Winfield Parks, "Craddock's First Pseudonym," *East Tennessee Historical Society's Publications*, VI (1934), 67-80; and *Charles Egbert Craddock*, pp. 41-43.

13. The once recalcitrant *Scribner's* welcomed "the new writers to the great republic of letters with all heartiness" and proclaimed that "The South and the West are hereafter to be reckoned upon in making up the account of our literary wealth" (XXII [September, 1881], 786). The *Atlantic Monthly*, however, could not resist a touch of condescension. "We have had our laugh at the florid, coarse-flavored literature which has not yet disappeared at the South, but we are

witnessing now the rise of a school which shows us the worth of
generous nature when it has been schooled and ordered" (review of
Where the Battle Was Fought, LV [January, 1885], 125).

14. Spence, p. 19.
15. Isabella D. Harris, *Charles Egbert Craddock as an Interpreter
of Mountain Life* (unpublished Master of Arts thesis, Duke University, 1933), p. 4.
16. See Parks, *Charles Egbert Craddock,* pp. 74-79.
17. Miss Murfree wrote in muscular black strokes of Gothic thick-
ness and pellucid legibility. The St. Louis *Globe-Democrat* printed a
facsimile of her writing with the comment: "Miss Murfree's manuscript was the delight of many a printer's declining years. The characters were bold and clear as poster type" (Mooney, p. xix). Thomas
Bailey Aldrich told her he supposed she wrote with one of those
brushes used by mountaineers for dipping snuff; and, when he re-
quested a serial for the *Atlantic,* he hoped "the young man" had laid
in a winter's supply of ink.
18. Stahl, p. 322.
19. Parks, *Charles Egbert Craddock,* p. 119.
20. *Ibid.,* p. 71.
21. *Ibid.,* pp. 118-19.
22. Mooney, pp. 33-34.
23. Parks, *Charles Egbert Craddock,* pp. 142-43.

Chapter Two

1. Parks, *Charles Egbert Craddock,* p. 118.
2. ". . . a manner that fortunately she was soon to outgrow."
Ibid., p. 63.

Chapter Three

1. George E. Vincent, "A Retarded Frontier," *American Journal
of Sociology,* IV (July, 1898), 18.
2. Horace Kephart, *Our Southern Highlanders* (New York, 1936),
p. 18.
3. John Fox, Jr., "The Southern Mountaineer," *Scribner's,* XXIX
(April, 1901), 388. M. T. Adkins in "The Mountains and Mountaineers of Craddock's Fiction," *Magazine of American History,* XXIV
(October, 1890), 305, speaks of "a people and a life that seemingly
belong to the last century."
4. Killebrew and Safford, p. 748.
5. Fred Lewis Pattee complains that "The mountains of eastern
Tennessee are only moderate ridges, yet in the Craddock tales they
take on the proportions of the Canadian Rockies or the Alps." *A History of American Literature Since 1870* (New York, 1916), p. 311.

6. Isabella D. Harris, *The Southern Mountaineer in American Fiction* (unpublished Doctor of Philosophy thesis, Duke University, 1948), p. 212.

7. Harry Aubrey Toulmin, *Social Historians* (Boston, 1911), pp. 62, 63.

8. Typical of the remarks made about Miss Murfree's lack of fine discriminations is Frank Waldo's in "Among the Southern Appalachians," *New England Magazine*, XXIV (May, 1901), 241: "She very properly makes a marked distinction between the mountain and valley folks; but she does not always keep them in their right places."

Chapter Four

1. *The Advance of the American Short Story* (New York, 1923), p. 158.

2. *Atlantic Monthly*, LIV (July, 1884), 131-33.

3. Harris, *Charles Egbert Craddock*, p. 73.

4. Spence, p. 26. She has a supporter in Edwin Mims (ed.), *History of Southern Fiction*, volume VIII of *The South in the Building of the Nation* (Richmond, 1909-13), pp. lix-lx: "By unity of impression nature and human nature are constantly present in her, and even when some bold action is in progress she can not help feeling that the mountains, the trees, the sun, moon and stars are not merely spectators, but participants."

5. Anonymous review of the *The Mystery of Witch-Face Mountain* in *Nation*, LXII (February 27, 1896), 182.

6. *Southern Writers: Biographical and Critical Studies* (Nashville, 1897), I, 388-89.

7. *Outlook*, CXXXI (August 16, 1922), 626; *Atlantic Monthly*, LXIV (July, 1889), 123.

8. See "Mountain Whites" in Olmstead's *A Journey . . .*; Kephart's *Our Southern Highlanders*; Waldo's "Among the Southern Appalachians." All corroborate many details of mountaineer habitat and habits from personal observation.

9. Mandy Tyler appears in "The Dancin' Party at Harrison's Cove"; Clarsie Giles in "The 'Harnt' That Walks Chilhowee"; Celia Shaw in "The Star in the Valley"; Selina Teake in "The Romance of Sunrise Rock"; Cynthia Ware in "Drifting Down Lost Creek."

10. Spence, p. 26. From firsthand experience Kephart reports: "Many of the women are pretty in youth; but hard toil in house and field, early marriages, frequent child-bearing with shockingly poor attention, and ignorance or defiance of the plainest necessities of hygiene, soon warp and age them. At thirty or thirty-five a mountain woman is apt to have a worn and faded look, with form prematurely bent—and what wonder? Always bending over the hoe in the corn-

field, or bending over the hearth as she cooks by an open fire, or bending over her baby, or bending to pick up, for the thousandth time, the wet duds her lord flings on the floor as he enters from the woods—what wonder that she soon grows short-waisted and round-shouldered?" (288-89).

11. "Southern Dialect in Life and Literature," *Southern Bivouac*, n.s. I (November, 1885), 346-49.

12. Anonymous review of *Down the Ravine* in *Nation*, XLI (August 20, 1885), 158: "It is doubtful if the word dialect, in any strict sense, can be applied to it. This has been used for want of a better, but it is too exact, too restricted. These people in their mountain solitudes are not preserving an ancient speech like the northern dalesmen or the Dorset peasants. It is simply the deterioration, by illiteracy and isolation, of the language carried there a century ago, now and again reinforced by some strong imagination, or by the half-learning of men like the circuit-riders."

13. Mrs. Johns appears in "The Dancin' Party at Harrison's Cove"; Celia Shaw and Mrs. Peel in "The Star in the Valley"; Mrs. Boker in "Electioneerin' on Big Injun Mounting"; Cynthia Ware in "Drifting Down Lost Creek."

14. Rick Pearson appears in "The Dancin' Party at Harrison's Cove"; Rufus Chadd in "Electioneerin' on Big Injun Mounting"; Simon Burney and Reuben Crabb in "The 'Harnt' That Walks Chilhowee"; Selina Teake in "The Romance of Sunrise Rock"; Celia Shaw in "The Star in the Valley"; Cynthia Ware in "Drifting Down Lost Creek."

15. *The Development of the American Short Story* (New York, 1923), p. 272.

Chapter Five

1. Mooney, p. 126.

2. E. F. Harkins and C. H. L. Johnston, *Little Pilgrimages Among the Women Who Have Written Famous Books* (Boston, 1902), pp. 88-89.

3. William Dean Howells, "Editor's Study," *Harper's*, LXXII (January, 1886), 322.

4. *Ibid.*

5. During her delightful journey to the Great Smoky Mountains, Miss Murfree proceeded to the top of Gregory Bald. When she spoke with customary fervor, the unresponsive guide declared that "he had seen enough of mountains to last him a lifetime." Spence, p. 18.

6. *Ibid.*, p. 67.

7. Waldo, p. 241.

8. Spence, p. 47.

9. *Ibid.*, p. 23.

Chapter Six

1. Parks, *Charles Egbert Craddock*, p. 79.
2. See letter to Osgood in R. Baird Shuman, "Mary Murfree's Battle," *Tennessee Studies in Literature*, VI (1961), 35.
3. *Southern Writers*, p. 381.
4. According to Spence, p. 33, Miss Murfree read Angell's *Treatise on the Limitations of Actions at Law* until the volume had to be rebound.
5. Bentley, p. 24.

Chapter Eight

1. Letter of July 6, 1910, quoted by courtesy of Cyril Clemens.
2. *Atlantic Monthly*, LIX (February, 1887), 267.
3. Miss Murfree releases the same sentiment from an entirely different angle. Out of rage and futility over his constant humiliation at the hands of power and money, Jed Knoxton shouts at his wife: "It is allus the way! The big folks is safe, an' high, an' dry, while us pore folks take water, an' skim the edge of hell."
4. Letter of July 6, 1910, to Robert Underwood Johnson.
5. Mooney, p. 158.

Chapter Ten

1. Quoted by permission of Duke University Library.
2. *Critic*, XXIII (June 15, 1895), 440.
3. *Nation*, LXVI (February 17, 1898), 135.
4. *Heroines of Fiction* (New York, 1901), II, 234-35.
5. "Recollections of an Atlantic Editorship," *Atlantic Monthly*, C (November, 1907), 598-99.
6. Parks, *Charles Egbert Craddock*, p. 172.
7. *The Rise of the American Novel* (New York, 1948), p. 593.
8. *Charles Egbert Craddock*, p. 83.

Selected Bibliography

PRIMARY SOURCES

In the Tennessee Mountains. Boston: Houghton, Mifflin & Co., 1884.
(Contains: "Drifting Down Lost Creek," "A-Playin' of Old Sledge
at the Settlemint," "The Star in the Valley," "Electioneerin' on
Big Injun Mounting," "The Romance of Sunrise Rock," "The
Dancin' Party at Harrison's Cove," "Over on the T'other Moun-
ting," "The 'Harnt' That Walks Chilhowee.")
Where the Battle Was Fought. Boston: J. R. Osgood & Co., 1884.
Down the Ravine. Boston: Houghton, Mifflin & Co., 1885.
The Prophet of the Great Smoky Mountains. Boston: Houghton,
Mifflin & Co., 1885.
In the Clouds. Boston: Houghton, Mifflin & Co., 1886.
The Story of Keedon Bluffs. Boston: Houghton, Mifflin & Co., 1887.
The Despot of Broomsedge Cove. Boston: Houghton, Mifflin & Co.,
1888.
In the "Stranger People's" Country. New York: Harper & Brothers,
1891.
His Vanished Star. Boston: Houghton, Mifflin & Co., 1894.
The Mystery of Witch-Face Mountain, and Other Stories. Boston:
Houghton, Mifflin & Co., 1895. (Contains: "The Mystery of
Witch-Face Mountain," "Taking the Blue Ribbon at the County
Fair," "The Casting Vote.")
The Phantoms of the Foot-Bridge, and Other Stories. New York:
Harper & Brothers, 1895. (Contains: "The Phantoms of the Foot-
Bridge," "His 'Day in Court,'" "'Way Down in Lonesome Cove,"
"The Moonshiners at Hoho-Hebee Falls," "The Riddle of the
Rocks.")
The Young Mountaineers. Boston: Houghton, Mifflin & Co., 1897.
(Ten short stories for children.)
The Juggler. Boston: Houghton, Mifflin & Co., 1897.
The Bushwhackers, and Other Stories. Chicago: Herbert S. Stone &
Co., 1899. (Contains: "The Bushwhackers," "The Panther of
Jolton's Ridge," "The Exploit of Choolah, the Chickasaw.")
The Story of Old Fort Loudon. New York: Macmillan Company, 1899.
The Champion. Boston: Houghton, Mifflin & Co., 1902.
A Spectre of Power. Boston: Houghton, Mifflin & Co., 1903.
The Frontiersmen. Boston: Houghton, Mifflin & Co., 1904. (Contains:
"The Linguister," "A Victor at Chungke," "The Captive of the
Ada-Wehi," "The Fate of the Cheera-Taghe," "The Bewitched
Ball-Sticks," "The Visit of the Turbulent Grandfather.")
The Storm Centre. New York: Macmillan Company, 1905.

The Amulet. New York: Macmillan Company, 1906.

The Windfall. New York: Duffield & Co., 1907.

The Fair Mississippian. Boston: Houghton, Mifflin & Co., 1908.

The Raid of the Guerilla, and Other Stories. Philadelphia: J. B. Lippincott Company, 1912. (Contains: "The Raid of the Guerilla," "Who Crosses Storm Mountain?," "The Crucial Moment," "Una of the Hill Country," "The Lost Guidon," "Wolf's Head," "His Unquiet Ghost," "A Chilhowee Lily," "The Phantom of Bogue Holauba," "The Christmas Miracle.")

The Ordeal; A Mountain Romance of Tennessee. Philadelphia: J. B. Lippincott Company, 1912.

The Story of Duciehurst; A Tale of the Mississippi. New York: Macmillan Company, 1914.

SECONDARY SOURCES

I. *Genealogy*

HARDEMAN, MARY MOORE MURFREE. "Brickell and Murfree Families." Typed manuscript in Tennessee State Library at Nashville, 1840. Extended by Mrs. E. M. Bowman, 1885.

II. *Biography*

PARKS, EDD WINFIELD. *Charles Egbert Craddock (Mary Noailles Murfree).* Chapel Hill: University of North Carolina Press, 1941. The only full-length biography, with extensive documentation, bibliography, and critical evaluations of the major works.

III. *Biographical and Critical Materials*

In unpublished theses:

HARRIS, ISABELLA D. *Charles Egbert Craddock as an Interpreter of Mountain Life.* Master of Arts, Duke University, 1933. Classifies types of mountaineers, folk characteristics, and mountain scenery.

————. *The Southern Mountaineer in American Fiction, 1824-1910.* Doctor of Philosophy, Duke University, 1948. Chapter III is devoted to the peak years of MNM's writing career.

MOONEY, MARY S. *An Intimate Study of Mary Noailles Murfree, Charles Egbert Craddock.* Master of Arts, George Peabody College for Teachers, 1928. Studies four facets: biography and personality, the writings, personal notices, book reviews.

REICHERT, ALFRED. *Charles Egbert Craddock und die amerikanische short story.* Doctor of Philosophy, University of Leipzig, 1912. A commendatory view of MNM's practices in the short story, particularly her suggestive use of locale.

Selected Bibliography

SPENCE, ELEANOR B. *Collected Reminiscences of Mary N. Murfree.*
Master of Arts, George Peabody College for Teachers, 1928. Intimate glimpses of MNM by a cousin, "made with the approval and cooperation of Miss Fannie N. D. Murfree."
See also: *Southern Literary Culture, A Bibliography of Masters' and Doctors' Theses,* edited by Clyde H. Cantrell and Walton R. Patrick. University, Ala.: University of Alabama Press, 1955. Lists thirty-six unpublished studies which deal wholly or in part with Miss Murfree's life and works.

In books:

BASKERVILL, WILLIAM MALONE. *Southern Writers: Biographical and Critical Studies.* Nashville: M. E. Church, 1897. First substantial survey-analysis of MNM's art in the mountain phase; generally defensive of her better qualities but not unaware of her important faults.
BASKETTE, G. H. "Mary Noailles Murfree," in EDWIN A. ALDERMAN (ed.), *Library of Southern Literature.* Atlanta: Martin & Hoyt Co., 1909. Biographical and critical review based on the assumption that MNM is among the creative authors of America as distinguished from merely popular ones.
BENTLEY, BLANCHE S. *Sketch of Beersheba Springs and Chickamauga Trace.* Chattanooga: Lookout Publishing Co., [1928]. Historical data and physical description of the region in which MNM and family spent many vacations, and which reappeared in her stories as New Helvetia Springs.
BROOKS, VAN WYCK. *The Times of Melville and Whitman.* New York: E. P. Dutton, 1947. Synthetical review of MNM's life, materials, and methods, mostly favorable.
COWIE, ALEXANDER. *The Rise of the American Novel.* New York: American Book Co., 1948. Examination of the qualities of MNM's novels, with chief attention to *The Prophet of the Great Smoky Mountains.*
DEMENIL, ALEXANDER N. *The Literature of the Louisiana Territory.* St. Louis: St. Louis News Co., 1904. Frequently cited for its exposition of MNM's writing habits, this sketch contains several biographical errors.
FISKE, HORACE SPENCER. *Provincial Types in American Fiction.* Chautauqua: Chautauqua Press, 1903. Brief survey of the mountain fiction preceding a long synopsis of *The Prophet of the Great Smoky Mountains.*
HARKINS, E. F., and C. H. L. JOHNSTON. *Little Pilgrimages Among the Women Who Have Written Famous Books.* Boston: L. C. Page & Co., 1902. Largely biographical, with emphasis on MNM's *nom de plume.*
HENDERSON, C. C. *The Story of Murfreesboro.* Murfreesboro, Tenn.:

News-Banner Publishing Co., 1929. Brief historical, geographical, biographical, and anecdotal account of the city from its earliest days.

HOLLIDAY, CARL. *A History of Southern Literature.* New York: Neale Publishing Co., 1906. Generalized, overenthusiastic appraisal of MNM as the epic poet of Southern mountaineer life.

KEPHART, HORACE. *Our Southern Highlanders.* New York: Macmillan Co., 1936. Highly informative study of the Southern Appalachian chain and the ways and speech of its inhabitants.

MASON, ROBERT LINDSAY. *The Lure of the Great Smokies.* Boston: Houghton Mifflin Co., 1927. Vivid, anecdotal presentation of the stamping grounds, occupations, and customs of the mountaineers MNM converted into fictional characters.

MOORE, JOHN TROTWOOD, and AUSTIN P. FOSTER. *Tennessee, the Volunteer State, 1769-1923.* Chicago: S. J. Clarke Publishing Co., 1923. An account of the battle between Union and Confederate armies at Stone's River, scene of *Where the Battle Was Fought.*

PATTEE, FRED L. *A History of American Literature Since 1870.* New York: Century Co., 1916. Best of the early analyses; demonstrates MNM's affinity with Thomas Hardy and Bret Harte.

————. *The Development of the American Short Story.* New York: Harper & Brothers, 1923. MNM's short stories not really of short story texture; she fails in the ultimate techniques of the genre.

QUINN, ARTHUR HOBSON. *American Fiction.* New York: D. Appleton-Century Co., 1936. MNM is a romantic idealist who achieved realism by the sheer potency of a primitive type.

RUTHERFORD, MILDRED LEWIS. *The South in History and Literature.* Athens, Ga.: Franklin-Turner Co., 1907. Brief biographical appreciation with the two outstanding anecdotes of spelling "Popocatepetl" and the disclosure of identity.

STAHL, JOHN M. *Growing With the West.* London & New York: Longmans, Green & Co., 1930. Personal description and accounts of MNM's status and activities during her residence in St. Louis.

TICKNOR, CAROLINE. *Glimpses of Authors.* Boston: Houghton Mifflin Co., 1922. Incident of MNM's revelation of identity in Boston, somewhat at variance with other versions.

TOULMIN, HARRY AUBREY. *Social Historians.* Boston: R. G. Badger, 1911. MNM's investigation into the generic psychology of Tennessee mountaineers is a genuine contribution to the science of social organization as well as an artistic success.

In periodicals:

ADAMS, OSCAR FAY. "The Prose of Mr. Craddock," *Literary World*, XV (October 4, 1884), 330. Shows the essential poetic measures of MNM's prose by recasting into free verse several passages from *In the Tennessee Mountains.*

Selected Bibliography

ADKINS, MILTON T. "The Mountains and Mountaineers of Craddock's Fiction," *Magazine of American History*, XXIV (October, 1890), 305-9. A native of Tennessee defends MNM against the allegation that she sought easy fame by portraying in dialect "the outlandish and grotesque in the low life of a small section."

BASKERVILL, WILLIAM MALONE. "Charles Egbert Craddock," *Chautauquan*, XXV (June, 1897), 294-98. Same as his introduction in *Southern Writers*.

DILLINGHAM, WILLIAM B. (ed.). "'When Old Baldy Spoke,' by Charles Egbert Craddock," *Emory University Quarterly*, XVIII (Summer, 1962), 93-106. Rates this hitherto unpublished story not an eminent addition to the canon but representative of the mountain tales for which she is remembered.

MOSES, MONTROSE J. "Charles Egbert Craddock: A Study of Mary Murfree in her Southern Home in Tennessee," *Book News Monthly*, XXXIII (October, 1914), 69-71. MNM's fault lies in idealization of the mountain spirit; the social and economic conditions are portrayed with relentless realism.

PARKS, EDD WINFIELD. "Craddock's First Pseudonym," *East Tennessee Historical Society's Publications*, VI (1934), 67-80. Analysis of the probationary period of four years during which MNM shifted from writing polite society sketches to mountaineer realism.

SHUMAN, R. BAIRD. "Mary Murfree's Battle," *Tennessee Studies in Literature*, VI (1961), 33-37. Reproduces in manuscript the letter to Osgood & Company which led to the publication of *Where the Battle Was Fought*.

SMITH, CHARLES FORSTER. "Southern Dialect in Life and Literature," *Southern Bivouac*, n.s. I (November, 1885), 343-51. MNM is not successful with characters from higher life, can see the harder life of the mountaineers but is weakest in rendering their dialect.

TAYLOR, ARCHER. "Proverbs and Proverbial Phrases in the Writings of Mary N. Murfree," *Tennessee Folklore Society Bulletin*, XXIV (March, 1958), 11-50. A compilation from twenty-two of MNM's books which demonstrates that she used no very large number of characteristic local sayings, especially after 1890.

WALDO, FRANK. "Among the Southern Appalachians," *New England Magazine*, XXIV (May, 1901), 231-47. Points out discrepancies in customs and characterization which arise from MNM's indiscriminate blending of the Cumberland and Great Smoky mountain regions.

WRIGHT, NATHALIA. "A Note on the Setting of Mary Noailles Murfree's 'The "Harnt" That Walks Chilhowee,'" *Modern Language Notes*, LXII (April, 1947), 272. Internal evidence indicates the precise locale of this story: on Chilhowee Mountain in Blount County, Tennessee, above the site of Montvale Springs Hotel.

Index

Index

Date Due
